NATIONAL SECURITY

NATIONAL SECURITY

The Israeli Experience

Israel Tal
Translated by Martin Kett

Westport, Connecticut
London

Library of Congress Cataloging-in-Publication Data

Tal, Yisra'el.
    [Bitahon le'umi. English]
    National security : the Israeli experience / Israel Tal
; translated by Martin Kett.
        p. cm.
    ISBN 0–275–96812–X (alk. paper)
    1. National security—Israel. 2. Israel—Military policy. 3.
Arab-Israeli conflict. 4. Israel—History, Military. I. Title.
    UA853.I8 T3513 2000
    355'.03305694—dc21   99–036593

British Library Cataloguing in Publication Data is available.

Library of Congress Catalog Card Number: 99–036593
ISBN: 0–275–96812–X

First published in 2000

Praeger Publishers, 88 Post Road West, Westport, CT 06881
An imprint of Greenwood Publishing Group, Inc.
www.praeger.com

Printed in the United States of America

The paper used in this book complies with the
Permanent Paper Standard issued by the National
Information Standards Organization (Z39.48–1984).

10 9 8 7 6 5 4 3 2 1

R0403587869

CONTENTS

Part Three: Security Doctrine and the Test of Time

PREFACE

The basic principles and ideas that underpin Israeli security doctrine took shape in the 1950s. The fundamentals of that doctrine were formulated by a relatively small group of commanders and staff officers under the direction of David Ben-Gurion, Israel's first prime minister and minister of defense. The members of that group and the commanders and staff officers who continued in later years to elaborate and expand upon their original work deserve the credit for developing an original and unique Israeli doctrine of security.

The leaders of Israel saw from the outset that the future did not augur well. The security horizon was likely to remain cloudy for a long time to come, and Israel would have to continue to rely upon its sword until the Arabs gave up their hope of forcibly extirpating it from the region. The country thus had to develop a doctrine of national security and consolidate its military strength.

A model of national security appropriate to the reality of Israel's circumstances simply did not exist. What was needed was an original solution to the unique situation in which Israel found itself: a situation in which the few faced the many, in which a David faced a demographic and geographic Goliath, in which a minute island was surrounded by a sea threatening to engulf it.

The solution took shape gradually. The strategic principles adopted were dictated, on the one hand, by the military legacy inherited from the prestatehood Jewish community in British Palestine and the experience acquired in World War II and the 1948 War of Independence, and on the other hand, by objective geopolitical circumstances. At first glance, the strategy seemed virtually impossible. However, it proved itself over the years and served as the basis for successfully dealing with the difficult problems confronting Israel. From these strategic principles a methodical, daring, and well-founded plan for national security doctrine came into being. That doctrine is set forth in this book.

Israel's security doctrine has not been crystallized into a single, set plan. It is in part an oral doctrine and in part a formal, written one, its scattered contents included in various laws; decisions by the Knesset (Parliament) and government; and standing orders, such as high command and General Staff directives and the training manuals used by the various arms of the Israel Defense Forces (IDF). The strategic, military, doctrinal, and organizational principles set forth in these sources constitute a security doctrine that has been relevant to Israel's circumstances for many years.

The first part of the book deals with the universal issue of national security. The second part presents the basic theory of Israeli security doctrine, and the third part its actual realization, setting forth the historical development of the military struggle Israel has waged since its establishment. This book was not intended as a complete historical account of Israel's wars; rather, it discusses them in the context of the nation's security doctrine and the lessons derived therefrom.

In this work, I have endeavored to set forth, according to the best of my comprehension, the fundamentals of Israel's national security thinking, as I learned it from my commanders, my comrades in arms, and my experience. This book makes no pretension to being a research work and hence does not rely on authoritative sources or quotations. In the course of surveying the development and implementation of Israel's national security doctrine, the book presents my own outlook on the subject, as well as various theories I have developed over the years in the field of military thought. Some of the material was originally delivered as lectures to audiences of the IDF and other armed forces, and some has been published in various journals related to military and security matters.

THE MIDDLE EAST

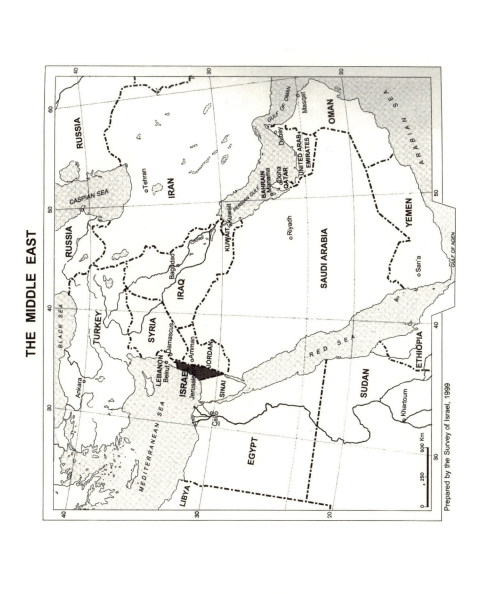

Prepared by the Survey of Israel, 1999

ISRAEL AFTER THE SIX DAYS WAR

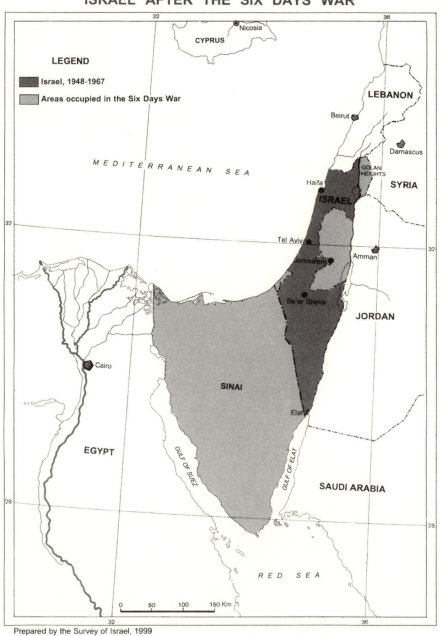

LEGEND

Israel, 1948-1967

Areas occupied in the Six Days War

NICOSIA

CYPRUS

LEBANON

Beirut

Damascus

MEDITERRANEAN SEA

GOLAN HEIGHTS

Haifa

ISRAEL

SYRIA

Tel Aviv

Jerusalem

Amman

Be'er Sheva

JORDAN

Cairo

SINAI

Elat

EGYPT

GULF OF SUEZ

GULF OF ELAT

SAUDI ARABIA

RED SEA

0   50   100   150 Km

Prepared by the Survey of Israel, 1999

PART ONE

NATIONAL SECURITY AND INTERNATIONAL SECURITY

CHAPTER 1
BACKGROUND

The concept of national security deals with safeguarding a nation's existence and defending its vital interests. Existence is the basic objective of security. It means, quite simply, physical survival; it constitutes an objective, primal value, one that all nations hold in common. By its very essence, it requires no justification. It is an unvarying element of the interest that every people has in physical existence and sovereignty—hence its objective nature.

Vital interests are a subjectively determined element in the totality of a nation's goals, and they derive from such background factors as the nation's political culture, dominant ideology, traditions, prevailing conditions, aspirations, and circumstances. Hence, they are unique for each nation and each regime. Every society periodically defines those vital interests that justify a nation's girding itself for conflict, with the purpose of preventing, or bringing about, particular results or developments.

There is no point in extending the discussion to include all the various kinds of violent national undertakings and their possible attendant outcomes, successful or otherwise. Some nations, for instance, have waged colonial wars with the aim of enhancing their security. However, as a rule, one should limit the concept of national security to what is directly existential or is perceived as such.

The subject of national security, in its modern sense, is related to three historical developments—those of the nation-state, of total war, and the industrial revolution. Until the American Revolution (1775–83) and the French Revolution (1789), most wars were fought between rulers or dynasties, with professional, mercenary armies. The question of security from the standpoint of existence, if it arose at all, pertained solely to the ruling classes.

The formation of the modern nation-state as an entity that gives expression to sentiments values and goals held in common by society as a whole altered the meaning of war. Now, war had direct implications for entire populations, not mainly for the personal fates of rulers. It is from this point onward that the concept of national security has meaning.

The age of total war commenced with the appearance of the nation-state. Total war meant armed states, mass citizen armies, total mobilization of resources, and the viewing of enemy populations and vital strategic sites inside hostile territory as legitimate targets. The identification of the people with the state has rendered all citizens potential combatants. The morality and rules of warfare have been influenced by the new nature of the art of war; with all the citizens of hostile states either combatants or active participants in the war effort, belligerent states have reserved for themselves the right—within certain limits—to view the populations of hostile states and the infrastructures that maintain them as objectives the conquest, neutralization, or destruction of which would further the attainment of a military decision.

Total war is not merely the outcome of the great revolution wrought by nationalism, as a result of which the importance of peoples in historical processes has grown and states are no longer the exclusive provinces of absolute rulers. This social process has been interwoven with a towering technological and industrial development—the industrial revolution. Mass production and the creation of national wealth and resources have served to underpin war efforts. Such things have made possible the raising of large citizen armies, the stockpiling of weapons, munitions, and spare parts, the equipping of armies, and the shifting of forces from place to place with unprecedented rapidity. Without trains and the internal combustion engine, it would not have been possible for the nation-state or the phenomenon of total war to engender such far-reaching change in the art of war.

Furthermore, the means of warfare and logistics have come to be increasingly dependent on natural resources. Coal, for instance, is used to drive rolling stock and steamships, rendering both railway lines and mining regions strategic targets. The industrial revolution has not only led to the development of sophisticated new weapons but has made possible, with the development of aircraft, attacks on population centers and other targets in the heart of enemy territory.

Thus, the development of technology and industry has been intimately linked with the essence, and the image, of total war.

The general conscription law enacted by the French National Assembly in 1792 was a harbinger of total war. When the French mobilized the revolutionary, and later Napoleonic, army, they were the trailblazers of the mass citizen army. However, in the Franco-Prussian War of 1870–71, as the French reverted to a professional army, the Prussians took their cue from the earlier French example and built up an army based on the principle of citizens in arms. It has been said that the Franco-Prussian War was won by the German grammar-school teacher; after all, Prussia based its military prowess on its rank-and-file citizenry. Young men, who had been imbued with patriotism and received their physical training as part of their education, went directly on from school to military training and service. Thus, after it defeated France, Prussia came to be held up as the final arbiter of, the ultimate source of inspiration in, military science.

Prior to the First World War, the United States learned the lessons of its own Revolutionary War and Civil War (1861–65), as well as from the Boer War (1899–1902) and the Russo-Japanese War (1904–5). It came to realize that traditional methods of warfare were no longer applicable. The American outlook was treated with contempt in Europe, which refused to implement those lessons or even take notice of them.

For instance, in the U.S. Civil War and the Boer War it became clear that cavalry no longer provided battlefield mobility, but Europe, in its conservatism, refused to see this. It took the carnage of the static trench warfare of World War I to shock Europeans into facing the facts. The loss of mobility and the freezing of the front lines jolted European military thinkers. It finally became clear to them—they could have foreseen this in advance but chose not to—that technological developments had destroyed the foundations upon which mobility in warfare had been based. Machine guns, shrapnel, craters left by exploding shells, barbed-wire fences, and trenches forced infantry to keep close to the ground and rendered cavalry useless as the means of battlefield mobility, maneuver, and assault. The old strategy had been neutralized.

However, while some technological advances were rendering the old strategy inoperative, others—the development of the airplane and tank—revived it. These new tools proved to be harbingers of modern war, and of the revolution in the art of war that took place between the two world wars.

The airplane added to warfare its third dimension—the arena of the skies—while the tank brought back the element of mobility to the land arena. Use was also made in the First World War of chemical weapons, although they failed to leave a lasting imprint on the art of war, as their use had been discontinued. In that war, submarines were also put to widespread and significant use.

After the First World War, in the interwar period, European theoreticians formulated new theories of warfare and set out to predict the nature of the wars of the future. A number of such thinkers were convinced that the total war of the future, in which hostile populations would be legitimate targets, would be decided by terror bombings by air forces before land and sea forces would even have the chance to go into action. The apostles of this doctrine, the most prominent of whom was an Italian officer, Colonel (later General) Giulio Douhet, assumed that a nation's will to fight could be broken by massive bombings of its urban population centers, above all of its capital. Such pounding would induce the people to force their government to sue for peace.

In his book *Command of the Air*, which appeared in the 1920s, Douhet contended that in the era of the airplane, mobility on land or sea was no longer the decisive factor in warfare. In future wars, Douhet felt, the firepower of the airplane would decide the issue before land and sea forces could get involved. He believed that firepower would supplant mobility as the decisive element in war, since the aircraft made it possible to bring overwhelming firepower to bear on vital enemy targets.

This doctrine was implemented in World War II and proved an utter failure. The Germans tried, with massive strategic bombings, to break the will of the British people to fight, but the British stood fast. Later, Allied bombings of Germany caused widespread devastation; nevertheless, German war production rose, and the Germans did not buckle under to the enormous aerial firepower that rained down on them.

The belief that the element of firepower, as embodied in the airplane, would supplant that of movement has been repeatedly disproved in other areas as well, such as armored warfare. Every new antitank weapon ever developed has led to erroneous assertions that, as the embodiment of the element of firepower, it would put paid to the supremacy of the tank—the embodiment of the element of mobility—as the decisive weapon on land. Time and again, and not only on the level of theory and strategy but also at the tactical level, in actual military engagements, reality has proved wrong those who have claimed that primacy on the field of battle has passed from movement to firepower.

Nevertheless, though decisions are not attained by air power, it is the single most important form of power in modern warfare, whether on land, in the air itself, or at sea. Air supremacy, if not a sufficient condition for forcing a decision in war, is nonetheless a necessary one. The prophets of modern warfare who made their forecasts between the two world wars foresaw the future course of warfare correctly. Their prophecies concerning the revolution that the airplane and tank would bring about proved correct. Mechanized and armored forces brought the elements of mobility and maneuver back to military strategy. The aircraft expanded the scope of firepower in warfare from merely the tactical level to the operational and strategic as well. A new era dawned in the annals of warfare, in the wake of historic revolution engendered by innovations and changes that dwarfed anything that had preceded them.

Until the airplane made its appearance in warfare, tactics were based on mobility and firepower, and strategy solely on mobility. The airplane, as a long-range firepower platform, represented a combination of mobility and firepower in the operational and strategic spheres—an advantage that had hitherto existed in the sphere of tactics alone. The prophets of air power were before their time; their only mistake was in ascribing to air power the ability to force a decision.

With the appearance of weapons of mass destruction, namely atomic bombs, at the end of World War II, another revolution was wrought, one that transcends discussion of the art and conduct of war. The change wrought by the advent of atomic weapons was one of essence, not just of degree: for the first time in history, firepower supplanted mobility as the decisive element in warfare. However, the full significance of this fateful development is the new reality that the few can deter the many, and even hold them in dread.

For the first time in the history of man, small states can attack great powers and annihilate millions of their people. This means the end of the art of war as we have known it, since it is now possible to force clear-cut military decisions. The weapons of mass destruction that already exist and those to come can be expected to bring a new and dangerous age, one of increasingly acute mutual dread and deterrence and of enhanced capabilities for mutual assured destruction. The critical factor is now "mutuality," not "superiority" or "balance." Furthermore, the arena of deterrence and war has already extended beyond the earth into space.

Taking into account this new reality and the proliferation of weapons of mass destruction, even a military decision by conventional means can be fraught with peril—if the losing side possesses weapons of mass destruction, its reaction could escalate uncontrollably. The new history of warfare in the age of weapons of mass destruction will be underpinned by the art of deterrence rather than the art of decision.

These historical processes and factors explain the development of the field of security. From time immemorial, kings and emperors have striven to assure the sovereignty, the territorial integrity, the assets, and the highways of their realms. However, security as an existential concern, both national and international, of the highest order, as a basic social and political concern, has been an outcome of the appearance of the modern nation-state and of the development of military technology. The nations of the world face bleak prospects for their security. The progressive acquisition by various states, some developed and others not, and some fanatical, of advanced weapons systems and military technologies poses a threat not only to national interests but to national liberty, sovereignty, and survival. This development poses a threat to the actual, physical survival of entire nations; it even involves the danger of the extermination of the human race by a human hand. This development, that of the proliferation of weapons of mass destruction, has been taking place under the backdrop of increasingly acute religious, national, and existential struggles.

The question of national security in the future has become increasingly intertwined with the condition of international security—the security of the entire human race; it is no less than the physical survival of humanity that hangs in the balance. Thus, national security and international security have become synonymous, their attainment being conditional upon the general world order. The appearance of the nation-state and developments in science and technology have engendered the field of national security. Yet the problem of world survival and security in all its acuteness is the product of the development of weapons of mass destruction: the power to wreak devastation and death that these weapons possess cannot be ameliorated, limited, or contained by geographic or political boundaries.

CHAPTER 2
COMPONENTS OF NATIONAL SECURITY

NATIONAL GOALS

National goals comprise a varied aggregate of values, some of which derive from beliefs and opinions, and are hence controversial. Nevertheless, this aggregate contains a basic, unvarying goal, the defense of the nation's very existence. Therefore, it is possible to reach a consensus on national security both in a pluralistic, democratic country and a totalitarian one.

National goals are not constant. They are set by vital interests and existential challenges, but are also often determined to a considerable extent by a nation's myths and ethos. Rational motives and instinctual-emotive urges work together in a complex way to forge national yearnings and desires. Religious principles, social and political values, such powerful ideas as justice and honor, all exert their effects on the behavior of peoples and states, no less than do their existential needs; they are even liable to tip the scales toward courses of action that clash with existential national interests.

This being the way of the world, the security of a people is liable to be threatened not only by the national aspirations of other peoples but also—and sometimes mainly—by the goals it sets for itself. The greater the national pretensions, the more their realization involves threatening other nations or actually harming them; the resistance of the threatened or harmed nations increases, the prospects for coexistence decline, and the problem of security is heightened. Thus, excessive national pretensions, those that engender confrontation, threaten even the parties that entertain them. It is a matter of keeping a proper sense of proportion.

OVERALL NATIONAL BALANCE OF POWER

The overall balance of power between nations is determined by the basic national strength of each. Such strength comprises two components: staying power, and assault power.

Staying power embodies potential strength, the totality of the human and material resources of a nation. These include a country's area, its geography and topography, and its assets, spiritual and physical—its national ethos and culture; the state of development of its science, technology, and industry; its economic strength; the quality of its regime, social and political; the organization and management of its affairs, at all levels and in all spheres; and the weight of, and policies pursued by, its allies. But most important of all is the strength of a nation's motivation. This in turn is the product of a sense of shared fate, as well as of the degree of general agreement on goals—a national consensus on vital national aspirations, and a willingness of individuals and the body politic to apply themselves to their realization.

Assault power reflects actual military strength. It is potential that has been brought into being, in part or in full. Basically, these two components of strength are two sides of the same coin. Staying power reflects the overall balance of power between nations, assault power the balance of military power between them.

The importance of such large, quantifiable factors as area, population, natural resources, and the state of development of industry is determined by human quality, individual and social. Human quality, however, though among the most important elements of staying power, is not the most important of such elements. In the final historical analysis, it is quantity, more often than not, that is the decisive factor.

The balance of concrete military power between states is determined by the strengths of their armed forces, to wit, by their assault power. The way a state allocates its national resources determines the ratio between the two components of its strength, its assault power and staying power. The establishment of a large army enhances the assault power but at the expense of the staying power, that is, the ability to persevere in a war effort over the long term. In other words, the building up and maintenance of large armed forces require the mortgaging of a large portion of a nation's resources to its military power, at the expense of investment in social, economic, scientific, and technological development—in other words, at the expense of staying power and the enhancement of its national potential. Such a policy is tantamount to living off the capital of national resources.

Conventional total war usually takes on the character of a "war of attrition," since it essentially is a clash between resources. Assault power alone cannot decide the issue in such a war. It is decided when, as a result of the very war effort itself, resources and manpower are used up and staying power fades.

A war can also take on the character of "a war of decision." One may readily assume that an unconventional war, being a war of extermination, would be a war of decision and not one of erosion; assault power, in the form of unconventional weapons, would be what decides the issue, immediately upon their employment. In a conventional war, the chances of effecting a decision are greater when one side commences hostilities with an assault; it may manage to attain an immediate result. Without such a decision, the war becomes one of erosion, and its outcome is determined by relative powers of endurance.

The degree of security a nation enjoys, to judge from the perspective of history, is a product of the overall balance of power. This balance is largely constant, while the balance of military power at the outset of hostilities is a variable, a temporary factor in an emergency; no nation can persevere over many years or even generations in maintaining strong assault power. Such a force would have to be at the expense of staying power—at the expense of general development in all spheres and at all levels of national life. Military superiority that derives from superior staying power is natural superiority; military superiority that derives from exhausting most of a nation's staying power is temporary.

States arm themselves and maintain large military forces in the face of perceived threats to their security, trying thereby to frustrate the threat by deterrence or by effecting a military decision, should deterrence prove inadequate. The transition from the path of deterrence to that of seeking a decision involves rendering potential power actual—turning staying power into assault power. There are states that build up powerful armed forces with the aim of attaining military superiority and employing it to pressure other states or to take military measures against them, in order to attain their national objectives at the expense of those of other states. Potentially threatened parties perceive such a build-up of power as an immediate threat. Thus, actual military aggression is not necessary to upset a geopolitical system in balance, whether local, regional, or global; it is sufficient that a single state in such a system divert its center of gravity from staying power to assault power.

In the dynamic circumstances of international relations, the states of balance between the elements of probability, danger, and balance of power are constantly being upset. Sometimes crises are solved, but sometimes they break out, threatening vital interests of entire nations, be they objectively or subjectively defined. The result is a new set of circumstances, one that could be the outcome of resignation to the inevitable compromise, deterrence, or war.

THE LIMITS OF POWER

The limits of power are affected by the following three paradoxes:

1. The attainment of ambitious war aims requires military superiority. However, the more grandiose the aims, the greater the resistance of the adversary, thus changing the balance of power to the detriment of the party entertaining the pretensions.
2. A military build-up, an enhancement of assault power, detracts from national power, staying power, thus changing the overall balance of power between the nations involved to the detriment of that engaged in the build-up.
3. Unrestrained use of power causes the contraction of that power, because national consensus and motivation are weakened.

In a democratic state, the employment of force arouses opposition. Yet even in an authoritarian state, opposition may develop that can shake a regime's stability, especially in the event of failure.

The objective limits of a state's power derive from a variety of factors: the relative strength of contending parties, the power of direct allies, and the deterrent power of interested great powers. To these factors must be added subjective considerations, such as the importance of a particular interest to a state compared to its importance to the adversary, the strength of national and religious myths, and the nature of the national ethos.

The degree of willingness of a people to pay the price entailed in going to war over an interest is directly proportional to the extent to which they perceive that interest as vital to their nation. Conversely, the more acute the threat to a vital interest of an adversary, the greater the price the adversary would surely be willing to pay, in human and material resources, to thwart it. Thus, the limits of power of a given state are likely to expand as those of a rival state contract, and vice versa, all in proportion to the extent to which the conflicting interests involved are vital.

National motivation has a direct bearing on the limits of power, since when there is general agreement among a people on the need to use power, willingness and even desire to use it rise. Under such circumstances, a nation's leadership senses it has public support and feels free to take whatever measures, political or military, it sees fit without having to worry about domestic opposition. Since the degree of motivation is directly proportional to the perception that an interest is vital to the individual and nation, that perception determines the price the individual and nation are willing to pay to attain it. In a democratic society, basic instinct guides the decision that people make as to what is worth endangering their lives and those of their sons, and what is not. People are willing to pay the ultimate price for their very physical and national existence.

Motivation, then, stands in direct proportion to the degree of general agreement concerning national goals. The strongest motivation is that which derives from existential goals. The greater the feeling that a vital interest hangs in the balance, the greater the motivation, all the more when an existential interest is under consideration. Concerning the existential goal there is an absolute consensus; it is the only goal that touches upon each individual, being both private and collective in nature. The limits of power are flexible and relative; they expand when an interest is more vital and contract as war aims become more ambitious and diverge from the existential. In a democratic society, people sense that lives may be risked, to say nothing of sacrificed, only in the defense of life and liberty.

The dialectic of the paradox of power is at work here: a grandiose broadening of the compass of national goals engenders a reduction in motivation, and hence a contraction of power, while perseverance in existential goals broadens the limits of power. Thus, uninhibited willingness to employ force engenders, paradoxically, its contraction. The converse obtains as well: it is just when much force is required to attain ambitious goals—which reduce motivation—that an adversary has a more vital interest in fighting and his motivation is thus the greater.

The concept of "limits of power" is thus relative and dependent on context. In brief, the overall balance of power and, in contrast, the concrete military balance are determined by a variable, subjective factor known as "the limits of power."

Nations ordinarily develop a sense of unity of destiny and of common goals, as well as a steadfast national will, in times of trial brought about by historical necessity. It is in such times that a people produces valiant soldiers imbued with a high sense of motivation. There are periods in the history of a nation in which its people develop warlike patterns of behavior, and there are periods when the martial spirit fades. Fear and panic, bravery and daring—these are all traits that change with historical circumstances. The same state may reveal itself as a nation of warriors in one set of historical circumstances and as a nation of defeatists in another.

Conduct on the field of battle is determined by the pattern of national behavior prevalent at a particular time. A martial pattern of behavior, which seems stamped on the character of some nation or other in a particular period, is not unvarying or inherent; rather, it derives from historical necessity. When a nation fights for its very existence, for the realization of clearly vital goals—its freedom, for instance—it fights with desperation. Thus, no security doctrine should be based on the idea that "steadfastness of spirit" distinguished the combatants of one camp but that its rival is marked by low morale.

The force a nation can bring to bear is limited. It may never exceed the sum total of the general and military aspects of its strength, including the components of national morale and motivation, augmented by the power of its allies.

DEGREES OF NATIONAL SECURITY

The security of nations and states is based on various elements and combinations among them. It would be theoretically possible to classify degrees of national security in four principal levels—although in practice the division is not so clear cut, as a particular state may derive its security from a combination of several circumstances and degrees of security. The four principal levels are:

1. The ideal model, involving optimal security, is that which derives from conditions of calm, balance, and stability. States enjoying this level of security are those that have attained the proverbial "promised land" of peace and prosperity. Such states make no claim upon others liable to arouse their hostility, and other states make no such claims upon them. Exempt from the exigencies of any proximate threat, they can invest virtually all their resources in developing the various components of their staying power. Such power is a healthy underpinning of national strength, enhances a nation's weight in the international arena, and, in the event of an emergency, is the source of its assault power.

2. The second level of security is that which is based upon superiority. In this case, security derives from the fact that a state is so much stronger than potential rivals that its vital interests are not menaced.

3. The third level is security based on mutual deterrence and a balance of terror. Many states, in fact all those involved in conflicts of vital interest with other states, belong to this category. Among these are states that enjoyed military superiority before the advent of weapons of mass destruction and had once relied on that superiority. In other words, they once belonged to the second level of security but have regressed to a lower one—that based on a balance of terror.

4. A special level of security involves giving in and adjusting. This level includes states that forgo a material part of their sovereignty, as well as of their national aspirations and goals, and meekly accept the superiority of others in exchange for continued national existence.

CHAPTER 3
RESPONSIBILITY FOR NATIONAL SECURITY

At the dawn of the age of total war, the full import of the revolution in the art of war was not fully understood; nor were the changes eventually wrought by that revolution in the fabric of political and security affairs foreseen. Only gradually did national security become a central concern in the affairs of nations, a salient part of social and political life, or an integral part of the existential experience, which it has become in our own time.

The first to grasp the incipient changes in the art of war and the new vistas opening up in the field of strategy were the Prussians. It was they who adapted the use of military force to the new means and possibilities ushered in by the industrial revolution and conscript militaries, possibilities, such as rail transport and large military formations. They were also the first to adapt their military institutions to the new reality, including the formulation of the concept of a modern general staff.

However, a narrow view still prevailed. Neither governments nor military leaders immediately grasped the full extent of the social and political changes about to make themselves felt in the wake of the transformation to total, national wars. In the new reality brought about by the advent of the total national war, overall security considerations took precedence over those of a purely military nature; political considerations now took priority. It was only gradually that the idea that social and political factors, and popular legitimization (consensus), were sometimes more important than the military balance of power began to permeate military thinking—that only staying power, assault power, and motivation, in combination, are capable of assuring balanced national power.

In conflicts between states in the age of the total national war, it is the overall balance of power that decides the issue. Military superiority alone is no longer sufficient; what is required is an overall perspective of national life. Hence, the military leadership should not take priority over the political; in fact, the opposite should be the case. Only they who possess the means and authority to influence all spheres of national life, to direct and coordinate them, are able to make a comprehensive appreciation of the situation, to set meaningful national goals, and to formulate and conduct policy accordingly. Indeed, the setting of national goals and the conduct of security policy, including the general conduct of war, must now be in the hands of political leaders. However, this was not always self-evident.

In Prussia, and later Germany, theories were prevalent that whereas in times of peace a country's political leadership should dictate policy and political moves, in the event of war the baton must pass to the military. These theories did not deny that the political leadership possessed sole authority to set war aims and to impose their attainment on the armed forces. However, they did claim that from the moment aims were set and the task of their attainment imposed on the military, the involvement of the political leadership in the actual conduct of the war came to an end. From here on, everything became subject to military judgment. War, after all, is a decisive, fateful contest, one of life and death; hence, all the resources of a nation at war, spiritual and material, must be committed to the attainment of war aims. Judgment in war, in this view, is synonymous with military judgment and must be left to the discretion of specialists, to the military leadership, who alone bear responsibility for attaining a favorable outcome in the field of battle. Thus, "irrelevant" considerations, those of a nonmilitary, such as a social or political, nature, must not be allowed to get in the way of military activity; they must not shackle those engaged in military work. Only at war's end would place of pride revert to the political leadership, with political considerations once again becoming paramount.

Such theories produce a strident militaristic approach to the affairs of state, whereby the military rules the nation. Most states, especially the democracies, were reluctant to establish a domineering general staff on the Prussian model. One may assume that the thinkers who came to such sweeping conclusions concerning the primacy of military judgment over the civilian would in the present day of national security and total war come to different conclusions, even with the same methodology and logic that they had used before. It seems, though, that some of their latter-day followers in various countries have pursued their theories without having inherited their talents.

Existential concerns, including those of national security, are salient features of life in a modern state. This state of affairs, which is felt in all spheres of life, requires constant vigilance in matters related to national security, and not just in times of war. Thus, security in our age depends increasingly on the overall strength of a society, deriving as it does from all aspects of national life, not just, or even primarily, military power. Hence, military considerations must not be allowed primacy over the totality of other considerations. The military element is only one component in the multifaceted character of total war. The leadership of the armed forces represents a part, while the political leadership represents the whole, the broad perspective of the nation's resources in its fight for survival. Therefore, he who bears responsibility for national leadership and the conduct of the affairs of state, he who both has authority and controls the totality of national institutions and wherewithal, must also bear the responsibility for leading the nation and governing the state—including the nurturing and employment of its military power, and the setting of its war aims.

Most militaries are marked by conservatism, by thinking based on precedent, and as such they are hostile to new developments and innovation. Not for nothing has it been said that war is too serious to be left to generals. Strategy is no longer a narrow, military discipline. It is a multidisciplinary endeavor, involving multifaceted considerations and effort, both national and international in scope, and involving all spheres of life.

If one bears this in mind, one may understand why twentieth-century wars, wars of the modern age, have been conducted by the supreme leaderships of nations, both in democracies and dictatorships. It can be argued that when the national leadership happens

prerequisite for their very survival. Leadership ought to motivate people. The actions of a true leader are not dictated by the momentary whims prevalent on Market Square but by an objective view of goals, against the backdrop of an uncompromising consideration of the limits of power.

The leadership of modern armed forces is expected to embody ethical values and professional excellence. At the same time, though, it does not necessarily have a comprehensive perspective. The military echelon is subordinate to the political national leaders, yet in the final analysis there is an ongoing dynamic, a synthesis of mutual influence between the two levels of leadership, the political and the military. The boundaries between them are neither well defined nor clear and distinct, but relative.

CHAPTER 4

THE PURSUIT OF WORLD PEACE AND INTERNATIONAL SECURITY

World War I was a total war, one that extracted a heavy price in blood. People were horrified at the dreadful, senseless carnage, and their horror engendered a yearning that this be the last war, "the war to end all wars." At war's end there was a widespread feeling that mankind could not bear the bloodshed caused by total war. Thus, out of the rubble and death rose hope and optimism, and the establishment of the League of Nations, an organization expected to confer peace and security on all nations and to usher in a new age.

Until the establishment of the League of Nations, international law had considered war a legitimate vehicle for the advancement of national policy. In the nineteenth century, states based their security on alliances with other states. With the establishment of the League of Nations in the second decade of the twentieth century, an attempt was made to attain collective, multinational security and to limit war as a means for attaining national goals.

Reality disproved the vision. The hopes pinned on the League of Nations were not realized; World War II was more horrible than its predecessor. At the end of that second war, when the victors established the United Nations, mankind once again based its hopes on an international organization and authority that would underpin collective security, maintenance of peace, and respect for the liberty and rights of all nations. However, even after the establishment of the League of Nations, the product of hope and optimism, and subsequently of the United Nations, the product of realism and pessimism, nations nonetheless, in their pursuit of security, continued to rely on alliances (such as NATO and the Warsaw Pact), on balances of power, and on deterrence.

Implicit in the idea of a social contract is the concession by the individual of part of his freedom or sovereignty to a central authority—a state and its institutions—in order to facilitate social order. In like manner, the twentieth-century world order demands of the state a part of its sovereignty in order to facilitate the establishment of a central world authority, like the League or UN, that is able to guarantee the existence, the security, and the integrity of all states.

In an earlier day, Immanuel Kant preached the idea of basing the security of nations on such an international order. However, experience has shown that nations do not accept international authority, all the more so since international organizations, which are supposed to constitute a sort of federal world authority, do not represent an objective entity guided by the principle of international justice. In fact, the idea that "might is right" still rules. The UN was not established on a proportional or egalitarian basis, either in principle or fact. Its member states operate in blocs based on interests—political and regional, at times permanent, at times ad hoc. States considered "great powers" at the time of the UN's establishment serve as permanent members of the Security Council and have unilateral prerogative to veto its decisions. The UN is neither a federation that rules its member states nor a confederation subject to their rule.

Kant believed that the division of the world into states is the natural state of affairs. He felt that a necessary condition for a permanent peace between states ("eternal peace") was a supreme world authority to guarantee their security. He saw the establishment of republican governments—democracies, in today's terminology—as another necessary condition for a permanent peace.

The problem of international security has not been solved in the twentieth century by the establishment of a Kantian world order, through the League of Nations or the UN. Yet a number of scholars have found that Kant's second condition for peace has proved valid: it is an incontrovertible fact that democratic states have not waged war against each other in the twentieth century. Their need for consensus might explain this. Matters of war and peace, the matter of the survival of the human race in the face of the dangers it faces from itself, depend on the mass of the citizenry, not just on leaders. Matters of war and peace between states depend to a great extent on their internal regimes, since the extent of a leader's freedom of action depends on it.

Leaders of nations, both authoritarian and democratic, are guided by values, impulses, and personal aspirations. However, when they want to implement a plan of action, they must mobilize popular support, convincing the people of the necessity of their proposed course of action. This is especially the case when the plan under consideration involves a collective effort and the sacrifice of life. In a state under an authoritarian regime, it is easier for the ruling elite to impose its will on the people by means of propaganda, intimidation, lies, and coercion; hence, the threshold of difficulty for initiating wars is lower in an authoritarian state than in a democracy. As war always involves social disruption and risk to life, under the conditions of freedom of information, discussion, and political organization that mark the democratic state, it is not easy for the governing elite to persuade the citizenry to fight a war that is not waged for clearly existential ends.

Another difference between authoritarian and democratic regimes is that in the former, whether they are ruled by cliques devoid of values or by ideological-religious elites, the idea that the ends justify the means generally underpins policy. Thus, these leaders view war as a legitimate vehicle for attaining goals—personal, ideological, or national—while democracies can only go to war to defend their existences, basic values, or vital assets. Keeping this in mind, one can understand that the two types of regime foster not only different national goals, cultures, and ways of life but different strategic goals—the one offensive, the other defensive.

A liberal democratic regime is almost always unable, by virtue of its defining characteristics, to wage an offensive war if it cannot convince most of its citizens of the justice of such a war. This inhibition is particularly strong when what is under consideration is war with another democracy. A circular condition obtains here: for a war to be just, it must be for the defense of national existence or vital interests, defense against an aggressor; otherwise, a people that lives in a democracy would not be convinced of the necessity of such an extreme measure. Thus, a democracy is not able to initiate hostilities with another democracy—just as the second democracy is inhibited from initiating hostilities, for the very same reasons.

If Kant is right, and the conditions for peace (that is, security) are to have a world authority whose judgments are binding and to have democratic regimes, the key to national security lies in international security. The key to international security, in turn, lies in the establishment of a binding, democratic world federation, in which the democratic states are represented on a regional basis and the great powers possess no veto power. In this way, a double system of democratic checks and balances will be created, one on the national level and one on the international. These principles have many ramifications. For instance, the principle of nonintervention in the internal affairs of a sovereign state would lose its validity if it transpired that a certain state threatened the peace of other states. Outside intervention would be permitted in such a case, not only to check aggression and right a wrong but to bring about a change in regime in a "potentially aggressive" state as well, to guarantee peace and security. Under the ideal circumstances of universal democratic pluralism, a country's form of government ceases to be strictly its internal affair, and the principle of nonintervention loses its sanctity.

These conclusions are morally valid and correct in principle. However, actual intervention must be subject to as objective criteria as possible. Procedures, rules, methods, and principles governing decisions regarding international intervention in the internal affairs of a state must be set, and intervention must be undertaken only when doing so is necessary to preserve the existence and liberty of other states. In any event, no state, or group of states, must be permitted to act on its own.

A democratic constitution may be forced on a state from the outside. However, it would be difficult to cast genuine democratic values by coercing the use of democratic outer forms. Authoritarian and democratic temperaments are spontaneous, indwelling forces—the force of nature in the individual, and the force of culture and ethos in society. Still, just as an individual's character can be changed through long-term education in a binding framework, so a democratic constitution and modes of behavior can be forced on an undemocratic society; influence can be gradually brought to bear on its political culture and scale of values until they are eventually rendered democratic not only nominally but in fact. Instillation of the essence, and not just form, of democratic value patterns is possible, but only through a long process.

In the meantime, as long as such a pluralistic, democratic world remains a utopian vision, the security of nations will be increasingly based on the principle of concession and adaptation on the one hand, and on deterrence and counterdeterrence on the other. If a certain state is convinced, even if mistakenly, that mutual deterrence between itself and its rival, or rivals, has unraveled, is no longer symmetrical, then war is liable to break out.

At the approach of the twenty-first century, the world can be divided not only into West and East but also between militant, benighted regimes and those that are peace loving. All this transpires under the backdrop of the objective tension between poor, despairing nations and those that are prosperous. This process of polarization is taking place concurrently with a strengthening of the bloc of democratic states. This was the background against which measures for a "world order" were taken democratically, without veto, during the Gulf War of 1991. This model of international intervention to prevent threats to world peace should be more thoroughly worked out and institutionalized. World democratization, then, if it is achieved, can have important ramifications on world, as well as national, security.

PART TWO
NATIONAL SECURITY DOCTRINE

CHAPTER 5

THE PRINCIPLES OF WAR AND THE ART OF WAR

THE CLASSICAL THEORY

By generally accepted theory of war, military history proves that war must be conducted in accordance with certain fixed principles. According to this view, these principles are general rules, as it were; universally valid, they apply to all wars. Developments in military technology and the changes they have wrought in the means and methods of war do not, in this view, detract from the validity of these fixed principles; such developments merely influence the manner of their implementation.

The idea that principles of war exist and may be viewed as laws or axioms rests on both empirical and logical grounds. The empirical claim is that the long history of warfare proves that the more a plan of war is based on correct application of the principles of war, the greater its chances of success. The logical claim derives from the assumption that all sciences are derived from laws; therefore, it is claimed, war also has laws.

The standard theories view the principles of war as mandatory injunctions, to serve as guidelines in the planning and conduct of war at all levels—the tactical, operational, and strategic—as well as in formulating combat doctrine and national security strategies. The principles of war, in this view, are the criteria for deriving and analyzing lessons from wars; to disregard them is perilous and may lead to failure. This view recognizes that application of the principles of war is subject to contingent developments, changing times, and circumstances, to which they must be adapted. Furthermore, even though these principles are universal, enumerations of them vary: each military establishment draws up its own list of principles in accordance with the objectives for which it is maintained, its geopolitical environment, and conditions in its theater of operations.

Principles that have usually appeared on such lists include maintenance of the aim, surprise, concentration of force, economy of force, security, mobility, initiative, cooperation, morale, simplicity, flexibility, and unity of command.

THE PRINCIPLES—SUBSTANCE, NOT FORM

There are grounds for taking exception to the classical theory, which considers the principles of war as laws and rules. It would perhaps be more correct to view such principles as categories of the essential components of war rather than as formal rules. The term "principle" derives from the Latin *principium*, meaning "beginning" or "foundation." Indeed, the principles of war are simply the fundamental components of warfare—they are the substance, not the form; they are the properties of war.

No battle, campaign, or war is anything more than an individual case in history. What is not an "individual case" is the dynamic nature of war: every battle, campaign, or war is a continuous process, involving an infinite number of details, phenomena, events, and acts, such as the extent to which aims have been maintained, degree of alertness, concentration or dispersion of force in time and space, morale, and the like. The sum total of details, phenomena, and events is nothing but the "materials" that constitute war; they are its building blocks, its organic parts. The principles of war are not "laws" but the various groups of components that constitute war— they *are* war. For example, the number of instances of "maintenance of the aim" in a particular battle is equal to the sum of individual such instances by the combatants and commands. All such instances taken together make up a set termed "maintenance of the aim." Furthermore, every principle can be divided into subgroups. For example, the principle of maintenance of the aim consists of such maintenance by the high command, by the various combat arms, and by units down to the individual soldier. This example may, of course, be applied to every one of the other principles, while the list of principles themselves reflects the division of war into its primary principles (fundamental parts). It is possible to perform that division according to varying cross-sections. That is, one may sort war's components in different ways or reduce the number of principles. Planning for war at all levels and the conduct of wars and battles embody a synthesis of the principles of war, something of a "mix" of the various types of "materials."

The principles of war, then, are merely categories containing the entire spectrum of the main materials that determine the essence of a war and shape its character in accordance with their relative proportions in the overall mix. When emphasis in a battle is put on the element of surprise, for instance, it is difficult to implement a concentration of force and effort, since the process of concentrating forces is liable to be discovered by the enemy and compromise the element of surprise. Sometimes principles complement each other, while at other times one may be achieved at the expense of another. The relative weight of each, in every war and at every level, is determined by need, capability, and the experience and intuition of a command.

Over the ages, then, lists of the principles of war have derived from the particular military requirements of each nation's armed forces at a particular time. They are not laws, rules, or injunctions but categories of types—the various types of the constituent parts of war. They are its main substance, and they shape its many facets at every level.

THE ART OF WAR

The division of war into main categories, "principles," as well as the implementation of those principles, is subject to, and influenced by, many factors. Developments in science and military technology have had decisive impacts. Everything is subject to change except the nature of man and the nature of war: war is full of surprises, and its developments and outcome are impossible to calculate or predict in advance; the factors that engender it and the events that bear upon it exert their impacts in no clear-cut way. Some of these factors are rational, others are not; some are simply caused by nature. Neither are the enemy's moves and reactions predictable. The imprint these factors leave on war is, a priori, one of lack of certainty. Furthermore, misunderstandings, difficulties in communication, and lack of perspective also tend to render the circumstances of war hazy (thus the concept "fog of battle"). The exercise of leadership in war involves groping between fact and illusion; it requires experience, skill, daring, imagination, and sharp senses.

When military leadership sets out to assess a situation or to plan, or actually conduct, a war, it relies on professional know-how and specialization in all that touches upon the means of warfare, the motives and objectives of the belligerents, and a complex aggregate of social, political, and economic factors. However, all this is not enough; because of the extent to which chance in war is decisive, because of the "fog of battle" and the necessity of reacting to developments and making decisions on an ad hoc basis, it is impossible to plan or wage war according to formulas. Therefore, although systematic knowledge and proficiency in the principles of war are, in themselves, necessary to war planning and competent military leadership, they are not sufficient. Since there can be no set formula for quantifying the principles of war and assigning their relative importance when they clash, and no "recipe" for determining the optimal ratio between the various principles, the quality of military leadership depends on experience, courage, ability, inspiration, and genius. The implementation of the principles of war and the conduct of war depend more upon the force of leadership than upon formal command authority.

War, then, is not an exact science but the art of finding the right balance between its parts (the various principles) and achieving their optimal implementation. Science is merely a tool of the art of war; a war or battle, at all levels, can be planned and waged with the same scientific and technological means in diametrically different ways. The mix of parts in the different plans will be different, yet each could be brilliant and all their results excellent. The difference between them would be similar to the difference between the work of different artists who paint the same object differently.

Everything changes over time: the tools of warfare, historical data, fundamental strategic factors, the quality of the combatants, the list of the principles of war themselves. What does not change, what is fixed, is the art of war: the ability of the command that unifies, that creates a unity out of a multiplicity of parts and fuses them into an optimal whole.

Israel's national security doctrine, in all that relates to the principles of war, the art of war, and the proper measure of things, has been forged against a backdrop of constraints deriving from a disadvantageous ratio of forces. Because of that, Israel has chosen a defense strategy based on calculated risks. One of the most salient of such risks is that the IDF is structured mainly for the offensive, at the expense of its defensive capabilities. Another salient risk is reflected in a very high dependence on early warning from intelligence about developing military threats. These matters will be addressed in subsequent chapters.

CHAPTER 6
ISRAEL: NATIONAL GOALS, SECURITY DOCTRINE AND POLICY

THE ROLE OF THE STATE AND NATIONAL GOALS

The architects of Israeli national security doctrine knew that many nations would not readily reconcile themselves, without objections, to Jewish sovereignty, as something legitimate and self-evident, that does not require explanation or proof. The hostility and caution with which various Western states have regarded Israel have been influenced by their international political, economic, and military interests (legitimate in themselves). However, while such interests are usually what determine the relations between states, there is sometimes in Western countries, where Israel is concerned, the additional, background element of anti-Semitism—which also contributes to anti-Israeli positions. In Africa and Asia, whose cultures do not derive from the Christian tradition, the opposite seems to be the case—anti-Israeli interests are liable to engender anti-Semitism.

Opposition to Israel, whether the result of anti-Semitism or national interest, has had a direct impact on the role and purpose of the State of Israel. The dispersion of the Jews among the nations, the tragic results of that dispersion, and anti-Semitism resulted in the fact that the role of the State of Israel preceded, both logically and chronologically, the state's establishment. The Zionist idea, which engendered the state of the Jews, posited that this state must be a sovereign shelter and fortress for the entire Jewish people, a center of moral and physical strength under obligation to protect them, directly and indirectly, wherever they may be.

This concept has had many ramifications, including for Israeli national security doctrine and strategy. The State of Israel, as the state of the Jewish people, has a link to the Jewish Diaspora, and a considerable portion of the Jews in the Diaspora feel a strong attachment to Israel. The fabric of that relationship nourishes the force of Israeli nationalism; it is obvious that the strength of the State of Israel must be based not only on the Jews who live in it but also on the Jewish people in the Diaspora, who are the state's only permanent ally.

Concerning the balance of power, this is a source of great strength. At the same time, though, it is an important constraining factor, since this strength renders the Jews of the Diaspora de facto hostages of the State of Israel; that is, Israel may find itself subjected to blackmail over Diaspora Jews. This may hobble Israeli foreign relations—political, economic, and military—a state of affairs requiring its successive governments to navigate with caution the impediments related to specifically Jewish considerations.

The limitations of power that have bearing on Israel's national goals and manifest themselves in inability to force the Arabs, through a military decision, to end their conflict with it and reconcile themselves to its existence, can be seen in sharp relief: forcing an overall decision of the conflict by military means is an option for only one side—that of the Arabs. The quantitative balance of power precludes any chance of Israel's forcing a conclusive decision upon the Arab states, while the opposite case—that of a final decision over Israel by the Arabs—is credible; were they to attain an overall victory over Israel, they would seal its fate. The clear knowledge that Israel would not get a "second chance," that if it is defeated once it will not rise again, has added force, as if of a divine injunction, to the perceived obligation of Israeli society to devote itself to the range of security-related issues. The matter of security is perceived as a fundamental requirement of Israel's very existence, and it has been the main national consideration ever since the War of Independence.

Israel can and will remain able to win wars—this ability is a necessary condition for its existence—but it will never be able by a military victory to dictate its will on the Arab and Islamic domain, stretching as it does from the Atlantic Ocean to the Persian Gulf and beyond. The imposition of one's will on an enemy requires the forcible negation and withholding of his sovereignty, pending fulfillment of the terms dictated to him. This is beyond Israel's power.

From the outset, Israeli national security thinking has been predicated on the fact it is the fate of the State of Israel to be permanently and irreversibly in the position of the "few against the many," from the standpoint of the demographic and geographic balance of power between itself and the Arab world. The Arabs enjoy quantitative superiority in manpower, resources, matériel, geographic size, and potential allies. Since Israel lacks strategic depth—its area, as the theater of a modern war, is very small, basically constituting an operational rather than strategic zone—it does not enjoy the luxury of being able to choose between a "rigid defense" and a "flexible" one. The Arabs, for their part, enjoy strategic depth of the proportions of a great power.

Thus, there is an asymmetry between Israel and the Arab states that puts Israel at a distinct disadvantage. Israeli victories, as many as there have been, can only assure its simple existence, not necessarily the attainment of other national goals. However, an overall Arab victory would give the Arabs everything they ever wanted: what for Israel is a necessary and sufficient condition for its preservation is for the Arabs a sufficient condition both for forcing a decision and attaining their overall goals.

It was clear to the founders of the State of Israel—which was born in a war waged against it by the Arabs with the declared intention of exterminating it in its infancy as a national entity—that the Arabs would not readily reconcile themselves with an alien presence in a region they perceived as belonging to themselves. The founders knew that the long process of the Return to Zion would come about in three stages: a war to defend the Zionist enterprise, including its physical and national existence; the establishment of peace; and finally, establishment and integration in the region, while preserving its uniqueness as the state of the Jewish people, with the goal of becoming an exemplary state. Their intention was to make the 1949 cease-fire lines borders of peace, on the basis of which Israel would integrate itself into the region—this was the national goal Israel set for itself at the time.

However, it was clear that the age of peace and integration would only come after the Arabs despaired of ever destroying the state of the Jews by force of arms and reconciled themselves with its existence as a final, unchallengeable fact. No one in Israel deluded himself into thinking that as soon as the state was established, it would enjoy calm. In fact, it was obvious that the Arabs would not abandon their aggressive war aims, that they would take action against Israel in every sphere, diplomatic, economic, and military, and that aggressive conflicts including military harassment, wars of attrition, and large-scale wars could be expected. It was clear that the state would have to live by its sword for many years to come. Under these circumstances, the IDF was not going to be an ordinary military, one that awaits "D-day," but rather one for which it is always D-day, that is destined to fight continuously for many years. Faced with that vision, Israel had to brace itself for the long term and formulate a national security doctrine that was both realistic and to the point.

NATIONAL SECURITY DOCTRINE

Israel's security doctrine is its basic and permanent plan for preparedness, deployment, and war in the defense of the national existence of the State of Israel as the state of the Jewish people.

The term "national plan" points to an overall perspective of national security, not limited to or focused exclusively on its narrowly military component. The term "permanent" indicates that what is envisioned are basic, fixed geopolitical and strategic matters, not passing circumstances or particular cases. The concepts "preparedness," "deployment," and "war" relate to components of security, since preparedness and deployment apply to the organization of the state, the economy, and infrastructure for an emergency, and the concept of war points to the possible military aims of war and the manner in which a war must, or can, be directed and the military built up accordingly.

The doctrine, formulated in Israel's formative years, immediately after its appearance in the Middle Eastern arena, was distinguished by analytical and critical thought of a creative and generalized nature and of a high level of abstraction. The architects of this approach pinpointed the basic, permanent strategic factors that characterized Israel's circumstances, defined threats and constraints, and determined the goals and aims that could be adopted within the limits of its power.

As a plan for the overall organization of the nation for defense and war, Israeli national security doctrine derives from, and is composed of, various elements, the first of which is the purpose of Israel—that is, its national goal. To this element are added other factors and constraints, from the balance of power and war aims (those of Israel and its enemies) through the overall national organization of all resources (manpower, strategic stocks, dispersion of population and industry) and on to the build-up of forces and the organization of second-tier units.

As long as Israel faces the possibility of war with a large, even all-inclusive, Arab coalition, it must base its existence on its assault power and endeavor to maintain military superiority—despite its inferiority in the overall balance of power—by converting its entire staying power to that required to force a decision. Israeli national security doctrine can be summed up in the single phrase: an almost total forfeiture of the staying power in favor of optimal assault power.

The architects of the Israeli doctrine, recognizing that Israel's staying power is inferior to that of its enemies, understood that in everything related to assault power—military superiority—there was a chance for Israel to enjoy relative advantage. Given the vital importance of defending the country's existence, they invested all its resources in assault power, in military strength. The entire Israeli population is conscripted during war as a reserve. That Israel has built up its assault power at the expense of its staying power has become apparent in all spheres—from national expenditure on security to the nature of the defense budget itself. Israel invests in assault forces at the expense of vital stocks of ammunition and equipment. In that way, Israel can conduct offensive wars of decision, although this approach weakens its ability to wage defensive wars of attrition.

The IDF is the "Israel Defense Forces" by appellation but the "Israel Offense Forces" in substance. Because of the hair-breadth calculations involved, Israeli national security doctrine can be considered an epitome of military thought, worthy of inclusion among the classics of the art of war.

It was obvious to the architects of Israeli doctrine that such military superiority would derive not from quantity but from quality. Furthermore, they knew it could be maintained only at the expense of staying power, with all that implies: Israeli society pays a very heavy price in such areas as its economy, social needs, and education. These areas suffer from neglect because the national awareness, effort, and powers of creativity are mortgaged by security needs. Over the long term, Israel's moral and social strength may also be undermined. Nonetheless, its military superiority has made possible decisive victories over the Arab confrontation states and expeditionary forces of their allies. These expeditionary forces augmented those of the confrontation states, were integrated into their theaters of operation, and took part in their campaigns against Israel. Distant allies of the confrontation states that sent expeditionary forces were not vulnerable to Israel's deterrent power, and they accordingly never worried about it. That was another fact limiting Israeli power.

NATIONAL SECURITY POLICY

Security policy is derived from security doctrine, and its purpose is the current, flexible implementation of that doctrine. It is the translation of security doctrine into the language of day-to-day developments, of dynamic political and military moves and processes, as determined by national requirements. While security doctrine is an unvarying factor, security policy is a varying one—it is dynamic and undergoes flexible adjustment to changing circumstances.

When surveying the accomplishments of the State of Israel, one cannot but note that those in the field of defense are astounding; when one examines the early Jewish collective creativity, it would be difficult not to acknowledge the establishment of the IDF. The point is not just divisions and air and naval forces, but the original ideas, over the years, of the architects of security and combat doctrines; it is thanks to these ideas that the few can maintain military superiority over the many. In Israel, the concept of security deals with existence; hence, the Jewish military is a unique entity, which by its very essence reflects the totality of the nation's fate.

CHAPTER 7

THE AIMS OF WAR

There is a hierarchy of war aims: overall, military, strategic, and tactical. The relationship between aims is as that between cause and effect, between ends and means. Each of the aims is a means, as it were, for attaining an aim above it in the hierarchy.

War aims are political aims; they derive from a nation's goals and the overall balance of power. Military war aims derive from overall (political) war aims and from the military balance of power, and they have a bearing on the political aims. Victory, defeat, or stalemate in war are judged strictly by one criterion: the attainment of the political aims. The attainment of the military aims is not sufficient for victory, or even necessary. The logic of war can tolerate a situation in which the side that wins militarily is defeated in the war (it can win the battles but lose the war). The converse is also true: the side that loses militarily can conceivably win the war.

Israel's security doctrine serves its national goals, and its basic war aims constitute a fundamental element of its security doctrine. Overall war aims and military war aims are virtually synonymous with the term "security doctrine." Security doctrine constitutes the theoretical underpinning of the attainment of war aims. Thus, these aims determine, to a great extent, policy concerning the allocation of resources to security, national priorities, deployment and preparation for war, operational plans, and doctrine governing the structure of forces. That is, they have impact on the entire range of topics and areas dealt with by the country's security doctrine. Without a prior definition of basic war aims, it would be impossible to work out a security doctrine and adopt a purposeful security plan, one appropriate to the specific geopolitical and strategic conditions with which Israel must contend.

The aims of a war are only the basis for planning. Each individual case, whether political or strategic, and each instance of operational planning, calls for specific evaluation and a proper application of the principles that are contained in the security doctrine and security policy and are reflected in the basic war aims, both overall and military. Concerning Israel's war aims, it has already been mentioned that its staying power is weaker than that of the Arab world, that it cannot impose its will on that world. As long as the Arab world is united in its enmity toward Israel and maintains a potential war coalition against it, Israel's only option is reliance on its assault power, and its only conceivable war aim, basic and overall, is strictly defensive: the thwarting of Arab attempts to defeat it. The security strategy Israel has adopted is thus essentially a defensive one.

Israel's national goals and the limits of its power have dictated a strategy of compromise. A strategy of compromise is a rational strategy, rooted in an understanding of the limits of power and a reconciliation with those limits. A "rogue state"—a state that adopts an "absolute strategy" and sets out to attain ambitious war aims without paying attention to limits to its power—ultimately fails and pays a high price. A strategy of compromise derives from moderate national goals; it does not define rigid goals. One cannot predict the outcome of world trends, political or social; thus, compromise allows freedom of action within the historical dialectics that result from changing circumstances and opportunities. After all, an interest deemed vital today may seem less so tomorrow.

Since it was clear from the outset that the circumstance of being few against many would prevent Israel from imposing its will on the Arabs by means of a military decision, it followed that Israel's basic political war aim could not be territorial. The aim of war had to be mainly defensive: defense of its existence and freedom. This position set the bounds of the national war aims Israel could conceivably pursue. The truth of the matter is that the existential war aim "saved" Israeli security doctrine, since without ambitious war aims, security doctrine lacks a military component and is virtually meaningless. There is no choice but to rely on a "natural," intuitive aim that is indispensable and perceived by all as existential and not requiring proof. Hence, Israeli security doctrine is predicated on a defensive aim—deterrence, or prevention—and on the enhancement of Israeli bargaining power by means of military, territorial, and political attainments.

Thus, the war aims, derived as they are from such a defensive strategy, have but one purpose: the frustration of attempts to defeat Israel militarily. These aims are obviously defensive—their purpose is to prevent change, not to bring it about. They are not the result of Israeli military initiative but rather of Israeli reaction; they are not aimed at realizing goals but of thwarting them.

While Israel cannot attain an overall decision of the conflict by force, and its overall war aim is defensive, its military aims are offensive—inflicting stinging defeats on the Arabs and enhancing its own strategic position, as long as the Arabs wage war against it. Just as security doctrine is merely a basic national plan to defend a country and not a specific plan for a particular war, and just as that doctrine is related to the overall war aim and not to a specific aim, and just as military organization is merely the basic structure of units and formations, and not an a priori "order of battle" for a particular operation, so it is with military aims. The doctrine does not deal with specific aims but rather with categories of them, as described below.

DESTRUCTION OF FORCES

The perennial question in war deals with the choice between the destruction of enemy forces and conquest of his territory, and the reconciliation of the two. Destruction of forces usually confers temporary advantage. It reflects an immediate, short-term military decision; the balance of military power is altered only temporarily, especially if the injured side has a greater staying power—if it has the wherewithal rapidly to rebuild or rehabilitate its defeated forces.

Israeli security doctrine, for various reasons, has required planners to think in terms of quick and early military decisions; the enemy must be administered a painful defeat by destroying a significant portion of his forces and capturing a portion of his territory. Nevertheless, it was clear to the architects of Israel's security doctrine that in light of the theater in which Israel operates, the destruction of an Arab force would be only temporary and would not change the overall balance of power; the resources of the Arab world, in manpower and matériel, relative to Israel are limitless, and with the help of outside powers it would be quickly able to restore its armed forces. The petroleum-derived economic weight, purchasing power, and geographic size of Arab countries confer upon them a position of strength in the international community and also put the best military technologies in the world, quantitatively and qualitatively, at their disposal.

Israel had always known that it could never even temporarily negate its enemies' sovereignty or dictate peace terms by destroying their forces. The destruction of military forces means destroying their organization and preventing them from fulfilling their designated functions. Destroyed forces have sustained heavy losses in men and equipment; they have been worn down, are no longer in a functional condition, and usually have low morale. Even if such forces continue to fight, they cannot do so as they did when properly functioning; everything must be improvised. However, since men and equipment survive, it is only a matter of time before they are reorganized and again able to perform their originally designated tasks. The process of rehabilitating such forces—even entire divisions, and naval and air forces—is rapid. If arms and equipment are readily available, an entire military can be rehabilitated within two or three years.

However, the destruction of forces, even if its impact on the balance of power is only temporary, removes the direct, immediate existential threat; hence, it is obviously an important and "practical" objective. Furthermore, the more thorough the destruction of forces and the larger the force that has been mauled, the greater the deterrent effect achieved, since the enemy is more likely to be convinced he has no chance of attaining a decision by military means.

CONQUEST OF TERRITORY

The conquest of territory, in and by itself, does not constitute the attainment of viable war aims. However, it does confer political and military advantage, and it is a negotiating asset for a postwar settlement. Hence, it is sometimes more important than the destruction of forces. Nevertheless, the conquest of territory also raises the question of how long it can be held. An elementary assumption of the architects of Israel's security doctrine was that its ability to retain captured territory over the long term was limited. This was the case both from the standpoint of the international community, which would not reconcile itself to unilateral annexation within a world order reached after two world wars, and from the standpoint of Israel's weight in the Middle East and world relative to that of the Arabs.

The conquest of territory in war spurs the enemy to ask for a cease-fire, thus expediting an end to hostilities. The benefit for Israel in retaining conquered territory is that it improves the strategic position of the IDF; it adds defensive depth, and it enhances deterrence, since it positions the IDF closer to strategic targets in enemy territory.

The liability inherent in conquest is that in addition to strengthening the subjective motivation for revenge, it also gives the enemy whatever objective motivation derives from the criticality of the interest involved. The greater the importance to the enemy of the interest under contention and his willingness to exert himself to restore it, the more he is likely to step up the pace of his military build-up.

SPACE FOR MANEUVER AND DEPLOYMENT

Deployment of the IDF on vital operational ground, either inside Israel before the first shot is fired or inside enemy territory during the fighting, allows it to demonstrate its superior ability to force a decision in mobile, armored warfare. The attainment of such strategic advantage is likely to seal the outcome of a war even before the decisive blow has been delivered. The success of such a move sometimes constitutes a prerequisite for conducting a decisive campaign and thereby avoiding a war of attrition; the danger that the enemy could maneuver the IDF into a war of attrition after proper deployment is reduced. Given the proper deployment of forces, the effect of deterrence is immediate.

Deployment on vital operational ground produces an optimal balance, both from a defensive standpoint and an offensive one. Such optimality permits complete implementation of the classic principle of concentration of forces. On the one hand, the very deployment of forces creates a threat to a variety of objectives, permitting a choice between possible lines of advance. The enemy is forced to disperse his forces defensively, in order to meet a variety of potential threats. On the other hand, positioning forces deep in the enemy's territory prevents him from advancing into Israel; if he did so, he would expose the flanks and rear of his own forces. Thus, such deployment on vital operational ground deep in enemy territory confers both offensive and defensive advantage.

HITTING ALLIES OF CONFRONTATION STATES

This category of aims includes the destruction of the economic infrastructure and accomplishment of other vital strategic aims, as circumstances require, inside the territory of the enemy's natural allies, through strategic bombing. The IDF must have the capability to inflict painful damage to vital objectives in distant countries, to deter them from attacking Israeli population centers and from sending expeditionary forces when war breaks out. If the IDF did not maintain such a capability, distant states would enjoy immunity to painful counterblows.

DESTRUCTION OF INFRASTRUCTURE AND THREATENING CAPITALS

A danger to Israel's very existence could materialize if its assault power collapsed and all appeared lost. Under such circumstances, no doubt should be allowed about the choice that remained—the automatic waging of total war. Intermediate stages in escalation must be observed, though, before the IDF stops being selective about its objectives and means. In order to avoid the desperate possibility of escalating to total war, flexible choices are required, that is, military objectives that permit gradual, provocative escalation by progressively painful blows.

Among the extreme aims of total war are the destruction of economic infrastructure and other vital strategic targets, attacks on the centers of government, and threats to capitals and their possible occupation. From the early 1950s on, Israeli security doctrine has posited that conquering enemy capitals is undesirable. The conquest of an enemy capital would require overrunning much of his strategic depth. Since a war would almost certainly be against a coalition, the capture of one capital would not be enough to force the outcome. Nevertheless, such a possibility has been considered for certain conditions of escalation, as a deterrent measure.

CHAPTER 8
STRATEGY OF DETERRENCE

The purpose of the security doctrine adopted by Israel is to assure the states's existence by force of arms as long as the Arabs continue their efforts to weaken and destroy it. Israel has opposed aggressive Arab war aims with a strategy of deterrence, the intention of which is the prevention of hostile initiatives against itself. The goal of Israeli military power, according to this doctrine, is to deter the Arabs from going to war and, should deterrence prove inadequate, to defeat them.

The strategy of deterring Arab attack was adopted by Israel because the war aims Israel must attain are essentially defensive—the thwarting of Arab attempts to exterminate it. The objective of deterrence, then, is the prevention of war; wars are unnecessary, needless, and harmful, even when Israel wins them decisively. If war breaks out nonetheless, it must end in a quick, decisive victory by Israel alone, without the active military participation of allies, so as to enhance Israel's deterrent image and obviate a long-term war of attrition and to reduce, to the extent possible, loss of life and matériel. Furthermore, if Israel is fated to fight needless wars, it is necessary not only to reduce damage as much as possible but to try to derive some benefit from what is intrinsically a bad situation: to damage Arab war machines as much as possible, seize territory, and improve cease-fire lines for subsequent bargaining. The aim is to demonstrate to the Arabs that they can derive little glory from the path of war, that as long as they choose that path they will find there only shameful defeat. Ideally, their motivation to keep trying their luck with force of arms will wane.

The deterrent effect of the IDF is enhanced not only by victory in full-scale wars but by operations between wars, operations that are part of Israel's ongoing defensive activities. Such activities include security measures, painful reprisals, commando raids, special operations deep in enemy territory, and demonstrations of prowess in military technology. Such measures are also employed to increase a sense of frustration in the opposing camp and heighten the deterrent value of the IDF.

A dilemma arises concerning the proper degree of deterrence. Excessive deterrent measures cause the enemy to feel degraded, bringing home his military inferiority and helplessness and arousing a desire for vengeance. The idea is to achieve a meaningful deterrent effect, causing the enemy to think twice before embarking upon aggression; however, to inculcate an awareness of his own inferiority spurs him to learn the lessons from his failures and step up the pace of his military preparations. Furthermore, the enemy becomes familiar with the methods used against him, acquires relevant experience, and learns to develop countermeasures, thus developing his ability to deal effectively with threats he faces in actual war. The dialectic, then, is clear. Effective deterrence is liable to strengthen the enemy and increase his determination, thus lowering the effectiveness of future deterrence. At the same time, whereas the appearance of weakness on Israel's part may lull the other side into lowering his guard and not building up his forces, neither would it force him to worry about the consequences of aggression—he would be more liable to try his luck.

A state's allies are part of its deterrent power. The Arab world has considerable weight in the international arena and a plethora of potential allies: the Muslim world, the countries of Africa and Asia, and various powers and blocs, as well. Israel has one permanent ally, and that is the Jewish people. It also enjoys the support of friendly powers.

An important assumption underlying Israeli security doctrine is that Israel must, to the extent possible, integrate into the world and regional communities—morally, politically, economically, and militarily—so as to prevent isolation. Thus, its deterrent power has relied in various periods on cooperation with other powers, mainly France and, later, the United States. Aid from these allies, especially the United States, has been mainly in the form of economic aid, the supply of arms, and diplomatic backing, such as, until 1992, deterring the Soviet Union from intervening militarily against Israel. In general, it may be said that Israel can rely on its allies more in what concerns the balance of power and deterrence between wars—diplomatic backing and economic or military aid, and imposing sanctions on the enemy—and less in participation in fighting when war actually breaks out. States do not go to war quickly for other states, and alliances, by their very nature, are transient.

Thus, Israel's overall power of deterrence, as predicated on its security doctrine, is based on the cumulative effect of repeated successes in thwarting the attempts of the Arab world to realize its aims against Israel through war. Actual deterrent power, deriving from the power of the IDF, and the outcomes of actual wars and battles are what have determined Israel's overall historical deterrent power. Considered in broad historical perspective, Israel's deterrent power has fulfilled its role in the state's security doctrine. The outcomes of wars and of military operations between wars, as well as the positions taken by the great powers, are the main factors that have induced the Arabs to forgo war and reconcile themselves with Israel's existence.

Furthermore, Israel's security doctrine is an open book. The "rules of the game" are sufficiently clear to all as to obviate war through an Arab miscalculation. Israel has established principles of deterrence that serve as clearly understood "red lines." Only when the enemy really wants war will he fail to notice those red lines, and cross them. There are four red lines—military threat, military attrition, full-scale war, and total war.

MILITARY THREAT

In the event of a threatening concentration of Arab forces, the IDF must be able to mobilize immediately and, should the enemy fail to withdraw forthwith, launch a preemptive strike. The IDF is a citizen military, and Israel cannot call up reserves and keep them statically deployed for a long period of time; that would paralyze life in the country and only weaken Israel's deterrent image. The justification in principle of preemptive strike is an important principle, since the national consensus hinges on it. Such a measure is especially justified in the case of the few against the many, the question of war and peace being one of life and death. The ultimate principle from which all else derives is simple: life may be endangered only in defense of one's own life, existence, and liberty.

The yardstick in a democratic society is majority opinion. When a country under direct threat goes to war to defend its existence, matters are as clear as daylight. However, when public opinion is divided, when general agreement is not immediate, there is room to suspect that a "war of choice," sometimes termed a "preventive war," has been embarked upon. The people harbor doubt, because only one thing is beyond question, people get killed in wars. All else is nebulous: the point to the war, its aims, its necessity. Hence, preventive war is problematic. After all, there is no certainty that refusing it will produce disaster in the future, while setting out upon a preventive war involves certain loss and pain in the present.

In contrast to preventive war, the aim of preemptive war, where Israel is concerned, is to anticipate a blow that is clearly coming, to take the initiative so as to gain the advantage of being the one to deliver the first blow, all in the light of the clear intentions and concrete preparations and actions of the enemy. Anticipation by the IDF of enemy moves is not illegitimate. A preemptive war is a necessary war, one that has been forced upon Israel, and its aim is anticipation of the enemy—"If someone rises to kill you, kill him first," as the sages of old put it. Such an undertaking is not controversial. However, a preventive war *is* controversial, since it involves a choice.

MILITARY ATTRITION

The whole Arab strategy of attrition—by means of hostile acts, harassment, firing on settlements, terrorism, large-scale wars of attrition—is countered by determined IDF countermeasures, including bombings, reprisal raids, even war. The factors Israel takes into consideration in deciding on its reactions are, on the one hand, the requirements of self-defense and the prevention of damage to the nation's morale, its self-image, and staying power, and on the other, the restoration and enhancement of its deterrent power.

FULL-SCALE WAR

Given such a possibility, Israel relies on the overall military balance of power between itself and the Arabs, and the IDF's offensive capabilities. Israel will not hesitate to strike preemptively. All vital strategic targets and population centers in potentially belligerent Arab states are vulnerable to the IDF air arm, Israel's main deterrent means. The Arab states must realize that any attempt on their part to attack Israel on land while it is unprepared and its reserves are not yet mobilized will result in their being subjected to the full destructive firepower of the Israeli Air Force. They should know that even if Israel's striking power on land is not yet mobilized and ready, the state can bring its immense firepower in the air to bear on them within minutes, whether inside Israel, along its borders, or deep in their own territory.

Israel has also emphasized the distinction between the strategic designation of the IDF as the *Israel Defense Forces* and its operational designation as the *Israel Offense Forces*. More than once IDF commanders have let it be known that the purpose of their mobile and armored land forces, noted for their offensive striking power, is to drive deep into enemy territory to attain operational and strategic objectives.

TOTAL WAR

In the event that Israel is subjected to total war involving massive casualties and danger to its very physical existence, it would take uncompromising countermeasures and not be selective in the means it employed. While in the Jewish ethos the ends do not justify the means, the matter of existence itself does justify them. To survive, to defend its existence and the lives of its people, the state of the Jewish people would employ any and all means.

The power of deterrence is a function of assault power. After all, without the ability to effect a decision, or at least to inflict damaging blows to the other side and exact a heavy price from it, deterrence loses its force. What determines whether a deterrent threat is "covered" or is just a "paper tiger" is not objective reasoning but the other side's subjective assessments. Israeli security doctrine recognizes this and requires full exploitation of the nation's strength to maintain the strongest military force possible. It is not only the size and quality of armed forces that have deterrent effect; the nature of one's military power also determines its deterrent value and contributes to its deterrent capability, no less than it does to its assault power.

The size of one's military budget also has bearing on deterrence. When military budgets grow relative to overall national expenditures, the power of deterrence also increases. The opposing side perceives military expenditures as evidence of military preparedness and power; thus, such expenditures have deterrent impact. However, they can also be interpreted as a threat and spur an opposing military build-up.

The willingness to employ force is another important deterrence-generating element. Willingness and the ability to use force presume a national consensus and the implicit acquiescence of the important outside powers. In turn, such a consensus and the attitude of the powers both hinge, in Israel's case, on not adopting overambitious war aims. Israel must take flexible political positions, avoid provocative behavior, and obtain the support and goodwill of the international community. A goal no less important is to bring home to the Arabs that there is a basis for an understanding with Israel. Nevertheless, Israel's behavior must be assertive, so as not to lose its credibility and deterrent effect. The opposite approach must absolutely be eschewed, that of taking aggressive, uncompromising positions and then showing flexibility. With such an approach, Israel would lose in every way: it would antagonize the international community by "climbing up a tall tree" with much fanfare, only to back down, thereby losing face and credibility.

The effectiveness of deterrence should be examined separately at each level of threat, including total war involving Israel's very existence; full-scale war; war of attrition; war by irregulars; and terrorism, both inside Israel and worldwide.

The effectiveness of a power of deterrence is relative—every threat requires an appropriate response. It is a matter of the proper degree: sometimes it is enough to threaten like measures in return, on the principle of "an eye for an eye"; at other times an express threat should be made to hit back with all the assault power available. In cases of a total existential threat, all means are legitimate; the aim is to prevent the extermination of an entire people.

Yet the threats Israel employs to deter must not be excessive. Excessive deterrence is liable to cause diplomatic damage, needlessly fan Arab hostility, and damage the chances for a reconciliation with them. It is also liable to be unjustified morally, mar Israel's self-image, and compromise its national consensus on security.

Thanks to its powers to effect a decision and exert deterrence, Israel has managed to exist and develop, and even to make progress toward Arab transition from total war against it to reconciliation with and acceptance of its existence. The end of the Cold War between East and West has also contributed to that process.

CHAPTER 9
THE STRUCTURE AND IMPLEMENTATION OF FORCE

Israeli security doctrine has been predicated on the assumption that IDF experience in the War of Independence, operational and organizational, would be inadequate for the future; the Arabs would plan future wars and improve their performance. Israel would obviously have to continue to maintain the IDF's qualitative superiority and see to it that the quantitative gap between the Arab armies and the IDF did not widen.

The considerations of "the few against the many," as well as of economics, imposed on Israel the principle of armed forces based on a militia; a large standing military was out of the question. The founders of the state attached the utmost importance to all components of national security, and not just to military power. They knew they would have to invest heavily in education, health, the absorption of immigrants, settlement, development of the Negev, and improvement and expansion of public services. While they gave top priority to military power, they were aware that there would be tight budgetary constraints and that not enough resources could be allocated to the military. Life and liberty would have to be assured by courage, resourcefulness, and the willingness of the state's youth to make sacrifices. With no chance of a quantitative balance with its enemies, Israel's fate hinged on quality. In the final analysis, of all components of power, quality was deemed the most important.

Israeli security doctrine has accepted the principle that the IDF must be able to win a war involving the worst-case scenario, that of all Arab states launching a joint, surprise attack. In the parlance of Israeli security doctrine, this contingency is referred to as "Case All."

Israel lacks strategic depth. Its area is small, and in a modern war it would constitute more of an operational theater than a strategic one—with or without the areas captured in the Six Day War. Only in the south, when Israel controlled the Sinai, did it enjoy any real strategic depth. Vital strategic targets in Israel are, from the standpoint of an Arab offensive, nothing but tactical targets. In other words, short enemy thrusts would endanger Israel; the enemy does not even have to mount a series of deep penetration attacks, and neither would he need additional strategic moves and maneuvers. Initial success in an Arab attack could very well result in the loss of vital strategic targets.

Israel's lack of strategic depth forces it to mobilize its reserve military immediately upon the manifestation of a threat and try to deliver a preemptive blow. In that way, Israel can hope to avoid a defensive war after a long, exhausting wait for the enemy to take the initiative, during which the reserves, and economy, would be paralyzed. Lack of strategic depth also forces the IDF to adopt a strategy of rigid defense, the aim of which is holding ground, rather than a strategy of flexible defense, aimed at destroying forces and forcing a military decision. Without sufficient operational depth, or depth for early warning, the danger exists that the reserve military might not be mobilized in time in the event of a surprise attack. To anticipate such a development and obviate the risk of larger armies' achieving immediate, initial success that threatens vital strategic objectives, the IDF established its Area Defense System (ADS).

The ADS is based on a network of fortified border settlements, backed up by military units. The location of new settlements over the years has been influenced by the ADS plan, with a view toward thickening, and eventually completing, the overall deployment of settlement networks in the border sectors.

The ADS is intended as a permanent defensive operational infrastructure. It is meant to force the enemy to allocate forces at the outset of an attack to overrun settlements, defended positions, and ADS units, thus delaying his advance and constraining his freedom of movement and room for maneuver. The ADS is also intended to serve as a base for a rigid defense, wherefrom the IDF can hold off the enemy in the defensive stage of operations. The ADS has made an important contribution over the years to Israel's military activity between wars. The idea for the ADS was derived from the lessons of the War of Independence, in which Jewish settlements had played a crucial role. Their steadfast resistance and contribution to the fighting had created the conditions for victory.

The fixed quantitative constraint that has fated Israel to permanent inferiority to the Arabs in the overall national balance of power has underpinned the Israeli doctrine of force structure. It is a doctrine meant to provide an answer to this challenging question: What is to be done, from the standpoint of the few against the many, concerning large standing enemy armies?

Over the years, Israeli planners have been guided by the assumption, which has become a principle of the state's security doctrine, that the IDF has no chance of competing with the Arab armed forces quantitatively. Hence, Israel must exhaust all its national resources in war and rely on the high qualitative level of its society in all spheres, moral, social, and scientific-technological—that is, on professional excellence and original military thinking. The qualitative gap between Israel and the Arabs must be a difference of essence and not of degree. Israel's leadership has tried to make sure that its quantitative disadvantage does not decline below a ratio of roughly one to three. National leadership does not worry about building up the military excessively; it has constantly built up the largest military possible. After all, Israel's very existence does not permit a single defeat in war.

Quality and quantity complement each other. In Israel's case, the quantitative limit is fixed by what the state is capable of, not by what is "enough." The limit of that capability, however, is the delicate balance between the two sides of a single coin—quality and quantity. Quantity must not be permitted to interfere with quality. Excessive allocation to the military at the expense of education and economic well-being will, in the final analysis, mar quality.

The following are components of quality in security matters:

1. Human quality, motivation, and national patterns of behavior that mark youth in a given generation;
2. The willingness of the people to persist in maintaining a citizen's military;
3. Scientific and technological advancement, economic development, and

the establishment of a strong industrial and economic basis for military power. This last element is what sets the quantitative limits of military power.

All these elements hinge on the quality of national leadership, on the comprehension of that leadership, and on its ability to formulate and adopt moderate, pragmatic, national goals, and to pursue appropriate policies in foreign affairs and security.

Motivation is the most important element in security. A feeling, an awareness, of unity of fate among the people is a necessary condition for maintaining a high level of quality. A necessary condition, though, is not a sufficient one; a unity of aim is also required. It is only when both these conditions are met that there is general national agreement, or a consensus.

A feeling of unity of existential fate exists among the Jewish people in any event. However, it is only when that unity is augmented by a unity of aim that individuals and the community at large can be properly motivated. Such motivation is the multiplier of quality among the few who face the many. The power of matter is faced by the power of the spirit, the power of numbers and wherewithal by the power of necessity and determination. Hence, the importance of the quality of leadership, civilian and military. Chosen concrete national goals and war aims and questions of peace and war are what decide the degree of national consensus and the level of motivation.

Concerning science, technology, and industry: Israel is distinguished by much spirit and little matter—it has much motivation but little economic strength relative to its security needs and the quantitative superiority of the Arab world. Such strength is a prerequisite for security and military power. Its economic strength cannot derive from natural resources, of which it has been blessed with few. Only science, technology, and industry can form a basis for Israel's economic strength. They have the potential to confer upon it economic strength and unique military quality.

Israel has an advantage, relative and absolute, over its enemies in these qualitative areas. Its security needs in the areas of military and defense have forced it to invest enormous efforts over the years in research, development, production, and the establishment of industries.

Over the years, certain guiding principles have been devised as to which munitions Israel would be best advised to develop itself and which it can prudently procure elsewhere. These principles are:

1. To develop and manufacture weapons and military equipment based on original Israeli ideas and to avoid their exposure, both for political reasons and to add an element of technological surprise in war;

2. To develop and manufacture essential weapons and equipment that overseas powers refuse to sell Israel but that they sometimes sell to the Arabs;

3. To develop and manufacture in Israel when it is economically worthwhile to do so—when the added value of development and manufacture is high and the cost of the foreign currency saved does not exceed the exchange rate.

The Arabs have been able to obtain a plethora of modern weapons, for land, air, and sea warfare, from outside powers, while Israel has only been able to obtain limited quantities. For years, Israel has had to improvise or make do with obsolescent, World War II–era weapons. Only in the area of modern combat aircraft has Israel obtained weaponry comparable to, or better than, that of its enemies. While virtually all Arab weaponry is imported, Israel's land and naval weaponry is almost entirely the product of its own development and manufacture: once-obsolescent tanks, upgraded and made almost modern; Israeli-developed Merkava tanks; self-propelled artillery; various antitank weapons (recoilless guns, rocket launchers, missiles, high-power tank guns); and submachine guns and assault rifles. The Navy is equipped with patrol and missile boats developed and manufactured in Israel. Israel has been a pioneer in the use of naval surface-to-surface missiles, which it builds itself and which sank Soviet-made Syrian and Egyptian missile boats in the Yom Kippur War. Israel possesses for all branches of the IDF a wide variety of additional equipment and munitions that have resulted from domestic invention, development, and manufacture.

Here too it is possible to discern a dialectic by which quality builds quantity, and quantity engenders quality. The need to develop and manufacture in Israel has contributed to the growth of industries that have in many respects changed the face of Israel. Tens of thousands of technicians, engineers, and scientists take part in such activity. Israel has become a modern industrial country because, to a great extent, of its security-driven industries and the development, manufacture, and equipping of the IDF with Israeli weaponry. These industries have changed the face of Israeli society and its level of technology and industry, making in the process a very substantial economic contribution. These factors are important; they are qualitative elements of the highest order. The contributions of technology and industry to the existence of the State of Israel, and to the overall balance of power—not necessarily just the military balance—between itself and its enemies have been priceless.

Despite Israel's limited staying power and its inability to force the Arab states to reconcile themselves with its existence, it has assumed that its assault power will enable it to maintain military superiority and win wars. Nevertheless, while Israel knows that deciding the outcome in war is a necessary condition, even a sufficient one, for assuring its existence, it cannot force a decision of the overall issue and bring about an end to the conflict.

From the standpoint of the art of war, Israel bases its security doctrine on the advantage of interior lines, which make it possible to shift assets between its northern, central, and southern combat sectors; on the help of the Jewish people, at all times; and on the advantage of qualitative superiority—human, scientific, and technological, which makes it possible to offset Arab numerical superiority.

Qualitative superiority also has a moral dimension. Israel has been fighting for its existence: it is the threatened, the persecuted, party; it is the only party to the conflict that has been the object of plans for extermination. This reality is what determines Israel's moral superiority: it is persecuted, and its right to self-defense by all possible means is beyond dispute. As long as it fights for its existence, these moral factors are part of its overall qualitative superiority. Israel's wars, according to its basic security doctrine, have been imposed on it and are hence "wars of no choice." The profound necessity involved has engendered broad national consensus, strong motivation, and a pattern of national behavior of warriors that typifies the country's youth.

Another qualitative element is that of the citizen's military—the reserve military—which bears witness to societal quality. If the extent of soldiers' motivation derives from necessity, from the fact that they are fighting for their and their nation's survival, the capacity of Israeli society to exploit all its resources, to press them into service and channel them into a war effort, derives from the quality of its human assets. The principle of full exploitation of resources requires the state to exhaust all of its human and material means, to use them to the limit. That principle is an extreme manifestation of a primary characteristic of total war: in Israel the entire nation is the military, and all national resources are integrated into the war effort. The necessity of seeking victory in wars of decision through the assault power—not wars of attrition, based on the staying power— has mandated the investment of all resources in the power to effect a military decision, rather than in overall national staying power. Israel has preferred as large a combat force as possible, at the expense of its ability to wage long wars.

IDF forces are composed mainly of reserves. Again, the entire nation is the military: in times of peace everyone goes about his own occasions, but in war everyone is called to the colors. In that way, Israel has maintained one of the largest armed forces in the world relative to its population.

The IDF force structure is based on three elements: a career military force manned by regulars, a standing military force of conscripts, and a reserve military force. The Air Force and Navy are mainly standing forces, while the Army mostly comprises reserve units.

The standing Arab armed forces are existing war machines, while Israel's reserve military is a potential war machine. The standing Arab armed forces do not need time to mobilize and are hence less concerned than the IDF is about being surprised. The most immediate role of the IDF's standing forces—conscript and career—is readiness; they must be able to hold off an attack until the reserves are mobilized, and they must also protect that mobilization. The standing forces bear the burden of Israel's sustained security and readiness. They are charged with training commanders for the entire IDF, both standing and reserve forces, and with building and training reserve units.

The role of regular personnel is to provide what neither conscript military forces nor reserves can provide. They are expected to resolve the tension between the nonspecialist pole of conscripts and reserves and the other pole, the requirement for specialization. It must represent professionalism, inject consistency and continuity into Israeli military thinking, and formulate and develop IDF combat doctrines. It must specialize in force structure, derive lessons from the cumulative experience of the military in all spheres, and nurture the values and heritage of the IDF.

The regular military comprises the nucleus of the senior command, from chief of the General Staff down to brigade commanders in the reserves, and down to battalion commanders or lower in the conscript military. Furthermore, it also includes the IDF professional cadre: regular military personnel of all ranks and in all capacities requiring years of continuous specialization. Regular military personnel are responsible for training the soldiers and officers of both the reserve and conscript forces.

Israel nurtures the career military force. The conditions of service are good, with generous social benefits and terms of retirement after long service. Patterns have been developed for rotation, and traditions have been built of relatively long service, collectively permitting renewal in the ranks, along with a continuity that prevents jolts to the military. In brief, the regular military must make up for the lack of specialization among conscripts and reservists, meeting the demands of modern warfare for a high level of professionalism, as conscripts and reservists cannot. If the regular military is to fulfil its role, the IDF must persevere in the principle of professional specialization in all areas, in all service branches, and in all military professions. Commanders at all levels must be the highest professional authorities for their subordinates.

The fact that the land army is composed mainly of reservists and conscripts clashes with the increasing demand for specialization, as armies become more modern. One of the conditions for quality and excellence is professional specialization, which depends on in-depth study, persistence, and continuous, concentrated employment in the various technical, managerial, logistic, and operational disciplines relating to war. A militia-type army is the antithesis of specialization. However, this has advantages as well as disadvantages. While a standing military is usually superior in matériel to a reserve military, a militia is often superior in morale. In the matériel sphere, for instance, mobility is a function of the type and quality of equipment, and of professional specialization. Morale, though, is the product of motivation, initiative, daring, flexibility of thought, and the ability to improvise—attributes deriving from consciousness. A citizen's military can distinguish itself in all these areas, and even exceed a standing military, whose combat elements contain few educated men in their lower ranks—professionals, scientists, intellectuals. At all levels of the combat units in Israel's citizen's military, in contrast, may be found representatives of the entire range of society. The technological, scientific, and cultural elites are represented at all levels and in all arms of the service. As a result, the average human level in its citizen's military, all through the ranks, is higher than in a standing military.

Some claim that quantity comes at the expense of quality, that certain levels of quality cannot be attained because of the limiting effect of quantity. This is incorrect. Quantity is a curse only when quality is low, when institutions, organizations, or individuals are incapable of effectually performing their tasks. Then they claim quantity is the cause.

This issue should be examined in another way, as well. It is the task of quality to engender quantity. It has the power of fully exploiting the moral and material potential of the nation, thus narrowing the quantitative gap between the IDF and other armies. Quantity does not clash with quality. By means of quality, quantity can be obtained, from which will grow a new quality, and so on.

There is no more salient, or important, an example of how quality engenders quantity, and quantity engenders a new quality, than Israel's reserve military, which is the "military of the entire people." Not many societies have been able to attain such a military. The IDF reserve military is not a single episode, a nonrecurring mobilization of the nation's resources for a single war, in the period of a single generation. It is an effort spanning decades in which the entire nation has been an armed force. Within a few hours, hundreds of thousands of men can be issued arms and equipment stored in warehouses around the country, be placed on alert and ready for war, organized into units and large combat formations. Such a reserve military is a reflection of the highest national quality. In order to attain such a level, society must have a high degree of organizational capacity; each individual must have the most developed awareness and sense of responsibility. Each must feel that the existence of the nation hinges on him personally.

The reserve military is among the most important collective creations of the Jewish people. In only one respect does its quantity come at the expense of quality: the more complex the modern battlefield becomes, the more sophisticated modern weapons systems become, the more specialization is required. Specialization depends on perseverance over time, of single-minded involvement in one specific, defined field.

The prerequisite for being able to rely on a militia-type land army in the face of the large, mostly standing Arab armies, which deployed along Israel's borders and could attack by surprise, is the maintenance of a standing intelligence corps, air force, and navy.

Israel in particular is dependent on effective early warning. Intelligence must warn of impending threats or processes that could lead to threatening situations, so that the reserves can mobilize in time. The unique contribution of intelligence is in periods between wars. When the IDF is preparing for war, the Intelligence Corps is involved in its own war.

Overall staff responsibility for intelligence in the IDF rests with the Intelligence Branch, which is part of the General Staff. The Intelligence Branch is a critical component of the intelligence community, which includes the organs of state engaged in espionage and national security—the Mossad (Institute for Intelligence and Special Operations), the General Security Service, the foreign ministry, and the police. The Intelligence Corps is subordinate to the chief of the Intelligence Branch. The primary role of the Branch is to provide early warning of threats to prevent surprise attack. In Israel, military intelligence is also responsible for overall national intelligence appreciations, political as well as military; the chief of the General Staff Intelligence Branch, then, is the national intelligence officer. He must furnish the government, the minister of defense, the military, and various other bodies with information and assessments so they can wage war, formulate security policy, decide on the organization of military forces, and plan operations and ongoing security activity.

The Air Force is responsible for protecting the country's skies, for providing air cover for mobilization and deployment of the ground forces, and holding up an enemy attack until the reserves are fully deployed. The air arm is the IDF's most versatile, flexible, and quickly employable force; it is capable of operational intervention within minutes, in all elements—land, air, and sea. The Navy maintains a constant presence at sea, in order to emphasize Israel's sovereignty over its territorial waters and assure the safety of its coast. Professional and logistical considerations related to the nature of the Air Force and Navy, which are technologically sophisticated service branches, require them to be standing forces, with few reserves.

In accordance with the principle of effectuality that underlies investments in the structure and order of forces, priority in resource allocation has been given the Intelligence Branch and the air arm. The latter is perceived as a multipurpose vehicle that can also be used as a "flying artillery" in support of land battles. It is also perceived as an alternative to an air defense system, to air raid shelters for the civilian population, to coastal artillery, and in a certain respect, to the Navy as well.

ts of Israeli security doctrine realized that if for po-
reasons the IDF could not launch a preemptive strike,
to choose between a flexible defense and a rigid one.
s a difficult one: the risk of not conducting a flexible
Israel versus the risk of taking a rigid defense, in other
n-out battle. With no way out, that horn of the di-
be chosen that permits a quicker transition to a coun-

backdrop of Israel's security doctrine was its lack of
; the necessity of relying on assault power, rather than
wer; the importance of obtaining a quick decision,
likelihood of international intervention; the necessity
decisions clearly favorable to Israel, until the enemy
zing the future effects of war on his national morale.
he need to take the fighting quickly and deeply into
ry was adopted as an elementary principle.
n of what form of battle puts one in a stronger posi-
or attack—is as old as military theory itself. It is usual
the attacker should maintain a numerical advantage
der of three to one. In other words, the attacker should
strong as the defender (the IDF has held its own in
ses with even more disadvantageous ratios). All this is
only at the tactical level. At the strategic level, the ratio
ker and defender must be reversed. There it is usually
who needs numerical superiority. If the attacker enjoys
vantage—in other words, if the defender is in the po-
"few" against the "many"—the attacker can attack
force by the "center of gravity" method in all sectors.
numerous tactical and strategic targets along the en-
in depth at many points simultaneously.
rly be seen, then, from the overall perspective of the
s, time, and space, that at the strategic level more forces
for a defensive posture than for an offensive one. It can
hen, that while at the tactical level (that of a battle)
onger than attack, at the strategic level (that of a war)
posture is stronger than a defensive one. The terms
nd "defensive" deal with the strategic level of war,
" and "defense" relate to types of battle at the tactical

re are two basic strategies: that of the "many" and that

In the mid-fifties, a switch began from reliance on infantry as the decisive arm in land warfare to mechanized, mobile, and armored units. The transition to the age of modern warfare was completed in the Six Day War. Since then, IDF combat doctrine has been based on maneuverability and battles of movement aimed at causing the enemy to lose his operational balance. It is in mobile, armored combat that the qualitative edge of IDF personnel is most clearly manifest; the IDF commander is distinguished by his initiative, ability to improvise, and operational flexibility. IDF soldiers have shown determination and stoutness of spirit whenever Israel's wars have been perceived as having been forced on it, as wars of survival.

In the past, the Arabs did not have adequate forces for continuous deployment in strength along their entire borders with Israel. They were able to wage war against it only by the method known as the "main effort." This method requires prior selection of areas for decisive operations, to which most forces and resources are directed; secondary forces are sent to other sectors to keep enemy forces tied down, induce him to send reinforcements there, and keep him uncertain as to the point of the main effort. The IDF also operates on the principle of the main effort.

In the 1970s, however, Arab forces reached quantitative saturation relative to the area of confrontation with Israel; they can now deploy continuously along its borders. They are now capable of implementing an attack strategy based on the "center of gravity" method. That strategy involves balanced, simultaneous attacks at many points, continuously along a broad front, with the aim of effecting breaches. Forces from the rear and flanks are channeled where success is apparent until enemy resistance weakens and his forces eventually collapse. In this approach, points of decision are chosen on an ad hoc basis, as operations develop. Defending forces cannot be concentrated in a timely way against large forces that operate by the center of gravity method. There is no one main effort by the attacking force that constitutes a clearly perceived primary threat and can be met in advance; there are many such efforts and threats, any of which is liable to develop in the course of battle into the most threatening effort, the "center of gravity." Instead of concentrating his forces for a decisive effort, the defender is forced to scatter them, to counter the assault in all sectors, and fight a long war of attrition. Under these circumstances, the defender has no chance of achieving local superiority anywhere.

Hence, when an attacker employs the "main effort" method, a "stationary (rigid) center of gravity" is engendered, while the "center of gravity" strategy produces a "mobile (flexible) center of gravity," or several such centers. Against the Arab's quantitative superiority and their ability to attack simultaneously at many points, however, Israel enjoys the advantage of interior lines, which, as noted, make it possible to shift forces from one front to another, to shift efforts with relative ease, with the aim of meeting threats as they develop. Interior lines also make it possible to transfer centers of gravity from one front to another. In that way, it is possible to attain the initiative and local quantitative superiority.

Because of the large number of enemy units and formations and of Israel's long land borders, the IDF needs a large number of formations if it is to have optimal operational flexibility and be able to group formations of various sizes on an ad hoc basis, according to operational requirements in the various sectors. A land army that must be able to move forces to many different places and conduct numerous main operational efforts must contain a large number of elementary formations—brigades and divisions. For this reason, the IDF has preferred a large number of formations, even if they are small and deficient in weapons and equipment, to a smaller number of large, well-equipped formations.

In the past, the structure of the land forces in general, and particularly the organization of formations and units, had been influenced by the fact the Israel's main enemy was Egypt, which was stronger than all the other front-line states and expeditionary forces combined. Hence, the IDF was structured, from the standpoint of combat doctrine, organization, and balance between the service branches, according to the optimal model for war on the southern front. As for the eastern front, IDF doctrine mandated a combat doctrine and force organization based on improvisation, as the nature of developments on the front dictated. After the Yom Kippur War, the concept of force structure underwent a change. No longer would emphasis be put on a particular front; a basic, universal structure for IDF land forces would be adopted.

The first principle of IDF combat doctrine is that a war must be taken quickly and deeply into enemy territory, and for the following reason: its lack of strategic depth poses a danger to Israel, since initial success by a hostile attack means the loss of vital strategic

targets, such as populati
the war into enemy terr
fering, the destruction o
and to prevent disruptic
Israeli rear. Attack by th
victory. Another necessa
short; only by attack can
be brief and end before t
come to the Arabs' aid
enjoy superiority in stayir
employ their diplomatic l
is going badly for them. S
it does not have the optic
ities by diplomacy; it can
painful, humiliating terms.
can be short only if Israel
is going so badly for the /

A war must also be shor
which would make it diffi
of attrition. A defensive w
and the Arabs have longe
Israel would exhaust its res
war also involves heavy ca
strategic depth that would
defensive war of attrition
choice left open to Israel i
decision by means of assau

Israel must end a war wi
made to taste the bitter dre
wage war. The results of a v
impact on society and nati
individuals and of society is
immediate military, politica
clear military victory raises
security doctrine reflects a d
negative cumulative effects o
war a necessary evil, somet
for lack thereof. If there is in
to launch a preemptive strik
territory, and attain a clear-

The archite
litical or other
it would have
The dilemma
defense inside
words, a draw
lemma should
terattack.

Hence, the
strategic depth
on staying pe
given the high
of obtaining
gave up, reali
Accordingly,
enemy territo

The questic
tion—defense
to think that
over the defer
be thrice as
tactical defen
true, though,
between atta
the defender
numerical ad
sition of the
with superio
He can attac
tire front an

It can clea
ratio of force
are required
be claimed,
defense is st
an offensive
"offensive"
while "attac
level.

Hence, th

of the "few." The many have freedom of choice. They have the liberty of choosing either a defensive or offensive strategy, of implementing either the center of gravity method or that of the main effort. The few have no choice: their strategy must be offensive and employ the main effort method.

Within the framework of an offensive, as in that of the defensive, attacks and defensive battles are conducted in juxtaposition with one another. When an offensive is launched, not all of the engagements conducted by the attacking side are offensive. After all, the side in the defensive posture is not likely to be satisfied with conducting defensive operations aimed at merely parrying attacks; it also launches counteroffensives to thwart the assaults against itself. Hence, the attacking side is forced to conduct, along with its offensive operations, defensive battles as well.

When one side is on the offensive, the other is on the defensive. There is usually no direct attack against an opponent who is conducting an offensive in the same sector. The transition to a concurrent offensive usually takes place in another area; in other words, the concurrent counteroffensive is usually indirect.

In Israel, practice came before theory: in the 1930s, under Yitzhak Sadde and subsequently under the British officer Orde Wingate, the defenders of Jewish settlements lay in wait for Arab attackers outside the enclosed settlement areas. In World War II, the Jewish population in Palestine made preparations to defend the country in the event of a German invasion; at the same time, though, it sent tens of thousands of its sons to the British and other Allied military forces, to fight Germany far from the country's borders, in Europe and Africa. Later, in Israel's War of Independence, the Jews were successful only when they went over to the offensive. The tradition of taking the initiative, of the spirit of the offensive, has helped shape the pattern of behavior adopted by Israelis ever since, by force of historical circumstances.

When Mao Tse-tung was still among the "few," he said, "Pit one against ten, that is our strategy. Pit ten against one, that is our tactics." That is also Israel's choice. A basic principle of its combat doctrine is to endeavor to attain local superiority where a decision is to be made, at the expense of other sectors. Under the circumstances of the "few against the many," that can be achieved only through a basically offensive-oriented strategy. At the national level, that means concentration of forces in general, and of ground forces in particular, for an offensive on one front, with defensive operations on the other fronts.

Each level of strategy and security doctrine must be derived from the level above it. If tactics are mortgaged to technique, strategy to tactics, and politics to strategy, battles are sometimes won, but wars are often lost.

Progressive combat doctrines and military technology should influence the shaping of the art of war; they should provide answers to the requirements of tactics, campaigns, and strategy, and make available the best weapons possible. Yet technical means and technology should not be seen as everything, or as nostrums for the complex issues arising from the human and physical constraints, both objective and subjective, deterministic and indeterminate, under which a nation's military prowess and power confront its opponents. There are no fixed, universal criteria concerning the relative strengths that forces conducting offensive or defensive operations should have.

In the case of Israel, when rendering judgment on the quality of a defense or attack, or the superiority of either, one must judge by Israel's existential reality, taking into account the sum total of basic strategic factors in its theater, as well as the requirements of its security doctrine. Israel's strategic circumstances demand that priority be given to an offensive. The general IDF order of preferences is:

1. Avoidance of war
2. A war of decision, a preemptive war, and an offensive
3. Counterattack, defensive operations as brief as possible, going over to the offensive
4. A defensive war of attrition.

The last option is dangerous, and Israeli security doctrine endeavors to circumvent it.

The defensive and offensive are two sides of the same coin, the two basic elements of the conduct of war. Together, they constitute the whole. They are complementary opposites, which together make up the synthesis of war.

The strategy of reliance on assault power, by means of movement, attack, fighting deep in enemy territory, decision by assault, and a short war determine the skills required for Israel's armed forces, their composition, and the priorities in their structure. Those priorities are as follows: intelligence; the air arm; mobile and armored formations; special forces ("commandos") and elite infantry; all others. The art of war by the few is averse to static lines and wearying, inconclusive operations. The relevant question is, as far as Israel is concerned, no theoretical one concerning the intrinsically stronger form of warfare. It is: What is the preferable form of warfare in Israel's circumstances? The answer is unequivocal: attack—on land, in the air, and at sea.

CHAPTER 10
EARLY WARNING

The ability to provide early warning is a fundamental component of Israel's national security doctrine. Just as the military elements of security doctrine are unique, so too is its concept of early warning. The reliability of the state's unique security doctrine—which on the one hand permits the normal routines of life to go on, and on the other guarantees that the IDF will not be thrown off its operational balance if Israel is attacked—hinges on that concept of early warning and its effective implementation.

Israel's is a unique and daring security doctrine, one based on a calculated risk: a large part of its military strength, the reserve military, is not kept mobilized or ready for battle; it is in the fields, the workshops and factories, research and educational institutions, in the offices and engaged in sundry occupations. Furthermore, Israel's defensive capacity is limited because of its lack of strategic depth. Given this calculated risk, early warning is of the utmost importance: without it, necessary measures for preparedness and mobilization could not be undertaken in time to meet military threats. Surprise and a sudden transition from peace to war would be very serious; such a war could take on an improvised character, with the danger of developing into a defensive war of attrition, accompanied by the loss of strategic and operational balance. Such a development would be exceedingly dangerous.

Israel perceives itself to be under threat when firm information and intelligence analysis point to an expected attack. Early warning of this kind constitutes "warning of intentions." Enemy military deployment and preparations that may become a threat to Israel and make possible an attack constitute a military threat; early warning of the development of such a situation is termed a "warning of threats." Such early warning indicates that there may be an intention to attack Israel. However, it may also indicate other enemy intentions, such as a defensive deployment, resulting from anxiety that Israel is planning a military move; or it could be part of an effort to deter Israel, to threaten it and apply military and political pressure on it.

In Israeli security doctrine, the concept of early warning is never considered mainly as "warning of intentions" but as the formation of a threat as an objective reality. It would be dangerous in a country with no strategic depth and whose land forces are mostly not mobilized to base its security on subjective appreciations of "intentions." Trying to prophesy that way is more a gamble than a calculated risk. Early warning is derived from various indications that point to the formation of a threat. According to Israeli security doctrine, in such situations the threat should be confronted and an appropriate deployment of forces made. The rule is that when a military threat exists, the IDF must deploy in accordance with its severity in terms of time and space, and in proportion to the extent of the threat. The role, then, of intelligence is to provide early warning so that the IDF is able to deploy forces in time, in the face of a developing threat. The meaning of the concept of "early warning" in Israeli security doctrine does not depend on information or appreciations concerning a priori intentions but rather assessments of the feasibility of actions, based on information and the development of a threat on the ground that are likely to indicate enemy intentions to go to war with Israel. This attitude toward warning on intentions is simply a by-product of the general appreciation of circumstances— political, operational, and intelligence—based on information and discernible developments on the ground.

One must not evade the objective and unique concept of early warning in Israeli security doctrine. It is important to adhere to it and recognize it as a sufficient condition for early warning. It must be remembered that warning of intentions is problematic in many respects. Enemy intentions do not always precede a threat, but sometimes the opposite: the threat is what engenders concrete intentions.

One must distinguish between a warning of the intention to go to war and that of a threat. Early warning of actual military threats is more vital to Israeli security than subjective political warning about intentions. Intelligence fulfills its role when it warns of a military threat. Responsibility for assessing the acuteness of the military threat and for evaluating enemy military intentions and plans rests with military intelligence. Responsibility for taking the necessary measures to meet a military threat rests with the General Staff and the government. For them, a military threat, as brought to their attention by the Intelligence Branch, is a given. However, the accompanying intelligence appreciation regarding political or military intentions and undertakings by foreign governments is only an opinion, not a given or fact; the government is not exempt from its sole, absolute responsibility for making an assessment of the overall threat. Such responsibility rests with the national leadership, not with its subordinates. This is all the more so given the fact that the basic aggressive aims of the Arabs toward Israel have been long known.

The responsibility of the Branch for evaluating intentions is not all-inclusive. Actually, the opposite is the case; while the Branch must furnish all the objective information and an intelligence appreciation, overall responsibility for evaluating intentions rests with the government. It is the government that bears ultimate responsibility for evaluating diplomatic relations, the international situation, and the intentions of foreign states and governments toward Israel. The military Intelligence Branch and its head are responsible for undertaking a *national intelligence* appreciation, but not for undertaking an appreciation of the *national situation*. That is the responsibility of the government. In the face of a developing threat, the government must evaluate, with all the tools at its disposal—including the intelligence community, the foreign ministry, diplomatic channels, and the defense establishment, including, of course, the General Staff—the actual extent of the threat.

It is the government, not the Intelligence Branch or even the General Staff, that must decide the extent of calculated risk Israel should accept, or what extent of state of alert the country should assume.

The kind of professionalism required of the political leadership is different from that required of the military. It is important that both have a broad view of the national interest. However, the ability to see all the national risks and prospects, and all of the country's needs, including those of national security, is a necessary condition for national leadership.

The aims of war are political, and the decision of whether to go to war is a political one, to be made by governments. Thus, the appreciation of warlike intentions toward Israel by hostile states must be made by Israel's political leadership. An assessment of military threats and dangers is in the professional competence of the military, and for that the General Staff bears responsibility.

The contention that the mobilization of reserves must be based on warning of intentions, since otherwise the IDF would have to remain in a state of alert as long as an apparent threat existed, is groundless. Israeli security doctrine is specifically based on a distinction between normal conditions and the movement of forces—preparations and the deployment of enemy ground, air, and sea units—that actually threaten Israel. It is only on the basis of this distinction that in ordinary times the IDF permits itself to remain at a low level of alert, from the standpoint of the ratio of forces. Whenever the balance of forces is upset and the threat increases, the IDF must prepare itself, mobilize, and confront the enemy in a manner dictated by the balance of forces. If the enemy fails to remove the threat, if he invites war, the IDF, true to its strategy of deterrence, must take the operational initiative. In Israel's circumstances, warning of threats is what counts.

CHAPTER 11
ORGANIZATION

The principles governing the structure and organization of the IDF and its staff concept were formed in its early years. After the War of Independence, a plan was worked out for reorganization of the IDF. Its principles were implemented and have essentially remained in effect to the present. There have of course been changes in quantity and concepts, brought about by the passage of time and developments in military technology, conditions in the Middle Eastern theater, and the involvement of outside powers. However, the basic principles of organization and force structure, as then formulated, have been essentially preserved.

CONCEPT OF COMMAND AND STAFF

By the principle of unity of command, the IDF General Staff serves as an integrated staff for all three services—Army, Air Force, and Navy. The General Staff is subordinate to the government, through the minister of defense. Subordinate to the General Staff are the Army (involving three territorial commands, functional commands, and the various corps) and the air and sea services.

The air and sea services are functional commands and bear overall responsibility for their own doctrine and structure. They command the air and naval forces and conduct their operations. The General

Staff, in addition to its role as the high command of the IDF, also serves as supreme headquarters of the Army.

The concept of staff, throughout the various echelons of the military, from the General Staff down to the lowest-level formations and units, is based on the distinction between coordinating staff, special staff, functional staff, specific staff, and personal staff. At the General Staff level, there are four coordinating staff branches: the General Staff Branch, the Branch of the Adjutant General (Personnel), the Quartermaster's Branch (Logistics), and Intelligence (from the War of Independence to 1953, Intelligence had been a department of the General Staff Branch).

The chiefs of the various army corps and their headquarters constitute the special staff component of the General Staff. They are subordinate to the chief of the General Staff, and their activities are coordinated by the various coordinating staff branches of the General Staff. The Air Force and Navy headquarters comprise functional staffs within the General Staff, for all air and naval matters.

Specialized staff functions, such as advocate general, chaplaincy, the Women's Corps, IDF Spokesman, and finance, make up the specific staff component of the General Staff.

The secretariat of the high command, the offices of the chief of the General Staff, and the chiefs of the various staff branches constitute the personal staff component of the General Staff. Staff officers of the various corps make up the special staff of all staff levels in the Army, from the high command down to the lowest echelons of the forces.

THE LAND THEATER

The land theater is divided into subtheaters—the three territorial commands of north, center, and south. This organization makes possible effective command and control of military operations in war and of routine operational activity and engagements between wars, training and fostering the preparedness of forces, both standing and reserve; and area defense.

The territorial commands deal with organization, preparedness, and reserve mobilization. They provide logistical support for all IDF forces in their areas ("area logistical support"). Much of the effort of the territorial commands is devoted to the organization and preparedness of reserve forces. Each of the territorial commands includes units and formations, both standing and reserve forces, as well as area defense forces. The commands are directly subordinate to the General Staff.

A condition for being able to rely on a large reserve military, which is strategically in a constant state of readiness and accounts for the bulk of an army, is that it be organized in advance into permanent organic units and formations. These forces are subordinate to the territorial commands in which they are deployed. Their equipment is stored in depots, termed "emergency stores." Two methods of mobilization, concealed and open, are periodically practiced, and they are implemented as required.

LAND FORCES

In November 1947, the National Command and General Staff of the Hagana (the underground Jewish military organization during British rule in Palestine before the establishment of the state of Israel) issued an order concerning the reorganization of its forces. The order stated that given the likelihood of an attack by the armed forces of the neighboring Arab states, the Hagana was to organize itself as a full-fledged military force, its land forces divided into two groups:

1. Field Forces, composed of ordinary infantry battalions and assault battalions (based on the elite underground force, Palmah). The battalion was to be the highest tactical unit, and the area brigade was to provide the administrative and logistical support framework. The role of the Field Forces was to constitute the maneuvering element that conducted regular mobile operations.

2. Home Guard, composed of regional-based units and settlements. The basic administrative unit was the subdistrict, which was responsible for administration, training, and the defense of its own area. The role of the Home Guard component was area defense.

This Hagana order mandated the establishment of four area brigades, to be deployed in existing regions and districts. For purposes of command and control in war, each subdistrict command was to be operationally subordinate to the commander of the Field Force battalion that operated in the area.

These measures proved inadequate for the needs of the War of

Independence. The military force had to be expanded and organized into larger formations. Mobilization and training were intensified. Additional brigade headquarters were established, Field Forces were organized into brigades; by mid-1948, the IDF order of battle included twelve mobile brigades (pursuant to a General Staff decision to separate the brigades from specific territories). In August 1948, a decision was reached to establish territorial commands, termed "fronts." Brigades were assigned to fronts as operational requirements dictated and subordinated to the front commanders.

Until this reorganization, forces had been directly subordinated to the General Staff, sometimes several brigades being grouped into a task force under one commander for specific operations, such as Operation Nachshon, or Operation Danny. The following year, in late 1949, it was decided that the brigade group (a reinforced brigade) would be the basic formation of the IDF land forces. However, it was clear that in the future, forces involving several brigades would sometimes have to be concentrated for joint tactical or operational efforts. In such cases, it was assumed, the territorial command would not be able to command it and also direct its operations, if additional operations were simultaneously being conducted in its area. An additional command would be required—an intermediate echelon between brigade and territorial command.

In July 1952, a decision was reached to establish permanent divisional task force headquarters while retaining the brigade as the basic formation. Permanent divisions were not yet established, so as not to undermine operational flexibility and to preserve the ability to organize forces in accordance with operational requirements. Combining brigades into permanent divisions would compromise operational flexibility and produce redundant divisional headquarters. The idea of combining a few brigades into permanent divisions and maintaining the independence of the others was rejected on the grounds that the creation of two basic formations, brigade and division, would compromise the standardization of combat and organizational doctrine.

Two divisional task forces had already taken part in the Sinai Campaign in 1956, one on the northern (Rafa) and one on the central (Abu Ageila) axis. In the Six Day War, three divisional task forces operated on the southern front and one in the northern. The IDF had grown. Henceforth, it was in the age of modern warfare. Large, mobile armor formations had been waging war on land, and tactical and operational requirements had called for the concentration of large forces. This was the background for the IDF's decision in 1970 to organize its armored forces in permanent divisions. The division has become the basic formation of the armored forces. The brigade has continued to be the basic formation for infantry.

After the Yom Kippur War, it became clear that with the considerable increase in the size of forces in the Middle East, there would be a need to concentrate several divisions to decide operations. It was then that a new echelon in the land forces was added, a corps, which would include several divisions.

THE AIR AND SEA THEATERS

The Hagana Air Service, established in November 1947, became the Air Force upon the establishment of the IDF. The role of the Air Force is to protect Israel's skies, attack ground objectives, and provide air defense. It must provide fire support for the land and sea forces and it must provide them with assault transport, airlift, and general transport services. In its capacity as Israel's strategic deterrent, the Air Force must be capable of attacking and destroying military and economic infrastructure deep in enemy territory, including cities. In that way, it can both damage the war effort of Arab states, should they attack Israel, and deter them from attacking Israeli population centers.

The Navy was preceded by the Hagana Naval Service, established in March 1948. Until then, the Hagana's sea force had been the Palyam, a section of the Palmah. When the Naval Service was established, the Palyam was absorbed into it. The Naval Service became the Navy upon the establishment of the IDF. The role of the Navy is to guarantee Israeli sovereignty at sea; defend the country through deterrence and combat at sea; and attack land objectives from the sea by engaging targets on shore and by conducting amphibious landings and commando operations against both land and naval targets.

Because Israel's air and sea theaters are relatively small, the principles of "unity of theater" and "unity of command" may be applied to them. The headquarters of the Air Force and Navy are responsible for structuring the air and sea forces, as well as leading and commanding them, in both peace and war. In their case, the principle of unity of command is strictly observed.

HOME FRONT DEFENSE

In 1991, after the Gulf War, the Civil Defense Command, established in the War of Independence and charged with responsibility for civil defense against air attack and for overall protection of the civilian population, was disbanded. In its place a system of rear defense was established, under the Home Front Command. The system of rear defense is a distinct command subordinate to the General Staff and one of the ministries of government. The Home Front Command bears overall responsibility for preparation of the system of rear defense and mobilizing it during an emergency. The command is responsible for coordinating the activities of the police in matters related to rear defense, as well as those of various emergency organizations, local government, and civilian institutions and authorities. It is the Home Front Command that operates the forces responsible for civil defense, rescue activities, area defense, and the security of the country's interior and of its vital installations.

NATIONAL LOGISTIC INFRASTRUCTURE

A body has been established with responsibility for logistic infrastructure in an emergency—Emergency Economy. Its function is to assure the continued flow of goods and services and continued operation of enterprises vital to the civilian population, the war effort, and various essential areas the interruption of which would cause severe and lasting economic damage. Emergency Economy is directed by the interministry Supreme Board. The members of the board are the directors-general of government ministries, senior representatives of the IDF and Israel Police, the director-general of the Jewish Agency, and representatives of local government. The minister of defense is the board's chairman and usually appoints a permanent deputy chairman. The deputy has a special staff (the National Emergency Economy Staff), which is charged with guiding and coordinating the work of the various bodies engaged in logistics, in accordance with the policies and decisions of the Supreme Board.

The main bodies that make up the Emergency Economy system and are responsible for the arrangement of vital economic functions during an emergency are dedicated ministerial bodies, Emergency Economy boards in the territorial commands and various geographic areas, and local government authorities. The range of Emergency Economy–related activities is wide, encompassing such areas as energy, water, food, agriculture, transport (on land, air, and sea), communications, manpower, hospitalization, casualties (evacuation, welfare, fatalities), education, and public relations.

THE GENERAL STAFF AND THE VARIOUS CORPS

The reorganization of the IDF after the War of Independence included the establishment of a functional command called the Military Training Command. It was subordinated to the Training Branch of the General Staff (sometimes called the Training Department). It was the Training Branch of the General Staff that bore actual responsibility for the development of combat doctrine, and the various corps (e.g., infantry, armor, medical) were responsible for elaborating that doctrine. The Military Training Command was the executive arm of the Training Branch, and it constituted a powerful functional command. It was the organ that made it possible for the General Staff, in its capacity as the land forces high command, to decide on all matters of combat doctrine, including combined-arms doctrine. The Training Command made it possible for the General Staff to supervise and control the structuring and training of the land forces.

Over the years, the span of control of the General Staff in coping with its designated role as high command of the entire Army had become too great. Combined-arms operations and adequate response to the reality of the "unity of the battlefield" suffered. The Training Branch of the General Staff underwent various incarnations: thrice it changed back and forth between a branch and department of the General Staff, eventually settling on department status. The Training Functional Command became an administrative unit, eventually vanishing. Instead of integration of the various corps, the opposite occurred: military schools were gradually subordinated to the various corps, eventually becoming integral parts of them. A similar process occurred with manpower management, authority for which was delegated to the various corps, each of which became a law unto itself in manpower. Such a process was inevitable because of increasing demands to emphasize specialization, at the expense of intercorps integration.

The development of the various corps had not been uniform. Each had its own history. However, the overall thrust of their development had been the same—except for infantry and armor.

In February 1948, the high command decided to establish an Armored Service directly under the General Staff. It was to introduce armored units in all brigades, which at that time were all infantry brigades. In May 1948, the General Staff decided to abolish the service and to establish an armored department in the Transport Service. That same month, the IDF's first armored brigade was formed, the Eighth Brigade, and in September 1949 a decision was reached to established an Armor Corps and appoint a Chief Officer for Armored Affairs in the General Staff.

In August 1954, an order was issued for the organization of the Armored Troops Command Headquarters, and the function of Chief Officer for Armored Affairs was abolished. The role of the new Command Headquarters was defined as follows:

1. To constitute a dedicated headquarters responsible for formulating and developing armored doctrine in the IDF;
2. To organise and command all armored troops, regular and reserve alike, in the IDF.

Thus was established in the Army a functional command that served concurrently as a command of forces and headquarters of the Armor Corps. In its capacity as the body responsible for combat doctrine and the establishment of armor formations, the Armoured Troops Command Headquarters functioned something as an overall field headquarters for armor formations and bore responsibility for the integration of doctrines of the various corps. This organization proved to be efficient and contributed much to the structure, effectiveness, and enhancement of forces in the IDF's multi-arm armor formations. The success of the Armoured Troops Command Headquarters proves how important the principles of specialization and unity of command are.

Infantry was for many years the only arm of the IDF not organized in a corps framework. The institutionalization of infantry and the establishment of a staff for a chief of infantry in the early years would have involved placing authority for manpower for most of the ground forces in a single corps, an idea the general staffs in the early years recoiled from. The reason was that the Army was largely an infantry force then, and the General Staff members of the period were afraid of losing control over manpower management. This was a period of thoroughgoing change and organization of the country's manpower into military frameworks, whether standing or reserve. Eventually, the chief of the General Staff Training Department was charged with the function of chief of infantry in all that pertained to combat doctrine and training.

In early 1953, a special Infantry Corps Section was established within the Training Department of the General Staff. The section did not solve the problem, though, and in October 1956 it became a large staff element within the Training Department, headed by an officer who bore the title of Deputy Chief of Training Department for Infantry. His responsibilities were defined as follows:

The Deputy Chief of Training for Infantry has authority comparable to that of the other chiefs of corps concerning doctrinal development, planning of the training of infantry units, and providing advice on all related to the professional development of infantry officers. Within the purview of said authority are included all units whose corps designation is infantry, Area Defense units, special units for current operational activity, as well as infantry training and infantry equipment in all IDF units.

Despite the fact that paratroopers had been part of the infantry, a separate staff for the Chief of Paratroop and Airborne Forces was created in August 1954. In theory, the Paratroop Staff had the status of the staff of a corps, although in practice it had little influence, because it had no authority whatever in the area of manpower. Furthermore, the one standing paratroop brigade was under the authority of the Central Territorial Command, which jealously stood between the new Paratroop Staff and the standing airborne forces. In 1969, the Infantry and Paratroop Corps was established. At long last, the various types of infantry—ordinary infantry, paratroopers, special units, etc.—had a corps of their own. Yet even this new common corps did not have authority in the area of manpower management.

When eventually the relative quantitative weight of infantry in the IDF declined, the Infantry and Paratroop Corps Staff was recognized as an authority in matters of manpower management. Hence, only in December 1974, after the Yom Kippur War, did the infantry finally join the family of normal IDF corps. The endless birth pangs of this basic arm of the service were the result of a lack of consistency and of a hesitancy that for many years prevented following through on the IDF's concept of special staffs.

FIELD FORCES

Even in the early years of the IDF, there was a need for inter-arm integration and for a special command that would bear overall responsibility for combat doctrine and training in the land forces. The idea was broached at the General Staff in 1953, and a proposal was put forward to establish a common command for the field forces, charged with formulating combat doctrines, development of weapons, and training for the land forces. The thrust of the idea was to free the General Staff from the staff work involved in inter-arm coordination and combined operations in the land forces, so that it could concentrate on the strategic tasks of a supreme national command.

The proposal was rejected. However, in 1956, comprehensive discussions were held on the establishment of a Field Forces Command that would be responsible for military schools and training bases as well as for the establishment of new formations and units. Concurrently, a Logistics Command responsible for all Army logistics facilities was also considered. Eventually, in 1966 a decision was reached concerning solely the reorganization of the logistics system: the logistics depots were taken out of the responsibility of the staffs of the various corps and directly subordinated to the Logistics Branch of the General Staff. The logistics depots—such as Ordnance, Supply, Signals, Engineers, and Medicine—became centers operated by the Logistics Branch of the General Staff. The argument of the supporters of the reform was that the logistics coordinating staff in the General Staff could not fulfil its duty in an optimal manner because it lacked the necessary professional knowledge; but that could be gained only by subordinating the special depots directly to the General Staff. Hence, the proposal to establish a logistics command was not accepted, and the Logistics Branch was in effect also charged with fulfilling—in addition to its function as a coordinating branch of the General Staff—the function of an executive body.

Various proposals for disbanding the field corps and establishing a Field Force Command have been raised every few years, only to be rejected.

In the past there have been objective circumstances that made it easier for the General Staff of the IDF to fulfill its secondary role as the Land Forces Command. Periods of peace were relatively long. The assumptions that underpinned the IDF's annual work programs generally made it possible to give priority to the long-term military buildup, over maintaining a state of readiness. In such periods, the military had been engaged more in the structuring and training of forces (preparations) than in readiness and operational activity. The General Staff devoted itself to structuring the land forces up to the stage of formulating and integrating the doctrines of the various corps into a unified IDF doctrine. Such was also the case with General Staff activity in that period in the sphere of weapons development for the land forces and of the training of professional commanders at all levels. The General Staff was also involved in the formulation of combat doctrine for the various formation levels, directing and regulating manpower policy.

In the past, the distinction between the various corps had been based on clear-cut fields of technical specialization. Historically, the purpose for the creation of corps in the world's armies has been specialization, and this indeed is what underpins the concept of corps. Nevertheless, this concept has always over the years engendered a tension. On one hand there are the requirements that derive from the principle of "unity of the battlefield," leading to a "horizontal" organization (in accordance with the nature of military operations, namely, that they are always conducted by combined forces under common command and control). On the other hand, there are the requirements for the training and structure of force, emphasizing "vertical" organization (based on narrow professional specialization).

The need to resolve such tension, that between horizontal and specialized, vertical organization, led to the creation of coordinating staffs, the aim of which was a synthesis between the horizontal and vertical aspects. Over time, the "wings" of the corps were clipped, and authority for the command of forces was taken from them. Thus, the corps staffs became special staffs that provided professional guidance. The principle of unity of the battlefield and the requirement of inter-arm integration were reconciled.

Developments in military technology in the first half of the twentieth century lent increasing importance to the professionalism of the corps, because of their monopoly over technology; each corps became an authority in specific technological areas. However, weapons, equipment, and technologies gradually spread through all the various corps, becoming the domain of all corps and units, which produced duplication. Different corps possessed the same technologies and weapons. The distribution of specializations became artificial, as had the management of manpower. The coordinating staffs—whose function it was to achieve a synthesis that created intercorps integration and a balanced horizontal structuring of forces—became paralyzed.

The corps in the IDF have fulfilled, and continue to fulfil, decisive roles in the structuring of forces and nurturing of their quality, particularly since the IDF was established in the midst of a war and forged through continuous operational activity. Nevertheless, along with the contributions the corps have made, an inevitable process, one that has taken place in all armies, also developed in the IDF. The corps organization became anachronistic; the professional staff neutralized the coordinating staff with horizontal organization becoming the ultimate loser. It is under this background that voices have been raised in recent years against neglect of "the combined battlefield."

The relatively long periods of military buildup have been succeeded by a reality that calls for both preparation and readiness, and the General Staff, which plays the role of a unified staff for the entire IDF, is burdened also with the tasks of operations and readiness. Furthermore, the size of the IDF and the intensiveness of its operations are immeasurably greater than what they were in the past. Thus, not only is the corps structure anachronistic, but a vast and growing range of technologies and weapons systems are used and maintained by several corps, rather than by a single, specialized one.

Clear, perceived criteria for the definition of corps by specialization were being lost. The specialization that derived from professional know-how was superseded by administrative decisions and conservatism. Over the years, in the normal course of things, the basic corps concept became twisted beyond recognition. Instead of bearing professional responsibility solely at the unit level, the corps staffs became large, independent headquarters, which in addition to their roles as special staffs of the General Staff also command General Staff reserves, installations, and schools. Some even bore intercorps responsibility for organization and doctrine.

One can almost say that the number of types of corps became as the number of corps themselves: one corps also became a functional command; one bore responsibility at the formation, but not unit, level; one corps was subordinate to the chief of General Staff, another to the chief of a branch; one was strictly a staff, while another bore inter-arm corps responsibility. These circumstances came about because the coordinating staff (the General Staff) consistently avoided implementing change, leaving the job of intercorps integration to unregulated processes, determined by the strength of the contending corps and their commanders.

At the end of 1977, a plan for the reorganization of the land forces was submitted at the behest of the minister of defense. It included a recommendation to disband the staffs of the corps and to unify the corps within the framework of two distinctive commands. The field corps (infantry, armor, engineers, and artillery) were to be under a Ground Forces Functional Command. The logistics corps were to constitute a Logistics Functional Command. The Ground Forces Command, according to the recommendation, would be responsible for the structure of units and formations, and for training them for their designated roles. The Logistics Command was to provide logistical support for the entire IDF.

The Ground Forces Command would have subordinated to it training centers, the units and formations of the General Staff reserve, and units and formations in the process of being established. The Ground Forces Command would be responsible for organization, combat doctrine, and research and development.

Intercorps integration, however important, was only the second most important consideration underlying the proposal for the establishment of the Ground Forces Command and Logistics Command. The main point was to transfer functions and tasks from the General Staff, as a coordinating staff, to the staffs of corps, thus releasing the General Staff, as the inter-arm coordinating staff, from that task. The intention was that the General Staff devote itself entirely to being a supreme national military headquarters, conducting war, commanding all three services with the help of the Air Force and Navy staffs, and concerning itself with current strategic matters. Such matters would include the current security effort and preparedness, operational planning, the development of military thought, strategic planning and deployment, development of doctrine concerning force structure, development of weapons systems, and the fostering of inter-arm integration. The transfer of some of the General Staff's authority as the staff of the Army, in the fields of force structure and training, to the Ground Forces Command, would also make it possible to assign more air and naval officers to various functions on the General Staff, thus contributing to its effectiveness as an integrated, interservice staff.

In February 1984, after much delay and internal struggle in the defense establishment, the Ground Forces Command was established; the recommendation concerning a Logistics Command was rejected. Expectations that with the new organization, the strategic functioning of the high command would rise to an altogether new standard have, however, been only partially realized.

CHAPTER 12
THE MINISTRY OF DEFENSE AND THE MILITARY

The State of Israel has managed to establish a military under strict civilian control, despite the fact that the state itself arose from divided society, replete with armed underground movements. At the time of Israel's establishment, its political parties were for the most part not opportunistic mass parties; they were ideological and dogmatic in character, their members willing to die for their beliefs and opinions. Ideological struggles were bitter; suffice it to recall the uncompromising rivalry between Left and Right, the split in the kibbutz movement, the heated controversy over the role of religious law in a secular state, and contention over whether the political orientation of the new state should be toward the Soviet Union or the West.

Under these circumstances, the very establishment of an apolitical military, as the only subject in a divided society over which there would be no ideological controversy, and that would be the focus of a broad national consensus, was no mean accomplishment. It would never have come to pass had the military not been effectively subordinated to civilian control in all operational activities. In the period just prior to the establishment of the IDF and in its early years, an excellent tradition of military subordination in all matters to the civilian authorities was indeed created. But what existed in all spheres in the IDF's early period has, over time, survived only in the sphere of operational control.

The principle of operational subordination has been religiously preserved and has become a firm tradition. The founders of the state were concerned that this national consensus on security not be compromised by the rivalry between political ideologies and military undergrounds that had dominated life in the prestatehood period. Therefore, they set norms for the IDF aimed at ensuring and nurturing the values of a democratic society, on the one hand, and on preserving a hierarchical, bureaucratic military organization, predicated on the principle of formal discipline and not merely an individual's inner convictions, on the other. Two elements constitute the guiding principle in all that relates to what is permitted and forbidden: freedom of opinion and discussion; but absolute compliance with, and obedience to, orders. Indeed, ever since its establishment, in the IDF command and staff concept the dividing lines of authority between the various levels of hierarchy have passed through the spheres of responsibility and seniority, not through the province of spirit and thought. Everybody has the right, even obligation, to think as if he were the one who must decide and to try to convince his superiors. However, after a decision has been reached, he must obey and do his utmost to advance the purpose of that decision, in letter and spirit.

Israel's first prime minister and minister of defense, David Ben-Gurion, described the principle underpinning the organization of the military, its internal regime, and discipline, as follows:

The military does not determine policy, the regime, laws, or the workings of the government of Israel. The military does not, at its own initiative, even decide on its own structure, internal regime, or its modes of operation, and it does not, of course, decide on peace or war. The military is nothing but an executive arm, the arm of defence of the State of Israel. . . . The organisation of the military, and the shaping of its character are all within the exclusive prerogative of the civilian authorities: the government, Parliament, and the voters. . . . The military is subordinate in every way to the government.

In that early period, there was also concern that with the transition from voluntary underground organizations to a professional, official military, based on compulsory service and military careers, militarism would develop in Israel. It was a specter that frightened many in that period. Ben-Gurion said then that

a military, as an armed force, is liable to become a violent, hobnailed boot that could endanger the security, internal and external, of the country and the people—should it not be kept in a framework of strict discipline, and if it is not absolutely subordinate to a civilian State authority, and if the actions of each soldier and his way of life, as long as he serves in the military, are not governed by the military regulations.

The defense system took on its present structure early in the process of the institutionalization of the defense organs, with the establishment of the IDF. Various facts and considerations constituted the basis for the model that came into being. The more salient of them were:

1. The need to subordinate the military to the elected civilian organs and to assure that it would accept their authority and obey them.
2. Since the defense system had not been created from scratch—its various elements, or the germs of such elements, had existed in the prestatehood underground movements—the factor of continuity had an impact on that structure in any event. This was all the more so since the entire transition took place continuously and at an accelerated pace under emergency conditions, in the War of Independence, with officials of the undergrounds continuing in their previous positions.
3. High sensitivity to the threat, real or imagined, of militarism. The founders not only made certain of civilian control of the military but also saw to it that some defense functions would be performed by the civilian establishment. Toward that end, the principle of division of authority and power between a civilian staff (the ministry of defense) and the military staff (the General Staff) was adopted.

The organization that took form was intended to detach military personnel from civilian concerns and to confer upon the civilian authorities the weight to countervail that of the military. Practical consideration of effectiveness also guided the organizers of Israel's defense system; they wanted that system to guarantee that military personnel would be able to concentrate entirely on the operational aspects of defense, by leaving the financial and public administration aspects to the civilian authorities. Furthermore, there were considerations of value. In order to assure the ethics and impartiality of uniformed personnel, an effort was made to prevent them from being engaged in commercial or financial activities, away from negotiations with interested parties, such as suppliers and contractors, and even away from direct working relationships with the various government ministries and other civilian institutions, except in what related to the military reserve units, area defense, and settlements.

A practice has developed over the years according to which the military decides in matters of procurement—what, how many, and when, while the ministry of defense obtains the means, deciding how and wherefrom.

Because of the principle of division of authority and power, and because of the historical reasons outlined above, no single integrated defense system was established at the outset. The defense system was composed of two separate staffs and two hierarchical pyramids—an integrated General Staff and a civilian ministry of defense—between which were tenuous areas of contact.

The clumsy bureaucracy thus created, with its duplication of functions, caused harm that outweighed the advantages of checks and balances between the General Staff and Ministry of Defense. A process developed involving the accumulation of power by the military side of the system, with the General Staff acquiring too much influence, direct and indirect, on industry and the economy. No synthesis was created that would engender a propitious balance between the conflicting interest represented by the General Staff and ministry. The scales had tipped (not always in a useful way) toward the demands for readiness and explicit military power, as advocated by the General Staff, at the expense of industrial and economic power—that is, at the expense of overall national power, which is within the purview of the Ministry of Defense.

Whether because of the type of organisation or for some other reason, fears of militarism have not been realized. Israeli democracy is strong, and the military is unqualifiedly subordinate to civilian authority in all that concerns its public status and defense-related employment. The military does not set policy, nor does it decide for itself its military assignments. Yet even so, the General Staff is a dominant center of gravity, one that is not under adequate guidance by the political authorities in what pertains to its character and values, patterns of organization, procurement, the balance between the various components of forces, long-term forecasts and build-up of forces, and security doctrine in general.

The IDF enjoys nearly total autonomy in such matters (even if it requires the formal authorization of the Ministry of Defense—an authorization it obtains almost as a matter of course). Thus, the military to a great extent dictates to the national leadership the essence, nature, composition, and scope of the country's military power.

The estimates and considerations of the General Staff should undoubtedly have considerable weight in the determination of national security policy. However, given the structure of the defense system and the nonexistence of other tools, such as an advisory staff to the government on national security, there is no mechanism in Israel for informed, balanced appreciation of the situation from an overall national perspective. In a survey of security matters to the government on 18 October 1953, Ben-Gurion said:

The military mind perforce sees everything from a military standpoint; it is not always able to properly evaluate the other essential needs of the country, and the minister of defence must not rely solely on the lone opinion of the chief of the General Staff. Because all defense personnel are subordinate to him, only one opinion will be heard in the military, which is by necessity structured on hierarchy and discipline. It is not easy for a military man—although not impossible—to see that the country has other needs of equal importance to military needs. Priorities must be discussed— between military needs and the other basic needs of the country—from a comprehensive and balanced perspective of all our historic needs.

In the survey, Defense Minister Ben-Gurion warned against a monopoly of the General Staff.

For years, there has been a certain degree of integration between the defense ministry and General Staff, which is manifest in common staffs, and in certain departmental sections that are staffed by both uniformed personnel and civilians. Such procedures are inevitable under the organizational background described above, and they should be encouraged.

Despite the distinction between the civilian ministry and military staff, the areas of contact between the two pyramids are such that they have some units in common. Some such units are subordinate to the ministry and some to the General Staff; in areas within the purview of ministry authority, they are directed by the ministry, and in areas of activity under General Staff authority, they are directed by the General Staff. The dividing line between the General Staff and ministry is in accordance with definition of function, not necessarily optimal organizational principles. In fact, things are even more complex than that. Ministry employees are subject to Civil Service Commission guidelines, while military General Staff personnel are under the authority of the Branch of the Adjutant General, on the General Staff. Thus there are two types of employees from the standpoint of manpower management. The existing organization calls for a greater degree of integration between the ministry and General Staff, but without compromising the principle of unity of command within the military system.

In order to avoid duplication and promote efficiency, it would be desirable to have staff functions within the purview of the Ministry of Defense and General Staff performed in joint staff units. Certain staff units should be subordinate to both the military and civilian staffs, in their own areas of responsibility, in order to perform their designated tasks. However, such units should always be subordinated in the chain of command to only one of the two bodies.

The integration of staffs streamlines defense work. Putting information in the hands of common staffs obviates extensive liaison and senseless disputes over the reliability of information. That is how the Ministry of Defense Budget Branch, for instance, works. The director of the Budget Branch fulfils a double function: in addition to his capacity as the Budget Branch director, he is also financial advisor to the chief of the General Staff. In his capacity as Budget Branch director, he is subordinate to the director-general of the Ministry of Defense; as financial advisor to the chief of the General Staff, he is subordinate to the latter.

The assumption that civilian control of the military is represented by civilian officials supervising uniformed officers, standing as it were between them and democratic institutions, thus keeping the "militarist bugaboo" in check, is baseless. The civilian official and his uniformed counterpart are both appointed and subject in the same way to the values of democratic control by the elected echelon. Civilian control is properly maintained when the *elected* representatives of the people oversee both appointed civilians and military personnel.

The establishment of the IDF as a national instrument that reflects a general consensus and is not ideologically controversial was without doubt an immense accomplishment. That accomplishment, though, would never have transpired, had the military not been effectively subordinate to civilian control. While no one in Israel would challenge the principle of military subordination to the civilian authorities, the IDF has over the years become a largely autonomous, self-perpetuating, and dominant institution. The responsibilities and authority of the military go beyond the qualifications put in place in the early years of statehood, even though the rules that were formulated, and were once in force, state explicitly that the military is not to shape its own image, its character, or even its organization. The General Staff has become more and more of a law unto itself, to the point where Israeli governments and ministers of defense are almost outside observers. For instance, in late 1994 the IDF General Staff issued a document entitled *The Spirit of the IDF: Values and Basic Rules.* The document set forth a list of values and rules, and it states that the *Spirit of the IDF* represents the collective military spirit, values, and identification. According to a General Staff explanatory note, this document constitutes an ethical codex for the IDF and reflects the position of the military leadership on the spirit of the IDF, concerning the basic norms that are its guiding principles. The values and basic principles that guide and obligate the IDF are explicit expressions of the elements that shape its image. Here the General Staff is determining them itself and applying them to the military, instead of the opposite: Parliament and the government should decide the character of the military and dictate its values.

Civilian control over military power and its use are firm in Israel. In that respect, Israel sets a good example for other democratic countries. An independent entity of "military will" vis-à-vis "political will" would be inconceivable in Israel in operational matters or in those pertaining to peace and war. The civilian authorities decide on the use of military force, on its operational employment; an exemplary model of military subordination to civilian authority obtains. This is not to say that no IDF commander has ever misled civilian authorities or initiated unauthorized military activity. Such instances, though, are rare exceptions to the norm.

In other spheres, though, such as national security doctrine, the characteristics and patterns of military power, the allocation of resources, and the economy and industry, civilian control over the military is less effective. The military is to a certain extent a kingdom within a kingdom.

In all that pertains to the essence of the military—to the role of the various arms and corps and the qualifications required of them, the order of forces, organisation, preparedness, combat doctrine, weapons systems, norms and discipline, promotion policy and the appointment of general officers—in all these matters, the virtually sole arbiter is the chief of the General Staff (CGS). The "opinion of the military" is nothing but the opinion of the CGS. Over time, ministers of defense have become dependent on CGSs. When General Staff decisions have been brought to a minister for confirmation, only rarely has he imposed his judgment on the military. It is because ministers of defense lack tools to check and analyze information independently that they almost always end up confirming the opinion of the CGS. There have, of course, been exceptions, and ministers have imposed their will on the military. Nevertheless, it would be fair to generalize that Israeli ministers of defense have controlled the military and imposed on it civilian will in all that pertains to operational employment and the neutralization of its political influence, but that they have not been sufficiently firm in matters of the IDF's organization, character, and efficiency. Ministers of defense have not dictated promotion policy, nor have they had a material impact on the education and training of senior officers or on the appointment of generals. Decisions concerning manpower establishments and the appointment of generals and other senior officers are in practice and for the most part, made by the military alone. The military makes appointments with the pro forma concurrence of the minister of defense, but the minister is not able to render an independent judgement.

Relations between the military and civilian authorities can be divided into two periods. The first period was from the mid-1940s to the Six Day War in 1967. The dominant figure in this period was David Ben-Gurion, who assumed the chairmanship and defense portfolio of the Jewish Agency Executive in December 1946 and who, two years later, upon the establishment of the state, took the defense portfolio concurrently with the prime ministership. It was he who largely shaped the relationship between the civilian and military authorities in this period. The second period is that subsequent to the Six Day War.

The patterns that arose in the beginning of the first period, with the establishment of the state, derived for the most part from the traditions and precedents of the Hagana. While the relative contributions of various groups in the creation of the IDF can be argued about—the Hagana, the Irgun, the Stern Group, former British

Army servicemen, and others—no one would dispute that the IDF General Staff has been a continuation of the Hagana High Command and General Staff. Hence, when the IDF was organized upon the establishment of the state, there was no need to define the subordination of the military to civilian authority or explain its critical importance. On the eve of the establishment of the state, the Hagana was subordinate to the elected Jewish political leadership, whose members had a broad perspective on national needs.

During Ben-Gurion's tenure of office as minister of defense, he had the General Staff branches at his disposal. The minister was not dependent solely on the chief of the General Staff. He himself was able to weigh and judge, on the basis of his wide-ranging and efficient work directly with the staff branches. The minister had the necessary tools, and the General Staff was not omnipotent. It often had to work hard to convince the minister in matters of organization, procurement, combat doctrine, and senior appointments.

As the competent political authority, Ben-Gurion was able to reach independent conclusions and make judgments and decisions in military affairs because he devoted himself to the various matters at hand and became proficient in their details. The advantage of Ben-Gurion over the military authorities in the strategic sphere derived from his mastery of all other matters of state. Such mastery is what confers a comprehensive outlook and an ability to set priorities.

In those days, the minister of defense commanded the IDF in the name of the government; the CGS was head of the military staff and acted at the behest of the minister of defense within the military. The minister of defense could command because he had a staff at his disposal—the General Staff. In the War of Independence, the various General Staff branches served the minister of defense directly, as required. After Ben-Gurion, General Staff branches and their departments gradually stopped being the staff of the minister of defense; since then, CGSs have not always enabled the minister of defense to work directly with General Staff officers. Toward Ben-Gurion, most of whose years in government had been as prime minister and minister of defense, there had been a special deference that prevented any change in the norm instituted in the War of Independence. But after Ben-Gurion left the scene, that norm atrophied; only the chief of Intelligence served as a staff officer to the minister of defense and the government in his capacity as the national intelligence officer.

Furthermore, CGSs after Ben-Gurion have exhibited varying degrees of antagonism toward the very idea of establishing a special assisting staff section that would work directly for the minister, verifying data for him, requesting additional information from both the General Staff and the Ministry of Defense staff, and analyzing the implications of their recommendations. CGSs have contended that ministers of defense do not need an extra staff, because they already have one, namely, the General Staff of the IDF. This contention is inaccurate, since the General Staff branches no longer work directly for the minister of defense, as they did in Ben-Gurion's day. Thus, the minister is neutralized and entirely dependent on the CGS, having no tools of his own that would enable him to reach his own decisions in the various spheres that call for his attention. The minister has no alternative but to choose from among the IDF recommendations offered by the CGS, and from among the recommendations offered by the director-general of the Ministry of Defense.

It is important that the minister have a staff of his own, composed of both civilians and uniformed officers. The purpose of that staff would be to study the reports and recommendations of the military staff under the CGS, and those of the civilian staff under the ministry director-general; to monitor the activities of the two staffs; to follow the decision-making processes; and to analyze recommendations for the minister and request alternatives from those who submitted them. Such a staff is needed to help the minister issue regulations and guidelines for both the military and civilian staffs.

Another reason why a minister needs a staff is the principle of the unity of command—because the military command and staff channels converge at the CGS, the military staff cannot serve the minister directly. The idea that underpinned the IDF at its inception was the division of power, as a part of keeping the military under civilian control. The control of financial resources and manpower, for instance, was removed from the military and given to the Ministry of Defense, although over time it has in effect reverted to the military.

The chief of the General Staff is perceived in Israel not as the supreme commander of the armed forces but as the chief of the military staff. The entity that commands the military is the government, through the minister of defense. The strengthening of the institution of CGS in Israel has been brought about in part by prime ministers and important government ministers who wanted to create a counterweight to the power of the minister of defense.

In the period between the Six Day War in 1967 and the Yom Kippur War in 1973, an additional factor was at work. The minister of defense, Moshe Dayan, contended after the Six Day War that his appointment under public pressure, without having been elected, had not conferred on him sufficient authority; hence, he tended not to impose his will on the General Staff. Even after the 1969 elections, when he was elected and reappointed minister of defense, the personal scenery in both the government and IDF remained unchanged, and it would have been difficult to reassert the minister's will over the General Staff.

The fact that Israel's ministers of defense have included "professionals"—former generals—shows, however, that the excessive independence of the CGS has not been caused by lack of qualifications or the weak personalities of ministers but rather by basic institutional and legal defects.

In May 1948, the law establishing the IDF, "The Israel Defense Forces Ordinance, 1948," was promulgated. It states that the military is subordinate to the government through the minister of defense (in the words of the ordinance, "The minister of defense is entrusted with implementation of this Ordinance").

Investigation of the events of the Yom Kippur War indicated a lack of clarity concerning subordination of the military to the minister of defense. In order to clarify matters and unequivocally define authority and the relations between the civilian and military authorities, Parliament enacted a constitutional law, "Basic Law: The Military," in March 1976. Even the Basic Law, however, tends to compromise the position of the minister of defense relative to the CGS: at one point the law states that the "CGS is subordinate to the minister of defense," at another that he is "subject to the authority of the government." The legislature meant that the CGS is subject to the authority of the government through the minister of defense and is hence subordinate to him; in other words, for the CGS, the minister of defense embodies the government. However, the wording is liable to mislead, because it is context-sensitive and liable to be interpreted incorrectly; if one argues that the minister of defense does not embody the government, the CGS would not have to obey him.

Under these circumstances, with the military at times enjoying unbridled independence and the institution of the CGS acquiring enhanced power, it would be highly inadvisable to give the CGS an opening through which to evade the authority of the minister by exploiting the swings of authority between the minister and government. It must be made clear that the CGS is responsible to the government through a hierarchy, namely through the minister of defense. However, in order to prevent the minister of defense from being a sole, final, arbiter in military matters, the CGS should be required to make his reservations about the minister's decisions known to the government in writing, through the minister of defense, whenever he feels that is necessary. That way, on the one hand, the government will be aware of differences of opinion, and on the other hand, the CGS will not be exempt from responsibility for the results of acts or omissions that result from a decision.

While the General Staff functions under the civilian authorities, the latter do not have the tools by which to make decisions or judge those of others. Hence, they almost always confirm General Staff recommendations, except those concerning the size of the budget. The level of the budget is determined by the government, and it is the outcome of power struggles between the military and the finance ministry. Therefore, decisions are the result not of comprehensive national appreciations of the situation but rather of ad hoc compromises. Arguments over the budget do not focus on security concepts and needs but rather on the ability of the public coffers, in the view of finance ministry officials, to satisfy the demands of the military.

It is not only at the civilian and military echelons that relationships have not been adequately settled institutionally. At the governmental level as well, that of the supreme national command, matters have not been sufficiently formulated and put on an institutional footing. For instance, on the morning of 6 October 1973, the day the Yom Kippur War broke out, a number of ministers, among them the prime minister, decided that Israel would not make a preemptive air strike; in other words, it would not commence hostilities but instead would risk absorbing a massive blow with its forces not mobilized or deployed. In fact, such an air strike could not, for various reasons, have been effective, but when the political authorities made their decision, they did not know that. A simple choice was put before them: to undertake a preemptive air strike or not to. The IDF recommended attacking only Syria, believing that the Syrian air force would be destroyed within two hours and its system of antiaircraft missiles within another three hours. If such a strike were carried out, the Air Force would be able to help check the Syrian assault on the Golan Heights until the reserves were mobilized.

This was the information the political leadership had that morning. After serious consideration, a decision was reached not to deliver a preemptive blow before war broke out. This group of ministers, which was composed of figures of the highest stature, was to take upon itself extremely critical decisions throughout the war, and to demonstrate courageous national leadership; nevertheless, it was constituted in an improvised manner, without any guidelines for its own conduct. It was an ad hoc "war cabinet." The entire government sat as a ministerial committee for national security affairs throughout the Yom Kippur War, but the fateful decisions were made by the improvised ministerial group.

On the night of 10 October, the "war cabinet" decided that the IDF would launch a counterattack on the Syrian front. On the following day, 11 October, 1973, at 11:00 A.M., Israel launched the counterattack against Syria, but it was only at 9:00 P.M. that the government as a whole, at a formal meeting, heard that Israel had done so that morning. The prime minister reported on the consultations that had taken place the previous night, and the government confirmed the decision retroactively. However, at that same meeting of the government, several ministers demanded that a crossing of the Suez Canal be brought up for governmental authorization in advance.

On 12 October, less than twenty four hours after a plenary session of the government supported the prime minister's position that a demand should be made that the enemy withdraw from all the areas captured in the fighting and return to his opening positions, the "war cabinet," on its own, accepted the recommendation of the military to accede to a "cease-fire in situ," in other words, in each side's current positions.

In the midst of the fighting, a constitutional argument raged within the government over what was permissible for the military, the prime minister, the "cabinet," and the government as a whole. It was a principled, legalistic argument aimed at working out basic rules for the orderly workings of a government in peace as well as war. Discussions that should have been conducted years earlier burst forth in the midst of a war.

The government was divided into two groups over the question. One faction contended that the prime minister and "cabinet" could not decide alone whether to cross the canal. This group was led by a member of the "cabinet" who, only the previous night, had joined his colleagues in supporting a counterattack against Syria without feeling any need to obtain authorization from the entire government. The second group contended that the military should conduct the war as it saw fit—including the matter of whether to cross the canal—without asking anyone's authorization. The argument ended in a temporary compromise: the "war cabinet" was authorized to order a canal crossing to conduct raids and destroy forces; a crossing to hold ground until a cease-fire would require a decision by the entire government.

In the Yom Kippur War, the autonomy of the General Staff was limited in the purely political sphere that touched on relations with the great powers, such as whether to deliver a preemptive strike before the outbreak of war, or to bomb Syrian airfields so as to prevent Soviet resupply aircraft from using them during the fighting. In all other matters, the General Staff enjoyed virtually automatic authorization of its requests: for instance, the day before the war the CGS recommended not mobilizing reserves, and the political leadership acceded to that recommendation. That was also the case in numerous other instances as well: the counterattack in Sinai on 8 October, the attack on the Golan Heights on 11 October, and the recommendation to request a cease-fire on 12 October even if the Egyptians and Syrians refused to return to their original positions as of the outbreak of the war.

The government of Israel does not avail itself of a special consultative staff—professional, objective, and independent—as is required of governments that bear responsibility for security and for the nurturing and use of military power. The government of Israel is dependent on only one staff—its unified, military General Staff. Therefore, when the government wants to weigh situations and alternatives, to pass judgment and take positions, it perforce relies on the very staff—the General Staff—that it must supervise, whose recommendations it must consider, and to which it must furnish guidelines. In other words, the process is circular. He who is charged with national security lacks adequate tools to discharge his function.

In order to enable the government properly to fulfil its responsibilities in national security and command of the military, it must have a consultative staff to examine and process data and recommendations in foreign affairs and security matters. Furthermore, an advisory staff ought to be established in the prime minister's office for evaluating the nation's circumstances. A complex web of factors bears upon national security: political, economic, military, demographic, social, etc. The consultative staff should collect information in these areas, prepare position papers, and analyze available options and alternatives, as well as their implications. Without such tools, it is difficult to pursue well-founded policies in foreign affairs and national security. Without such a staff, the government must rely on a military that has developed and functioned in a haphazard manner, and without control. Without such a staff, the government is doomed to being led on by its security apparatus, rather than leading it.

PART THREE

SECURITY DOCTRINE AND THE TEST OF TIME

CHAPTER 13
MYTHS AND LESSONS

THE FOG OF BATTLE AND THE FOG OF HISTORY

Israeli security doctrine has been shaped by national goals and objective regional circumstances—violent opposition to Israel's very existence, the ratio of forces, and certain unvarying strategic factors. It has also been shaped by the lessons of war.

In order to ascertain whether that doctrine has proved itself, it is necessary to ask whether it has fulfilled its expected goal, or if Israel has had to diverge from it and improvise, rather than implement it flexibly, according to circumstances. In order to answer that question, it behooves one to follow developments in Israel's security history, to learn the lessons of its wars and from the development of security affairs between wars. The answer to the question of whether the basic aim of Israeli security doctrine has been attained—thwarting Arab attempts to exterminate Israel and inducing the Arabs to seek political solutions—is self-evident. However, the question of whether the attainment of national security goals has been the result of adherence to the principles of an optimal security doctrine, or whether those goals have been achieved *despite* adherence to those principles, is a difficult one to answer.

An optimal doctrine is one derived from unvarying fundamental principles, principles that do not change frequently in the light of current developments, or for specific cases, but that can nevertheless be effectively applied in varying circumstances. The difficulty lies in deriving lessons from the various components of security-related processes in general, and from war in particular.

A necessary condition for learning lessons is a knowledge of the facts. One must check if known facts can be substantiated and if historical research on a given war and battles fought in it has been authoritatively established—or if imagination and reality have been interwoven. Hence, the drawing of conclusions involves certain information and the verification of historical memory. But verifying such matters is difficult, because studying the lessons of war is a transition from the fog of battle, saturated with the fumes of gunpowder, to the yet heavier mists of military history, overcast with the vapors of myth.

MYTH AND TRUTH

Fact relates to myth as rational cognition relates to intuitive cognition. Just as intuitive cognition cannot be dismissed out of hand, neither should myth be dismissed, even though it has no genuine claim to reflect the truth. Myth is the creature of the imagination, the offspring of man's preconceptions, his clinging to his past and his dreams. Impulse and ignorance may also be involved in myth. It is the absolute ruler over both defeat and victory, failure and success. The impulse toward both envy and competitiveness is ingrained in man, stimulating his quest for glory. In moments of triumph or success, such a force may undermine one's psychological balance, inducing one to magnify one's own part in events and belittle that of one's fellows. In defeat or failure, a self-defense mechanism is at work, inducing a person to blur his own part in events and magnify that of his fellows.

The first rumor spread about an event is what takes hold of people's minds. The first "news"—rumor—spreads with geometrically increasing speed. In short order, it becomes "common knowledge," henceforth attaining the status of "received wisdom." Thus, impulse combines with ignorance. Human nature, with its many impulses, and the nature of war—the fog of battle and the friction of war—generate myth and the fog of military history.

There is a difficulty in trying to be free of myths: the professional, who is privy to privileged information, is an interested party, while the layman, who is disinterested, is unfamiliar with the relevant details. Interested parties fight each other with myths. Myths are the weapons commanders use in the fight for glory and survival after a war; no one disarms as long as there is a "threat" to his place in history.

The goal of military history is the ascertainment of the truth. Truth can be sought, on condition that one recognizes two limitations to such an endeavor: first, the truth has a relative dimension, and second, even myths contain a kernel of truth about that which pertains to human nature. However, a myth is to be dismissed out of hand as soon as it purports to depict events and convey information in terms of space, time, and quantity.

THE FORCE OF MYTHS

Only systematic, critical, and objective research can determine if a particular event occurred at a particular time and place. However, even the most thorough and critical research cannot prove conclusively what reasons, moods, motives, or occurrences underlay the acts and omissions of men as they waged war. A myth has force, sometimes more force than the findings of scientific research, when it focuses on the subjective forces that underlie and motivate human-historical developments. No matter how much research is done, the picture of a historical process will essentially remain a matter of interpretation. The power of seemingly objective scientific research cannot exceed that of literature and art. Scientific historical memory is a framework, an infrastructure, based on events in time and space. Yet, this framework is enshrouded in the blanket of myth in all that concerns the interpretation of events.

Myths have acquired a bad name, yet from a broad historical perspective, it is often found that they contain profound truths. Scientific inquiry is superior to literary imagination in whatever involves fact, such as time, space, and quantity. But literature is superior to research in that which pertains to human nature and the human impulses that have brought about a process at a given historical time. The official military history of Napoleon's campaign in Russia is preferable to literature for learning dates, places, and quantities; yet Leo Tolstoy's *War and Peace* is a more complex and profound guide to the psychological forces, impulses, that motivated the decisive actions of individuals and groups in that great war and determined its outcome.

As historical studies probe more deeply into such matters as the size of forces deployed, timetables, and movements, they will surely get closer to the truth. Matters are different, though, when consideration is turned to something's significance, the explanations, reasons, urges, impulses, and fears that could have motivated those who took part in a battle or made decisions, or about their behavior or moves. Tolstoy can explain better than a historian why one course was taken rather than another, what could have led commanders or units to act as they did, from the standpoint of human nature. From that standpoint, a work of art can usually (although not always) come closer to the mark than a technical accumulation of fact.

Nevertheless, and surprisingly, what often arises is a dialectic in which both myth and substantiated fact are valid, both are relatively correct. For this reason, a literary genius like Tolstoy, who understands human nature well and knows how to get to the bottom of human behavior, can teach us more about the nature of war and its moves—what motivated its participants, how they reached decisions, whether rationally or irrationally, or simply by chance—than can dry research.

This is also the case when the source of a story is an individual's own real-life experiences. After the Yom Kippur War, a nineteen-year-old tank gunner, Ron Zohar, wrote a book, *War Story*, in which he described the war in the Sinai as he experienced it through the gun sight of his tank and his radio earphones. Even though his perspective was narrow—the perspective of one tank that fought in one company—his subjective book, written from one soldier's experiences, tells more about the nature of the war, about the prevailing qualitative ratio of forces, and about the fighting quality and heroism of the Israeli tank crewmen in general than all the erudite studies published in the wake of that war.

According to Carl von Clausewitz, an action in war is like a movement inside a constraining medium, the resistance of which causes "friction" in the war machine and erodes it. Combat experience, the "lubricating oil" of the war machine, may reduce the friction and erosion. The principle of Clausewitzian friction applies as well to national security doctrine. The various components of Israeli security doctrine have been put to the test of time and performance for many years. The development of a large part of that doctrine has been influenced by the lessons of routine operational activity and war. In order to assess its worth in the light of experience and the extent to which it has succeeded in overcoming friction, one must look through the fog of military and military affairs. One must review the events that have transpired over the years, focusing on those wars that have proved to be milestones, that have affected political and military reality and have changed (in the Israeli-Arab arena) the basic strategic factors underlying Israel's national security doctrine.

CHAPTER 14

THE WAR OF INDEPENDENCE, 1948

The Arabs went to war against the Jewish population in Palestine with the aim of exterminating it and taking control of the entire country. The aim of the Jews in that war was to defend steadfastly all areas of Jewish settlement in Palestine and to take control of whatever areas were allotted a Jewish state should the UN decide in favor of its establishment. Should such a decision not be made, the Jewish aim was to take control of the entire country, or as much of it as possible, and retain control of it pending a political settlement.

At the outset, the War of Independence was between the Jews and the Arabs of Palestine, but upon the declaration of the State of Israel it developed into a full-scale war between Israel and the Arab states that invaded the country. In the first stage of the War of Independence, Palestinian Arabs, some 1.2 million in number, fought a Jewish population of some 650,000. Palestine's Arabs obtained highly valuable aid from the Arab Legion, as the regular Jordanian army was then called. Thousands of volunteers from neighboring Arab states also rushed to their aid. The fighting was bitter; Israel sustained painful defeats, but it eventually prevailed. Afterward, the second stage of the war commenced, involving the regular military forces of the five Arab states that invaded Israel: Egypt, Jordan, Syria, Lebanon, and Iraq. That stage of the war also ended in an Israeli victory. In the beginning of each stage of the war, the Jews conducted a defensive campaign, and in both instances were pressed into difficult circumstances. Only when they went over to the offensive, first against the Palestinian Arabs and later against the coalition of Arab states, did the Jews attain a decisive victory.

In the overall balance of national power, the Arabs enjoyed overwhelming superiority in manpower, resources, and weapons. The aggregate population of the Arabs states that invaded Israel was some forty million, but not all of this potential was exploited. The number of combatants on each side was roughly equal, approximately one hundred thousand.

It was not the Arab quantitative military advantage, then, that weighed heavily on the IDF in the second stage of the war, but rather the advantage in weapons and firepower. The Arab armed services were standing military forces, equipped with individual weapons and organic, heavy support weapons within the various units and formations. They had tanks, artillery, and combat aircraft, at a time when the IDF had just been created from underground military organizations and was equipped with only a varied and improvised arsenal of individual weapons. In comparison to the IDF, the Arabs had immense firepower. Firepower was not a highly significant strategic factor at that time, but at the operational and tactical levels, it was vital.

Because of Arab superiority in weapons systems and firepower, the IDF at first took a defensive posture; had it continued to do so, Israel would have been defeated. An imminent danger of total, irreversible defeat hovered over the newly born State of Israel. Israel's wartime leaders managed to reverse the IDF's strategy twice—in the fighting with the Arabs of Palestine and again with the invading Arab forces. They realized that Israel must pin its hopes on its assault power and go over to the offensive, as its staying power was inadequate. When the IDF went over to the offensive, Israel was able to win the War of Independence.

At that time, the Middle East had not yet experienced the revolution in the art of war that had commenced in the First World War and reached its peak in the Second. Sophisticated weapons systems had elsewhere appeared on the modern battlefield, mobile and armored formations had become the decisive ground formations, and air superiority was a necessary condition for victory in modern war. Yet the War of Independence was not a modern war but mainly an infantry war, one in which infantry formations were decisive. In that war, the IDF had all of sixteen tanks, and the Arabs forty-five. (In the mid-1950s, Israel and the Arabs together were to have half a million soldiers, approximately five hundred combat aircraft, a thousand tanks, and 1,200 artillery pieces. In the 1960s, Israel and the Arabs would have one million soldiers, eight hundred aircraft, nearly four thousand tanks, and 3,500 artillery pieces. In 1973, the aggregate extent of Israeli and Arab forces would come to some 1.8 million soldiers, 1,650 aircraft, 7,800 tanks, and 4,800 artillery pieces.)

In the War of Independence, modern weapons systems played an insignificant, supporting role. Arab firepower, including air power, was unable to prevent the IDF from concentrating forces and carrying out approach marches and deployments; at the strategic and operational levels, Arab firepower had only harassment effect. However, at the tactical level, it was a critical factor. The stage of "fighting to the objective" is characterized by firefights; the IDF was not able to contend with the Arabs at that stage, because of the meager firepower it had had at its disposal in the early stages of the war.

The method the IDF adopted to overcome that limitation consisted of avoiding firefights by approaching objectives by stealth. Instead of applying covering fire to neutralize sources of enemy fire, IDF forces would move to their objectives at night, under the cover of darkness. IDF forces would thus bypass the stage of "fighting to the objective" and go directly to that of "fighting on the objective." This method reflected the qualitative superiority of the Israeli soldier in the War of Independence. In that way, close combat was forced—motivation versus motivation, man versus man, grenade versus grenade, bayonet versus bayonet; at that stage of a battle, supporting firepower is not significant.

Thus, in the early stages of the War of Independence, the optimal solution to the problem of inferiority in firepower was found: attainment of decisions based on night fighting by assault infantry forces. In the course of the war, the IDF managed to obtain weapons systems and in its later stages, it had combat aircraft, artillery, and mechanized forces at its disposal. From then on, the IDF conducted large-scale mobile operations, day and night, with mechanized formations and units.

Various lessons were learned in the War of Independence, among them:

1. Full use of national resources by reliance on a reserve military.
2. Offensive as a basic strategy, reliance on assault power, and eventually

the doctrine of preemptive attack and taking the fighting into enemy territory. The tradition of taking the initiative and the spirit of attack, which came into being by force of historical circumstances, influenced the development of the fighting values and offensive patterns of conduct that the IDF has adapted to its needs ever since.

3. Area defense as an alternative to strategic depth, and as the infrastructure for conducting a rigid defense.

4. Full use of force at all levels in combat, by not maintaining reserves but sufficing with one central reserve at the highest tactical or operational level in each sector.

5. Not evacuating the wounded using those engaged in assault, in order to avoid compromising the maintenance of the aim. Wounded are to be taken care of and evacuated by combat medical orderlies and by special maintenance and evacuation units of the Medical Corps.

The IDF's national security doctrine and doctrine of war formulated in the 1950s were influenced by both the mistakes and achievements in the War of Independence, and it was based to a very considerable extent on the lessons learned from that war.

The war ended with cease-fire agreements. Those cease-fire lines were to be the temporary borders of the State of Israel until the signing of peace agreements with the Arabs and the drawing of permanent borders.

CHAPTER 15
MILITARY ACTIVITY OVER THE YEARS

At the end of the War of Independence, the IDF was deployed along armistice lines. It was obvious that the Arabs had not reconciled themselves with their defeat and that more wars could be expected in the future. Israel prepared for a "second round" of the war against itself and deployed in anticipation of the wars to come.

Great Britain and other countries supported territorial changes that would have benefited the Arabs, including Israeli withdrawal from the southern part of Israel, the Negev. The armistice agreements left various matters aside from the question of final borders unsolved, among them freedom for Israeli shipping in the Suez Canal and the Straits of Tiran.

The war also left in its wake the problem of Arab refugees who had fled during the fighting to various Arab countries. Under the background of the Arab countries' refusal to reconcile themselves with the existence of the State of Israel, fertile ground was created for friction and military clashes: border disputes and arguments over land; conflict over freedom of shipping; infiltrators and armed bands who crossed the borders to commit sabotage and murder. Indeed, border clashes broke out from time to time between the IDF and the military forces of the confrontation states.

A concept of national security was forged. The IDF concurrently undertook the tasks of readiness and preparation—on the one hand, it engaged in wide-ranging operational activity related to continuing operations along the borders, and on the other, it worked hard on structuring its military power and building it up, working above all on the organization of the reserve army. The Arabs, for their part, licked their wounded pride, nurtured a desire for revenge, and invested considerable effort in their own military build-up, all the while taking action against Israel in every way possible: politically, militarily, economically, and culturally.

In the military sphere, they employed tactics of low-level warfare with the goal of harassing and damaging the morale and self-confidence of Israel's people. They would infiltrate into Israel, either as individuals or small bands, to gather intelligence, steal, commit sabotage, and indiscriminately murder men, women, and children.

From time to time the Arabs also challenged the status quo along the armistice lines by taking control of demilitarized areas and opening fire on civilians, settlements, or workers in the fields along the borders. The IDF would be forced to attack and evict them. Such incidents led to sporadic firefights between Israeli troops and those of Egypt, Jordan, Syria, and Lebanon. In particularly egregious cases of deep infiltration into Israel accompanied by murder, Israel would conduct retaliation raids.

In the early stages of its operational activity, the IDF used to attack civilian objectives, but it quickly changed its approach, switching to military forces, with the aim of undermining their self-confidence and deterring their governments from aggressive actions against the Israeli population and other objectives. Sometimes there was no choice but to undertake deterrent retaliation actions, simply because of the vital need to protect the Israeli inhabitants of frontier settlements and to help them to remain steadfast and not abandon their settlements. In some cases, there was no choice but to take action against Arab villages that had sheltered saboteurs who had set out from them to commit acts of sabotage and murder in Israel.

The operations the IDF had undertaken across borders, within the framework of the activity and the small-unit warfare they involved, forged a fighting spirit and contributed to the development of the patterns of conduct of its troops in battle and of its combat doctrines. In the 1950s, Special Unit 101, established to conduct special raids, and the paratroop forces developed the required methods of combat and undertook most of the retaliation raids over the border.

They set standards of combat and served as models for the entire IDF. Their contribution to the fostering of a fighting spirit in the IDF after the War of Independence was decisive. Ordinarily, IDF operations over the border were undertaken at night, in platoon to battalion strength. Sometimes there were larger operations, involving armor, infantry, and artillery, in brigade strength.

The IDF also conducted retaliation raids and various other operations with heliborne and amphibious forces. Such operations usually resulted in impressive success, excited the imagination and raised morale in Israel, while concurrently lowering the spirits of the Arabs and spreading a feeling of helplessness among them. There were also air and naval operations and battles between wars. The Arabs made attempts to intercept Israeli aircraft on reconnaissance and photographic missions, and the Israeli Air Force intercepted enemy aircraft that penetrated Israeli airspace on photographic or attack missions. In such aerial encounters over the years, the Israeli Air Force always overcame those of the Arabs. The Arabs would invariably suffer heavy losses in aerial combat, thanks to the qualitative superiority of the Israeli Air Force, a superiority that derived from the quality of Israel's pilots, its doctrines of aerial combat, its leadership, and the effectiveness of the Israeli Air Force's command and control system. The IDF also usually had superior combat aircraft.

The IDF made intensive use of the awesome firepower of its modern fighter-bombers, its reactions often involving massive bombing from the air. The tremendous firepower of the air arm spread terror in the Arab forces and had a not inconsiderable deterrent effect. Israel's uncontested command of the air deterred the Arab states over the years, to a considerable extent cooling their enthusiasm for war. As a result of the repeated blows they sustained, Arab governments realized it behooved them to think twice before any attack on Israel. The operations undertaken by the IDF repeatedly demonstrated both its superiority on land, in the air, and at sea, and Arab impotence. The retaliation raids shook the governments of Arab countries from which the terrorist bands had set out on their murder operations, and whose armed forces had fired over or crossed the border to attack targets in Israel. The deterrent impact of the reprisal raids and counterblows also derived from the fact that they threatened the stability of the regimes of Arab states that took aggressive action against Israel or that served as springboards for such action. Furthermore, these operations and battles contributed to Israel's deterrent image, were compatible with its strategy of deterrence, and comported well with the principles of its security doctrine.

Not everyone in Israeli society agreed with the strategy of retaliation raids and counterblows. There were also those who had reservations. They usually did not deny the need to deter and put pressure on Arab governments, but they claimed that the contribution of retaliation raids and deterrent operations was not commensurate with the attendant damage. They contended that the retaliatory and punitive raids could not root out hostile activity against Israel but did fan the flames of hatred; they were oil on the flames. Instead of lowering the profile of the conflict, they magnified it.

The argument, then, was not one of principle but over practical considerations. The disagreement was over the question of effectuality, not whether justice was with Israel—over the means, not the end. The argument was almost irrelevant, though, since there was no alternative course. If the possibility had existed of relying on the passive defense of Israel's people to prevent the indiscriminate murder of innocents, it would perhaps have made sense to agonize over the proper reaction. However, it was not possible to prevent hostile activity passively. The only avenue available was to hurt and deter those responsible for acts of murder and sabotage, those who sent the armed bands and those who gave them shelter in their countries. Israel had always held fully responsible the sovereign governments of the states that served as bases for saboteurs, and from which saboteurs set out on terrorist attacks in Israel or third states. Those governments of course also bore responsibility for the firing into Israel by their regular forces, and for any other kind of hostile activity by their forces, their citizens, or terrorist organizations within their borders. Retaliation raids in such cases were sometimes unavoidable, and they were an alternative to full-scale war.

The principle of deterrence is of the utmost importance in Israeli national security doctrine. There can be no doubt that the retaliation blows and the IDF's preemptive raids and bombings, on land, in the air, and at sea, contributed to deterring Arab governments and to inhibiting sabotage activity and firing into Israel from over its borders.

CHAPTER 16
THE SINAI CAMPAIGN, 1956

The aim of Egypt in 1956 was to preserve its territorial integrity and sovereignty after having provoked outside powers by nationalizing the Suez Canal in July and maintain a blockade of Israeli shipping in the Straits of Tiran. The aim of Israel was to break the naval blockade, remove the Egyptian threat in the Sinai Peninsula, and to put an end to terrorist raids by irregulars, the *Fedayeen*, who operated from the Gaza Strip at the behest of Egyptian intelligence, undertaking sabotage raids deep in Israeli territory. Israel also aimed to strengthen its power of deterrence by defeating Egypt, which was in the process of an unprecedented military build-up. At that time, it was receiving massive military aid from Czechoslovakia, on behalf of the Soviet Union, including tanks, aircraft, and naval vessels. Another important aim was to deal a painful blow to Egypt's president, Abd el-Nasser, who had become the dominant figure in the Third World, and even to bring about his downfall and perhaps effect a change in the orientation of the Egyptian regime.

Not everyone agreed that Israel should have allied itself with colonial powers, Great Britain and France. There were those who defined the war as preventive and therefore denounced it. There is room for disagreement over the political wisdom of the Sinai Campaign and whether the benefits it brought outweighed the damage it caused; however, there is no room for criticizing the blow to Egypt on moral grounds. A clear-cut justification existed for attacking Egypt and hitting it hard. Israel went to war in reaction to provocations made at Egypt's behest, and that had inflicted much harm to Israel's people. Actually, Egypt had been actively waging war against Israel. It had adopted a strategy of terrorism and small-tactics warfare, initiating raids into Israeli territory and committing acts of terrorism, indiscriminately killing children, women, and men. Israel had found itself confronted with an existential threat, one that was getting progressively worse. The Sinai Campaign was an answer to the homicidal policy implemented by Egypt, reflected in constant and intensive aggression against the State of Israel.

The Sinai Campaign, in which Israel had achieved an impressive victory, took place in the midst of a transition in the Arab-Israeli wars from the age of individual weapons to that of collective weapons systems. Subsequent to the Sinai Campaign, in which the fact was borne home that the decisive formations in war were now mobile armored units, the Arab-Israeli wars took on the character of modern wars, with large-scale clashes of aircraft against aircraft, tank against tank. Awesome firepower and electronics systems began to be wielded on land, in the air, and at sea, and combined formations waged land battles.

Thus the Middle East passed into the age of modern warfare, an age that had commenced between the two world wars and reached its highest expression in the second.

The campaign was conducted on the principle of operating deep inside enemy territory. However, the IDF delivered the first blow under the force of circumstances and a specific war plan, not because the doctrine of the preemptive strike had attained the status of a basic principle in Israeli national security doctrine. In fact, the opposite was the case; it was only after that war, the second in Israel's history, and in the face of an Arab military build-up, with modern weapons and mobile armored forces, that Israeli national security doctrine adopted the principle of the preemptive strike in the event of a perceived threat.

The main distinguishing characteristic of combat doctrine in the Sinai Campaign was the transition to mobile armored warfare. Israeli national security doctrine, based on the lessons of the War of Independence, had not changed. However, the principle of attack and carrying the war deep into enemy territory—with the flexible, multipurpose air arm, mobile armored formations, and special forces, the paratroopers—took on added force.

Until the Sinai Campaign, the Arabs had not attached much military importance to Israel. It seems that they viewed the outcome of the War of Independence as a mishap, a historical accident, not as a reflection of the balance of military forces or of the IDF's qualitative superiority. They thought that the outcome of that war reflected their own flaws and inefficiency, and thus they engaged in much mutual finger-pointing. At the conclusion of the War of Independence, Israel seemed a passing episode, the existence of which depended on the grace of others. Neither was Israel perceived elsewhere in the world as being of much military weight until the Sinai Campaign. Yet even though Israel did not fight alone in the Sinai Campaign, but with France and Britain, its deterrent image underwent a radical change, thanks to the lightning operations of its air, armored, and paratroop forces. From then on, Israel was perceived as an entity in possession of impressive military capabilities in its own right, its deterrent image strengthened accordingly.

Despite the defeat Israel administered Egypt—the Egyptian forces were routed, and the IDF captured most of the Sinai Peninsula, including Sharm el-Sheikh, and removed the naval blockade—the Egyptian president managed to present the outcome as an Egyptian victory. He claimed his country had fought a coalition of three states and held its own in the canal area against England and France. He did not remind his people that the two superpowers, the United States and the Soviet Union, had delivered an ultimatum to the three countries that attacked Egypt. Nasser created the impression among his people that Egypt alone had gotten the upper hand over the opposing coalition.

The lesson Israel had learned was that such possibilities must be taken into account and that it must endeavor in setting its military aims for future wars to attain clear-cut victories that cannot be misconstrued.

Before the Sinai Campaign, there were arguments in the IDF over whether tanks should be used in support of infantry or mobile armored formations should be the basic formations for attaining decisions in land warfare. Recalling the experience of the War of Independence, in which infantry had played the decisive role, the high command and senior officers of the IDF generally viewed tanks

as infantry-support weapons. The clash of views over the role of
tanks was mainly between the General Staff on the one hand, and
on the other, the commander of the Armored Corps and a handful
of tank veterans who over the years had kept the spirit of the Corps
alive—the pioneers of the IDF armored forces. Before the Sinai Campaign, the conservative view, which denied the decisive role of armor
in land warfare, prevailed.

The accomplishments of the armored forces in the Sinai Campaign
belied the established wisdom. The tanks of the two advance armored brigades refuted the conservative approach. The IDF learned
on the battlefields of the Sinai what others had learned in the Second
World War, namely, that armor bears the brunt of the war on land.
The doubters were now the first to laud the contribution of armor,
recognize their own misconception, and staunchly champion the fostering of the armored arm. Ever since, the centrality of armor in the
military thinking of the IDF and in its combat doctrine has been
assured. In the wake of the Sinai Campaign, an idea of the structure
and application of force was formulated and incorporated into Israeli national security doctrine. Armored power would be enhanced
and, along with the Air Force, would defeat the Arab armies in the
Six Day and Yom Kippur Wars. From then on, it would be Israel's
new armored power that would prove decisive in its wars.

CHAPTER 17
THE WATER BATTLES, 1953–1966

Even before the establishment of the State of Israel, various proposals had been made for the exploitation of the Jordan and Yarmuk Rivers. A number of plans, local or from overseas, had been studied. However, the two parties involved, Israel and the Arab states, had never been able to agree, and no plan had come to fruition. In the mid-1950s, the Jordanians began working on their own national plan, which was completed in the 1960s. They built a canal to divert water from the Yarmuk to irrigate the eastern bank of the Jordan Valley.

In the 1950s, Israel tried to exploit water from the River Jordan. The Arabs were violently opposed, and numerous battles resulted between the IDF and Syrian forces. The Soviet Union and the UN, with the concurrence of the United States, foiled the Israeli project. The United States categorically demanded that Israel cease work on the project, threatening a cut-off in economic aid. Israel had no choice but to submit. Israel decided to adopt a national water program of its own, one that was not dependent on cooperation from its neighbors: the construction of a pipeline to carry water from the north to the center and south of the country. The National Water Carrier, as it is known, pumps water from the Sea of Galilee, rather than directly from the River Jordan, and passes through the country from north to south.

The National Water Carrier was completed in 1964. The Arabs saw it as an indication of increased Israeli power. In January of that year, before the Carrier was completed, a summit conference was convened in Cairo. The leaders of thirteen Arab states met to devise a joint strategy against the "threat" of the Carrier. Syria demanded immediate military action to destroy it. The leaders of the other Arab states, though, felt the Arabs were not yet ready, because of their military weakness, to launch an all-out attack on Israel; they would first have to build up their military strength. Hence, they decided to establish a Unified Arab Command to coordinate the military build-up of the states to be involved in the conflict.

The Arab leaders believed that even without the military capability to launch a successful attack and immediately destroy Israel's National Carrier, they could conduct a successful campaign against Israel of a different kind. They decided to divert the Hatzbani and Banias Rivers, sources of the Jordan (which flows into the Sea of Galilee) that are outside Israeli territory (and are the source of 50 percent of the Jordan's water), into Syrian territory. They thus hoped to thwart the National Carrier without having to launch an all-out offensive against Israel. Denying half the water of the Jordan to the Jews, would, they reasoned, dry up Israel's National Carrier. Israel would have either to reconcile itself with the deprivation of its water or launch an all-out offensive to prevent the diversion of the water, which the Arabs felt they could contain by defensive action. The conference also established the Palestine Liberation Organization (PLO) and the Palestine Liberation Army.

In September 1964 another Arab summit conference convened, at which it was decided to commence implementation of the previous decision to divert the Hatzbani and Banias Rivers, with financing from the oil-producing states. In November of that year, the Syrians commenced actual work. They began digging a canal, with heavy earthmoving equipment, along a course that ran along the southern shoulder of Mount Hermon. The canal was intended to channel water from the Hatzbani and Banias, through the Golan Heights, to the Yarmuk.

In Israel, there was unanimity of opinion about the necessity of preventing the diversion and thus Arab control over the water. There were those who favored capturing the Syrian area through which the canal was supposed to pass; for them, there was no other way than war. The minister of defense ordered the chief of the General

Staff to prepare a plan of military action that would prevent the diversion without leading to a full-scale war.

In consultations among the military, under the CGS, the commanding general of the Armored Troops Command proposed to prevent the diversion with precise tank fire at long range without crossing the border. Many in the military discounted the possibility, on the ground that it would be impossible to hit such small targets— various types of heavy earthmoving equipment and the tanks that protected them—from ranges that in some places were twice, or even thrice and four times, the generally accepted effective range of tanks. After considerable persuasion, the government authorized the proposal of the Armored Troops Command, and in a series of operations involving fire from tanks in March, May, and August 1965, and an air attack in July 1966, the heavy earthmoving equipment the Syrians had been operating was destroyed.

IDF tanks went into action from Tel Dan against construction sites along the Hermon, a range of two kilometers; from the Kfar Hanassi area against sites in the area of the Upper Customs House, a range of six kilometers; and from Korazim (Almagor) against sites in a more distant area, at a range of eleven kilometers. The Air Force attacked the most distant construction sites, which were twenty kilometers from the border, to which the Syrians had moved to get out of the range of tank fire.

Fire from Israeli tanks knocked out eleven tractors and other pieces of heavy earthmoving equipment, as well as several Syrian tanks that protected them. Syrian tanks knocked out one Israeli tank. In the Israeli air attack, eight tractors and two pieces of heavy earthmoving equipment were knocked out. Israeli tank fire and air attack put an end to the Arab coalition's strategic plan to divert the sources of the River Jordan and deprive Israel of its water.

The Water Battles crystallized the Armored Corps's gunnery doctrine. The strategic necessity of hitting pinpoint targets at long range forced the Armored Corps to study and develop ballistic methods and special fire techniques. Thus came into being the Corps's unique gunnery doctrine. The techno-tactical nature of that doctrine left its mark on all the battles and wars Israel has fought since the Water Battles, contributing much to the qualitative superiority of the Israeli Armored Corps and to its victories.

CHAPTER 18
THE SIX DAY WAR, 1967

In the Six Day War, Israel achieved one of the greatest victories in the history of the Jewish people. It was a war in which the lessons of the Sinai Campaign were implemented, including the need to deliver an incontrovertibly devastating blow to the enemy, one that he could not construe as a victory after the event. The lessons in tank gunnery learned in the Water Battles were also implemented. It was proof that the IDF was capable of planning for the wars to come, not those of the past. Yet because by nature the Six Day War was a mainly air and armored war, and one involving only the offensive, with no defensive operations, not all of the IDF's combat and organizational doctrines were put to the test.

The war aims of both Israel and the Arabs had developed in the course of events that led to war. Arab harassment of Israel along the borders had become a constant feature of life. For example, in late 1966 three Israeli soldiers were killed and six wounded in Israeli territory south of Mount Hebron. Israel reacted with a combined tank and infantry raid, in broad daylight, against the village of Samu'a, on Mount Hebron, and blew up houses. The Arab Legion sent reinforcements, and a battle developed, leading to dozens of Jordanian casualties. In April 1967 the Syrians opened fire on Israeli tractors in fields of the demilitarized zone and on the settlements of Gadot, Ein Gev, and Tel-Katzir. Israel sent its air force against Syrian artillery. The Syrian Air Force was sent up to intercept the Israeli planes, and in the ensuing air battle six Syrian planes were shot down, two of them crashing in the outskirts of Damascus.

After that incident, the Egyptians began to receive reports from Soviet sources that Israel had begun to concentrate forces on the Syrian border, with the aim of capturing Damascus. Soviet leaders warned Syria and Egypt that Israel was planning to attack Syria and promised that the Soviet Union would back them fully should war break out. Israel actually had no intention of attacking Syria and had not concentrated forces; the claim was a deliberate Soviet provocation. Furthermore, the Jordanians had been openly baiting the president of Egypt, Nasser, after the raid on Samu'a about his remaining secure behind the UN forces stationed in the Sinai. Egypt was bound to Syria with a mutual defense treaty obligating it to come to Syria's aid, and to the aid of other Arab states, should Israel attack. Egypt felt called upon to act, to evict the UN force and concentrate its forces in the Sinai, and eventually to block the Straits of Tiran and impose a naval blockade of Israel. The closure of the Straits would constitute a casus belli. Egypt's ruling oligarchy knew what such a step would lead to; it had decided to precipitate a war. In short order, Jordan and Iraq joined Egypt and Syria. The leaders of the Arab world threatened Israel with annihilation.

The Arab war aims took form during these events. Egypt's aim was to deter Israel, impose a naval blockade on it, and to capture the southern part of Israel (the Negev). The Syrian aim was to capture the northeastern part of Israel (eastern Galilee) as a preliminary step, and to protect the Golan Heights. Jordan's aim was to protect the West Bank, grab pieces of Israeli territory, and neutralize Israeli air bases with artillery fire. Iraq prepared to send an expeditionary force for a joint war effort with Jordan.

The Israeli aim was to remove the threat to its existence, to capture the Straits of Tiran, the Gaza Strip, and at least the part of the Sinai adjacent to it, and to destroy the main part of the forces Egypt had moved into the peninsula, as well as to defend its borders against threats to the east and north. It thus hoped to restore its lost power of deterrence.

On 14 May 1967, Egyptian forces began moving into the Sinai, thus setting in motion a concentration of forces and positioning them for attack. The armed forces of Egypt, Syria, and Jordan were large, well armed, and well equipped on land, in the air, and at sea.

On 16 May, Egypt demanded that the UN Emergency Force with-draw from its border with Israel and, on the 18th, that it leave the Sinai. Also on the 18th, the commander of Egyptian forces in the Sinai issued an order of the day that stated in part:

Our forces are definitely ready to take the war beyond the borders of Egypt. Morale is high, because this is the day we have been waiting for—to set out on a Holy War, to return the stolen land to its owners. . . . The soldiers are asking when the Holy War will commence. Indeed, the time has come to fulfil this wish.

On 22 May, Egypt closed the Straits of Tiran to Israeli shipping. On 25 May, Cairo Radio announced that the determination of the Arab nation was to wipe Israel off the map and restore the honor of Palestinian Arabs.

On the following day, 26 May, President Nasser declared: "The Arab nation wants war. If we wage war we shall win and conquer. The closing of the Straits means war. After we have taken this step, we must perforce be ready for total war with Israel." On the same day, Hasnein Heikel, Nasser's mouthpiece, wrote in *Al-Ahram* that there was no choice but an armed clash between the Arab commu-nity and the Israeli enemy. This was the first time, wrote Heikel, that the Arabs had thrown the gauntlet with the aim of changing an existing fact and supplanting it with another.

In a press conference on 28 May, Nasser declared that Egypt had the power to change the existing state of affairs back to the way it had been before 1948—in other words, to destroy Israel. On 30 May, he declared that the armed forces of Egypt, Jordan, Syria, and Lebanon were deployed along the borders, and that behind them were the armed forces of Iraq, Algeria, Kuwait, Sudan, and the entire Arab nation. The Arabs were ready for battle, Nasser announced, the hour of decision had arrived.

The Arab rulers and masses all called for the destruction of Israel, and Arab capitals thronged with joyous crowds celebrating its im-pending doom. Other governments and peoples shook their heads in sympathy with Israel. They had a feeling they were standing at Israel's grave, only nineteen years after standing at its cradle. A sense of solidarity with Israel pervaded the world in the face of the tragic fate, so everyone thought, that awaited it. Nevertheless, not a single country or body on the international scene lifted a finger to help

Israel. The help Kuwait would receive during the 1991 Gulf War, Israel was not offered in 1967, and not only because it does not have oil—the Jewish people do not have natural allies. The existential danger that had hovered over the State of Israel proved once again that while other nations are occasionally destined to fight for their freedom, Israel must fight for both freedom and its very existence.

The ratio of forces in the war was as follows. The IDF had ten armored brigades, organized into four divisions, against eighteen Arab armored brigades; the IDF had nine infantry brigades against fifty-three for the Arabs; 1,300 IDF tanks faced 2,520 Arab tanks; the IDF had 746 artillery pieces, against 2,780 for the Arabs; 247 IDF combat aircraft faced Arab air forces that had 557; the IDF had five ground-to-air missile batteries, while the Arabs had twenty-six.

The Arabs thought they could wipe Israel out. They were deployed along Israel's borders, sure of themselves, yearning for battle, possessed by hatred. In the face of this palpable threat, no one in Israel waited for intelligence officers to say what to do. The government and General Staff called the people to the flag. In the face of the threat, the people of Israel rose above their internal quarrels. A feeling of unity of fate brought hearts together and a spirit of brotherhood reigned in the land. The people united, and a government of national unity was formed. As the people became united, the IDF was infused with the spirit of battle, a spirit that spread among all the people.

The Egyptian Air Force was destroyed by the Israeli Air Force immediately upon the outbreak of hostilities, on 5 June 1967. Ten hours after the fighting had commenced, armored units of the Iron Fist Division were on the outskirts of the capital of the Sinai, El-Arish. A record was set in the annals of modern mobile armored warfare: within ten hours armored forces had conducted two breakthrough battles against fortified enemy positions and had advanced seventy kilometers into enemy territory.

The IDF stormed. In the skies over Egypt, Jordan, and Syria, and in the battlefields of the Sinai, Judaea, Samaria, and the Golan Heights, Israel prevailed. Jerusalem was liberated.

The Six Day War put to the test the national security doctrine Israel had developed in the 1950s, after the War of Independence. The circumstances in which this war broke out and the manner in which it was conducted were classic examples of that doctrine: the sense of unity of fate and of goal, consensus and motivation, that permeated the people; initiative and delivery of the first blow; destruction of forces, capture of territory; and a short war. This doctrine had not yet been formulated in the War of Independence, and the Sinai Campaign of 1956 had been a limited war between Israel and Egypt. The Six Day War was waged against all the confrontation states and the expeditionary forces of their allies. According to its national security doctrine, Israel should have attacked first on one front and conducted defensive operations on the other two. The doctrine assumed that Israel would not have the strength to attain a decision simultaneously on more than one front.

In the Six Day War, Israel went to war under almost a "Case All" scenario. The difference was that Israel was not caught by surprise but had had a chance to prepare itself and meet the threat (during what came to be known as the "waiting period"); from every other standpoint, though, the situation accorded with the definition of Case All. Nevertheless, the IDF managed to launch simultaneous offensives on two fronts while defending a third, to defeat Egypt and Jordan, and then go on to the offensive against Syria. The Israeli Air Force demonstrated crushing superiority over the enemy's air forces, and Israel's armored formations were at their best, demonstrating outstanding ability in maneuver and mobile armored warfare. It was a modern war, in which numerous tank units and formations were thrown into battle, a war conducted between heavy force concentrations.

The principles of delivering the first blow and taking the war deep into enemy territory were implemented to the fullest. Modern weapons systems bore the burden of assault and achieved victory in all arenas, and the IDF enjoyed overall superiority in firepower, particularly in the air.

The principles of Israeli national security doctrine that derive from geopolitical, historical, and strategic circumstances were reflected in the war: lack of strategic depth, which mandated a rigid defense and quickly taking of the war deep into enemy territory; the need for a short war, a rapid decision. With these factors in mind, as well as the necessity of avoiding a war of attrition, Israel chose the offensive as the only possible course of action open to it. Because of the principles of force structure the IDF had adopted and implemented, it had been able to embark on that course of action; its order of battle had been designed to give first priority to the Air Force, its most flexible arm, which could be committed anywhere within a matter of minutes. Second priority had been given the mobile armored formations, and third to the paratroopers, to elite infantry, and special forces.

The principles of national security had stood the test—except in the matter of early warning. There had actually been no test of Israel's early warning capability, as the Arabs had openly deployed in strength. Egypt's strategy had been to operate in a deterrent manner, and its forces flowed into the Sinai in broad daylight. Thus there had been no problem of intelligence, the function of which is to discern a threat posed by stealthy movement and concentration of forces; Egypt instead took pains to publicize its threat to Israel, broadcasting its movement of forces into the Sinai far and wide. Egypt generously provided Israel with all the information and indications needed.

Israel had nevertheless been surprised, in that its intelligence appreciation before the war had been that an Egyptian initiative in the Sinai was not possible, since Egypt was preoccupied with a war in Yemen. In the face of Israel's great, historic victory and the successful test of its national security doctrine, however, public attention in Israel did not turn to the failure of intelligence to assess correctly the intentions of the enemy and his ability to concentrate forces in the Sinai despite the war in Yemen.

The war was decided by the Air Force and the mobile armored formations on all fronts—the Egyptian, Jordanian, and Syrian—in both desert and mountainous areas. From the Six Day War to the Yom Kippur War, Israeli military superiority over the Arabs continued to widen. Despite Arab quantitative superiority in artillery, the IDF had attained unqualified overall superiority in firepower, as a result of the growth of its air power and its qualitative superiority.

When Israel went to war, it seemed clear it would not be able to remain in conquered territory longer than it had remained after the Sinai campaign; captured territory would be used as bargaining chips in negotiations after the war. No one foresaw that Israel would hold onto these territories for many years. In the waiting period before the outbreak of war, as the IDF set about polishing its operational plans, it regarded the Gaza Strip as an area to hold onto for bargaining purposes. Nasser blocked the Straits; Israel would repay him by capturing the Gaza Strip and keeping it. Looking ahead somewhat more ambitiously, IDF planners added the adjacent areas of the Sinai, up to Jabil Livni and Abu-Ageila, but only for the purpose of attaining a military decision and additional territory to bargain with.

In the 1956 Sinai Campaign, both sides, the Israeli and Egyptian, had claimed victory. The fact that Israel had gone to war relying on two by no means inconsequential allies had irked Israel's military leadership. Thus the ambition arose to achieve a clear-cut victory over Egypt in the Six Day War, a victory that would restore to the IDF its lost power of deterrence and oblige Egypt to admit defeat without any opening to distort the outcome. The IDF leadership thought that end would be attained by realizing a limited military aim—the destruction of Egyptian forces in the areas of the Sinai adjacent to Israel and the opening of the Straits of Tiran to Israeli shipping. This was the basic aim; there was no intention then of reaching the Suez Canal, and certainly not of taking the West Bank and Golan Heights. All this came about in the course of the war, as a result of enemy provocations and the unfolding of events on the battlefield.

In the period of mobilization and preparation before the war, Israel's political and military leadership agonized over whether to initiate the war or wait for international diplomacy and the great powers to remove the threat. The fact that Arab forces had been allowed to concentrate aggressively along Israel's borders, impose the blockade, and display belligerent intentions, posing a serious threat to the existence of the State of Israel, cast doubt on the willingness of the powers to break the naval blockade of the Straits of Tiran and force Egypt to withdraw its forces. Yet the IDF high command realized that even if the threat to Israel were removed through the intervention of outside powers, it would not be able to recover the deterrent power it had lost with Egypt's dispatch of its military forces in strength into the Sinai in broad daylight, its closure of the Straits of Tiran, and its unrestrained, rampant behavior. The Egyptians were altogether familiar with Israel's deterrent strategy, and when they had not wanted war (as in an earlier flare-up, in 1960), they had immediately withdrawn. The members of the General Staff contended that the IDF must remove the threat and destroy the Egyptian military force. Neither did it believe that outside powers would get Israel's chestnuts out of the fire. The contention was also raised that the powers should not be allowed to break the naval blockade, that the IDF should do that itself, because only in that way could it recover its lost power of deterrence.

Lessons were derived from the Six Day War. However, it was clear that the only form of battle that had been tested was the offensive; the IDF had not conducted defensive operations to hold territory. Furthermore, the attacks had been carried out mainly by its armored formations. Those engaged in deriving the required lessons were therefore cautious. They realized that they must not come to conclusions about infantry combat or the IDF's infantry forces on the basis of the Six Day War. While mechanized and other infantry had fought valiantly—at Jirdi, Abu-Ageila, Radar, Ammunition Hill, Tel Fahr, and elsewhere—their operations had been limited. The assumption was that in other wars, wars different from the Six Day War—in which defensive battles to hold onto territory, or in which night attacks by infantry in built-up areas would have to be conducted—infantry and mechanized infantry could be of critical importance and would have to be employed in cooperation with tanks. The combat doctrine and organizational concept of the armored formations were adjusted and reformulated accordingly. It was decided that the armored brigade would be structured on the basis of an equal number of infantry and tank units—the number of mechanized infantry and reconnaisance companies would be the same as the number of tank companies.

However, this idea was later abandoned, without justification, and brigades composed entirely of tanks were introduced. As a result of this unbalanced concept, land combat in the Yom Kippur War was to be marked by lack of balance between tanks and infantry. In a like manner, the lessons learned from the Six Day War concerning certain weapons for infantry and mechanized infantry were disregarded. Some of these weapons were removed from the infantry arsenal, in violation of the lessons learned in the Six Day War, only to be needed in the Yom Kippur War.

If the 1956 Sinai Campaign had been a turning point in the art of war in the Middle Eastern arena, the Six Day War proved a revolutionary and far-reaching turning point in the field of national security. The results of that war proved fateful. They brought about a fundamental alteration in the basic strategic factors that for twenty years had largely dictated the main ideas underpinning Israeli national security doctrine. By war's end, the national aim had changed.

The armistice lines set at the end of the War of Independence had been viewed up to the Six Day War as possibly permanent borders. After the Six Day War, the national consensus changed. There was now wide agreement that there must be no return to the armistice lines, even in the event of complete peace between Israel and the Arabs. After the war, Israel was a conquering state, ruling over the Palestinian population and over the Gaza Strip, Judaea, Samaria, a united Jerusalem, the Sinai Peninsula, and the Golan Heights. The borders with the confrontation states had been pushed back, creating strategic depth.

These were far-reaching changes, but Israelis failed to see their full significance, to comprehend their full, profound implications. After the Six Day War, the nation slid into a deep slumber in political and security matters. It failed to adjust its foreign and defense policies, or its national security doctrine, to the new circumstances. This state of affairs accounts to a great extent for the political and military process that led, within six years, to the Yom Kippur War.

CHAPTER 19

THE WAR OF ATTRITION, 1967–1970

After the Six Day War, the Arabs once again chose the path of war. The Egyptian president, Nasser, set forth four stages on the long road to bringing Israel to its knees:

1. The stage of *steadfastness* would be devoted to rehabilitating the Egyptian armed forces and deploying along the Suez Canal.
2. The stage of *active defense* would be devoted to Arab reorganization aimed at deterring Israel, with the help of the Soviet Union. In this stage, also denoted the *stage of confrontation*, battles would be fought along the Suez Canal.
3. The stage of a *war of attrition* would involve the eviction of Israel by the Arabs from all the territories it had captured in the Six Day War, by means of military attrition all along its borders. This stage was also denoted the *stage of eliminating the results of aggression*.
4. In the stage of *final victory*, Israel would be brought to its knees and a Palestinian state created in its stead.

At the end of August 1967, the leaders of the Arab world convened for a summit conference in Khartoum (the Khartoum Conference). The conference confirmed the choice of the path of war, and on 1 September it adopted a resolution containing the three well-known "noes": no to peace with Israel, no to recognition of Israel, and no to direct negotiations with it.

The conference also decided to support the right of the Palestinian people to return to their homeland. The Arabs, under the leadership of President Nasser, realized that they did not have the military strength to evict Israel from the territory it had captured in the Six Day War. Instead, they chose the path of a limited military struggle, by means of a static war along Israel's borders with Egypt, Jordan, Syria, and Lebanon, the aim of which was the erosion of Israeli willpower. In the face of the casualties it would suffer in such a static war, the Arabs believed, Israel would eventually prefer to withdraw from the occupied territory, to avoid further losses. They also expected that with the tension such a war would cause and the danger of an overall conflagration in the Middle East, the great powers would intervene and force Israel to withdraw.

The Arab aim was to bring matters back to what they had been prior to the Six Day War and to solve the Palestinian problem, without giving anything in return or negotiating directly with Israel. The Egyptian president coined the phrase, "What has been taken by force will be returned by force," although the strategy he adopted was basically to conduct a combined military and political struggle and eventually to attain his goal with the help of the world powers.

The Israeli aim was to prevent the Arabs from any gains on the ground, bring about a cease-fire with a minimum of force, and avoid casualties. A military government was established in the occupied territories. Israeli policy was to deal harshly with terrorists, on the one hand, and to minister to the needs of the inhabitants of the territories, on the other.

Along its borders with Jordan, Syria, and Lebanon, the IDF strove to prevent infiltration into Israel and losses from cross-border fire on settlements. From Jordan, it faced the threat posed by the Jordanian army, the Iraqi expeditionary force, and Palestinian terrorist organizations, which wanted to settle permanently in Jordan and establish themselves in the kingdom, and which eventually became a "state within a state." From Syria, Israel faced the Syrian armed forces and terrorist organizations.

The policy of combatting the terrorists contained two elements:

1. An offensive initiative, administering preventive blows, and pursuing terrorists wherever they might be, as well as reactions that were not necessarily proximate in time and space with the acts of sabotage to which they were addressed.

2. Maintenance of the principle that the sovereign Arab states that served as bases for the planning, organization, and perpetration of acts against Israel bore the responsibility for such acts, without impunity. The IDF engaged in continuous combat against the terrorists in a variety of ways: routine patrols, raids, and ambushes across Israel's borders, along with air raids on the bases, training facilities, and concentrations of terrorists. Special methods of warfare were also developed, as required.

For example, on 8 May 1972, a passenger aircraft of Sabena (Belgian) Airways was hijacked and brought to Israel's Lydda Airport, and the passengers were taken hostage. An elite IDF unit succeeded in breaking into the aircraft, freeing the passengers, and killing the hijackers. On the basis of this experience, the IDF developed a combat doctrine for such situations and developed special weapons and established special military units for such tasks.

In the area of ongoing military activity, the IDF accumulated to its credit a large number of successes in frustrating terrorist activity, in disrupting deployment of terrorist forces, and in hitting their places of refuge. Such operations, though, have not gone without hitch. The most conspicuous of them had particularly tragic consequences—the downing of a Libyan passenger aircraft that accidentally penetrated Sinai airspace in February 1973.

EGYPT

The IDF deployed along the Suez Canal from the Mediterranean to the Gulf of Suez and established a line of fortified positions it termed "strong points." A military base that included ground, air, and naval units was built at Sharm el-Sheikh.

The Egyptians made attempts to penetrate east of the Suez Canal by land, air, and from the sea. Battles were waged, involving artillery, aircraft, and ships; battles flared over control of shipping in the canal and over the areas adjacent to it. In response to Egyptian provocations, the IDF struck at various objectives along the canal. Egyptian aircraft were shot down and Egyptian motor torpedo boats sunk. In October 1967, the Egyptians attacked the Israeli destroyer *Eilat* with missiles in the area of Port Said and sank it. In retaliation, Israeli artillery destroyed the oil refineries in the city of Suez. Oil tanks and petrochemical works went up in flames. There was loss of life, and the damage to the Egyptian economy and morale was substantial. The Egyptians held their fire.

Immediately after the war, in June 1967, the Soviet Union, ally to Egypt and Syria, had begun to supply them with large quantities of weapons and ammunition to replace what had been lost in the war. The Egyptian and Syrian armed forces recovered, and within a year and a half they reached their prewar quantitative strength. From the standpoint of quality, they exceeded their pre-war condition, with MiG-21 aircraft and T-54 and T-55 tanks replacing the MiG-17 and MiG-19 aircraft and T-34, T-54, and Stalin-3 tanks they had lost in the fighting. The Soviets began to deepen their penetration into Egypt and Syria. Thousands of their technicians and experts became integrated into Egypt's and Syria's military establishments, helping to rehabilitate their armed forces and train them.

The Egyptians busied themselves with restoring their forces, digging in and fortifying themselves west of the Suez Canal. In June 1969, President Nasser announced that while he could not recapture the Sinai, he could wear Israel down and break its spirit—thus the name, War of Attrition. Egypt's war of attrition was meant to implement the overall Arab strategy and, in addition, to bring about a national awakening in Egypt and renew its morale. It would be waged in place of a full-scale war. The Egyptians believed it would take years before their armed forces were fully renewed and able to wage a comprehensive war. But they also thought it would be dangerous to allow a long-term cease-fire and let their armed forces get used to Israeli control of the Sinai.

The purpose of a war of attrition was to maintain the tension of war with Israel, wear it down, inflict casualties on it, and erode its willingness to maintain the conquests of the Six Day War. The Egyptians systematically stepped up their attacks on the IDF: they laid ambushes along the canal, conducted commando raids on strong points, mined axes of transportation, attacked from the air, and laid down heavy artillery barrages on strong points and motor convoys along transportation axes. Egyptian frogmen sank vessels anchored in Eilat harbor. The IDF suffered much loss of life and many wounded. In response, the IDF took the fighting deep into Egypt, from raids on Egyptian forces and objectives on the west bank of the canal, to long-range heliborne raids deep in Egyptian territory, where objectives included Egyptian infrastructure, installations, and military forces. Israeli naval commandos sank Egyptian motor torpedo boats. An Israeli armored force moved by sea on the Egyptian

Red Sea coast, landed, and moving along the coast from north to south, destroyed guard and observation positions, military camps, and radar installations. Some one hundred Egyptian soldiers were killed in that raid.

The War of Attrition on the Egyptian front is usually thought of in terms of the period from March 1969 to August 1970. However, that war in reality commenced on the Egyptian front at the end of the Six Day War, lasting until August 1970, when a formal cease-fire was announced. However, the War of Attrition on the other fronts—Jordanian, Syrian, and Lebanese—continued.

From the beginning of the War of Attrition, land battles had been waged along the canal line; there had also been naval and air engagements. Commencing in July 1969, the Israeli Air Force came to be employed on a massive scale against Egyptian force dispositions and artillery on the canal line, in order to provide support fire for IDF forces on the eastern bank. The air cover reduced the pressure on Israeli ground forces, but the Air Force suffered losses, as aircraft were shot down by antiaircraft missiles covering Egyptian forces along the canal. The Egyptians adapted themselves to Israeli air intervention, and expectations that they would ask for a cease-fire came to nothing. In the light of IDF losses on land and in the air, criticism of its method of defense began to be voiced.

There were those in the IDF who wanted to deploy in the rear and control the water line with mobile forces, so as to reduce casualties on both land and in the air. Others favored crossing the canal in force, taking control of the western bank, and deploying there for defense. Both alternatives—withdrawal from the canal and deployment in the rear, or crossing it and holding on to the western bank—were rejected. With the aim of inducing the Egyptians to ask for a cease-fire by increasing the pressure on them, a decision was reached to expand the scope of Air Force involvement. In January 1970, the Air Force commenced deep-penetration raids against strategic objectives in Egypt, with the aim of forcing it to cease hostilities, of damaging the standing of its president, and even of destroying his regime.

In the wake of these bombings on targets throughout Egypt, including the vicinity of Cairo, its president made an emergency appeal to the Soviet Union for help. Russia decided to accept responsibility for the defense of Egyptian airspace, except in the vicinity of the canal. Three Soviet squadrons of combat aircraft were sent and took over the air defense of the Cairo, Alexandria, and Aswan regions. A Soviet air defense missile brigade was also stationed in Aswan. Israel did not want to provoke Russia and fight Soviet pilots, so it began to limit the scope of its air intervention to the vicinity of the canal. There was nevertheless an incident in which Soviet fighter aircraft penetrated the airspace over the canal; in the ensuing battle, the Israeli Air Force shot down five Soviet fighters.

Air Force operations were effective, but they also caused Israel not inconsiderable trouble: the Soviet Union had intervened in the War of Attrition, and thousands of Soviet servicemen took part in military operations at all levels. Israeli Air Force attacks brought about an acceleration in the pace of Soviet arms shipments to Egypt. The array of surface-to-air missiles employed by Egypt was enhanced both qualitatively and quantitatively. Some missile batteries were actually manned by Soviet personnel, as the Soviet presence, and intervention, in Egypt expanded enormously.

In time, Israel would pay a heavy price for that intervention. In the Yom Kippur War, Egyptian forces were able to rely on an awesome array of air defense missiles, which would largely neutralize Israeli airpower by covering Egyptian forces crossing the canal, and later, during the Israeli counteroffensive, by covering Egyptian ground forces deployed defensively.

The method of defense adopted in the Sinai after the Six Day War (rigid defense) was controversial. The task imposed on the IDF had been to hold the entire Sinai, right up to the canal line, and not to permit the Egyptians to evict it. This task derived from Israeli policy vis-à-vis Egypt. The General Staff was beset by a professional controversy over the best method of defense in the Sinai. The task set by the government had been clear: a rigid defense to avoid losing territory. Israeli forces defended the canal line by means of the strong points on its eastern bank. Each strong point consisted of a group of bunkers and fortified positions, inside a perimeter defense of minefields and barbed wire. Thirty strong points were built. They controlled the water line and transportation axes to the interior of the Sinai.

Mobile forces operated between the strong points, and an armored reserve was deployed to their rear. The strong points were separated by a distance of several kilometers; they were not expected to support one another, nor could they have. The line of strong points had been intended, along with armored forces and the Air Force, to function in the event of a full-scale war as a defensive deployment along the canal. Its aim would be to prevent a crossing of the canal and an enemy advance into the interior of the Sinai until the IDF managed to bring its forces up in strength. In a static war of attrition, the line had been intended as a base for operations and ongoing military activity, and as a way to prevent Egyptian forces from crossing the canal and establishing themselves on its eastern bank. Later, a second echelon of fortified positions was built along a ridge line some ten kilometers to the rear.

A group of high-ranking IDF officers had opposed construction of the strong points along the canal. The grounds for their opposition were that the strong points would not be able to prevent the Egyptians from crossing the water line, either during the day or at night; they were very distant from one another, with no possibility for mutual observation. The defensive contribution of the strong points in the event of all-out war would be negligible, because they were small, easily neutralized by either direct or indirect fire, isolated, and unable to rely on mutual fire support. Neither could they expect massive artillery support, because the IDF did not have enough artillery. These critics further contended that the strong points constituted convenient, static targets for enemy raids and tank and artillery fire, and that they were very costly relative to their operational worth. But above all, in a full-scale war, with an all-out Egyptian assault that included a canal crossing, the strong points would make no contribution to halting the enemy. Furthermore, the IDF ground and air forces, instead of operating in the most effective manner possible to outmaneuver and destroy enemy forces and achieve a decision, would have to extricate the men in the strong points.

The solution proposed by opponents of the strong points was based on the following principles:

1. No housekeeping activity was to be conducted within range of Egyptian artillery. Support forces (artillery and air defense) must also, to the extent possible, be kept out of the effective range of Egyptian artillery. The fighting forces charged with actual defense of the canal line had, of course, to operate within the range of Egyptian artillery; yet when not actually engaged in operational activity, such personnel were to remain beyond enemy artillery range, where they would undertake the routines of life, such as rest, cooking, diversion and entertainment.

2. Deployment of forces would be such as to permit full execution of their mission of ongoing defense along the canal line in a war of attrition, and the comprehensive defense of the Sinai in the event of an all-out Egyptian attack, even if the Air Force was not able to provide air cover and ground support. The IDF had to be able to conduct a defensive even without air superiority; the land forces had to permit the high command freedom of choice concerning use of the Air Force on the basis of broad considerations, military and political—technical and tactical constraints could not be permitted to force the high command's hand in strategic considerations.

In the light of these principles, the opponents of the strong-point concept recommended reliance on tanks and other mobile forces, such as mechanized infantry, to maintain observation forces of required density along the canal, day and night. Such forces would operate with artillery support and under the cover of Hawk antiaircraft missiles and air defense artillery. These critics also recommended bringing additional standing armored forces into the Sinai from permanent tank unit camps in the center of the country.

Experience had indeed proved that the strong points had not fulfilled expectations of them; the Egyptians crossed the canal day and night and laid ambushes. Egyptian artillery fire controlled the area east of the canal and prevented intensive IDF activity, such as laying ambushes and conducting nonarmored patrols between strong points. Most of the forces that had set up ambushes at night between the strong points had come from bases in the rear, not from the strong points themselves—contrary to the concept of the strong points, namely, that they would serve as firm bases from which forces would operate.

The system of strong points produced in the area of the canal, which had hitherto been devoid of vulnerable Israeli targets, a plethora of prominent, static Israeli targets where transportation axes necessary for the maintenance of the strong points converged. Constant service and supply activity had to be conducted in the vicinity of the strong points, exposing vehicles and people, including civilians, to enemy fire. The IDF had provided the enemy targets both static and soft. The IDF suffered over a thousand casualties on the line of strong points. The vast majority of these losses were not incurred in combat, on guard duty, or observation, but as men traveled between strong points and the rear, as they set out for or returned from leave, as they brought up supplies, or as they performed housekeeping tasks in or around strong points.

Concerning the defense of the Sinai in an all-out war, the method of defense by means of the line of strong points had not been tested in a meaningful way, because the reserves had not been mobilized, and the forces that should have been in the Sinai, ready to take part in the defense of the canal, were not there. However, on the other hand, the strong points were put to the test in the War of Attrition, and its failure had led to Air Force intervention, and in turn, to the massive introduction of Soviet surface-to-air missiles in Egypt. This, in turn, would eventually lead to a severe curtailment of the ability of the Israeli Air Force to perform effectively its designated role of providing tactical fire support for the ground forces in the Yom Kippur War.

The controversy over the method of defense in the Sinai was two-fold: over the value of the line of strong points along the Suez Canal as a static line of defense in a war of attrition; and over its defensive value in the event of an all-out Egyptian attack to recapture the Sinai. After the Yom Kippur War, the claim would be made that the line of strong points had never been intended to defend the canal in a full-scale war, only in a war of attrition. This was not the case. The General Staff had decided unequivocally, when the defense of the Sinai had come up for discussion and the decision to establish the line of strong points had been taken, that its purpose would be to defend the canal and the Sinai under all scenarios, ongoing military activity, a war of attrition, or full-scale war.

The line of strong points proved a disappointment in the War of Attrition. The IDF had suffered a considerable number of casualties, and the line did not fulfill its intended purpose. The ground forces absorbed painful blows, were not able to defend themselves, and did not deter the Egyptians or force them to seek a cease-fire; rather they had been static targets along the length of the canal, providing gunnery practice for Egyptian artillery. Nor did the daring raids deep into Egypt deter the Egyptians, and neither did they blunt the momentum of pounding by Egyptian artillery or the attrition of IDF ground units along the canal front.

It was the Air Force that deterred the Egyptians. It jolted Egypt and grounded the Egyptian strategy—their War of Attrition became a War of Counter-Attrition. The president of Egypt, panic stricken, felt compelled in his impotence to turn to the Soviets, throwing the doors to Egypt and its armed forces wide open to them. They came in the thousands, took over command of Egyptian air defense, and became integrated into all spheres of the Egyptian military, down to the unit level. Soviet naval vessels regularly berthed at Port Said.

Thus, the IDF was able to wage the War of Attrition, in the manner it waged it, only by reliance on the Air Force. The IDF held onto the canal line by means of a rigid, static, unprofessional defense in which all echelons, including service support and rear echelon personnel, were kept in the line of direct contact with the enemy. It was only airpower that prevented the Egyptians from making more massive and effective use of their own firepower and drove home that the element of fire in the art of war cannot be ignored. There was no alternative to reliance on the Air Force with the ground forces disposed the way they were. The ground forces had conducted a defensive tactical battle of attrition all along the front line, from the Mediterranean to the Gulf of Suez, without any possibility of attaining a decision. The Air Force was the decisive factor in the war—it was what forced Egypt to end that war.

JORDAN

Palestinian terrorists operated from bases in Jordan, from which they would infiltrate into Israel and perpetrate acts of murder and sabotage. They would fire across the border at civilians and soldiers alike, and shell settlements. Neither did the Jordanians let themselves be outdone; they shelled both military and civilian targets in Israel. On more than one occasion, Israeli and Jordanian forces engaged in heavy firefights.

In February 1968, seven Israeli settlements were fired upon by Jordanian artillery. The IDF returned fire with mortars, artillery, and tanks, and air strikes, hitting Jordanian military bases and outposts, Jordan's water pipeline, and villages that had served as bases for terrorists, all along the Jordan Valley, from the Yarmuk to the Dead Sea. Jordanian civilians living in the Jordan Valley began to flee eastward. Terrorist activity accelerated in March. In response, the IDF launched raids with tanks and helicopter-borne paratroopers, with artillery and air support, on terrorist bases south of the Dead Sea (three police stations, and the village of Tsafir) and north of the Dead Sea (opposite the Allenby Bridge in the area of the village of Karame) that had served as major bases for terrorists. Jordanian infantry and armor took part in the fighting alongside the Palestinians. In these operations, twenty-eight Israelis, twenty-five Jordanian soldiers, and 150 Palestinians were killed. The IDF took 128 terrorists prisoner.

The IDF responded decisively to shelling and rocket attacks on Israeli settlements by terrorists, and terrorist raids in Israel. It hit military and economic targets in Jordan, and the stability of that country's regime began to become undermined. The terrorists did not operate just against Israel. They attempted to assassinate King Hussein, and they hijacked the civilian airliners of several countries: Israel, the United States, Germany, Switzerland, and Britain. They held passengers hostage, murdering several, and blew up aircraft. Increasing friction developed between Jordan and its armed forces, and the terrorists. Finally, full-scale fighting erupted between the Jordanian army and the terrorists, and the latter were evicted from Jordan to neighboring countries.

SYRIA

Syria also took action against Israel, through both its regular military forces and terrorists operating from bases in Syria. The Syrians initiated attacks on IDF positions on the Golan Heights, employing aircraft, tanks, and artillery. They shelled IDF positions and forces, inflicting casualties. In response, the IDF used its air force, tanks, and artillery, and raided Syrian forces and other objectives in deep-penetration raids into Syrian territory, including the Damascus area. Among the more daring of such operations was the seizure of five senior Syrian officers on a reconnaissance mission along the Israel-Lebanese border, on 21 June 1972. This operation, after which the Syrian officers were exchanged for three IDF airmen in Syrian captivity, reflected a high level of planning and execution.

The Syrians suffered heavy casualties. Syrian aircraft were shot down in aerial combat by the Israeli Air force, and Syrian tanks were knocked out in engagements with Israeli tanks. Israel caused damage to economic infrastructure deep inside Syria and inflicted hundreds of casualties on Syrian forces.

LEBANON

In the first year after the Six Day War, the Lebanese border was quiet; except for sporadic instances of sabotage and fire across the border, an attrition front did not develop there. In October 1968, terrorists began to concentrate in southern Lebanon, in the vicinity of Mount Hermon. From there they fired across the border, laid mines, and engaged in acts of sabotage. They had transferred themselves to Lebanon and established themselves there because of the blows they had sustained in Jordan. They gradually obtained a hold over the rest of Lebanon, where they did as they pleased. They operated from there against Israel, engaging in terrorist operations, the taking of hostages, murder, and the shelling of settlements. It was from Lebanon that they came to direct their terroristic and homicidal activities around the world: blowing up the airlines of different countries along with their passengers; hijacking aircraft, attacking Israeli and other targets in Europe, and other such acts. Israel responded with massive air attacks and raids against selected objectives, command headquarters, and terrorist forces. For instance, an IDF force took control of Beirut's international airport and destroyed passenger aircraft belonging to Arab national airlines. It conducted other large-scale raids with infantry, armor, and artillery deep in Lebanon, along with sea and helicopter-borne commando raids on objectives inside Lebanon, including Beirut.

In April 1973, an IDF commando force raided the apartments of Palestinian terrorist leaders in the Lebanese capital of Beirut, as well as buildings that housed terrorist headquarters and a workshop for the manufacture of munitions. Three terrorist leaders and four other terrorists were killed, and dozens were wounded. The raid was a classic commando operation; its reverberations were heard long afterward in Arab countries and terrorist organizations.

Another operation worthy of note was carried out on 16–17 September 1972 in southern Lebanon. A force of infantry and armor raided nine villages of terrorists, while the Air Force attacked targets and provided close air support, inflicting heavy losses on the terrorists. During the operation, reinforcements began flowing in to the terrorists from northern Lebanon; the Air Force knocked out the bridges over the Litani River, isolating the battlefield. This operation also had a deterrent effect on the Lebanese government, which thereafter limited the terrorists' freedom of movement.

CONCLUSION

As a whole, the principles of Israeli national security doctrine met the test of the War of Attrition on all fronts. This method of limited warfare, small-scale offensive actions, and massive fire on forces and settlements did not place Israel into a purely defensive posture. The opposite proved to be the case: concurrently with conducting a passive defense, the IDF operated deep inside Egypt, Jordan, Syria, and Lebanon, delivering hard blows that proved painful and to have deterrent effect. The Arab governments were forced to watch their moves carefully and control their appetites. The principles of deterring and frustrating the enemy, as adopted by Israeli national security doctrine, proved their worth.

CHAPTER 20

THE ROAD TO THE YOM KIPPUR WAR

The Arabs did not achieve their aims in the War of Attrition. Israel continued to rule all the areas it had captured in the Six Day War. In the Sinai, a cease-fire was in effect along the Suez Canal after August 1970, while in the north, the Syrians discontinued operations against the IDF. The activities of the terrorist organizations along Israel's borders, in the occupied territories, and inside Israel itself declined, and for the most part were transferred overseas.

The great powers did not want war in the Middle East. The Soviet Union wanted to avoid war, because of the risk of confrontation between the blocs, and also for fear of another Arab defeat. The United States, for its part, had an interest in reaching a settlement of the conflict through diplomacy.

Between the Six Day and Yom Kippur Wars, various initiatives by the UN and the world powers were undertaken with the aim of reaching a settlement between Israel and the Arabs. The fruit these initiatives bore proved unripe. In this period Israel indicated a willingness to withdraw from territories captured in the Six Day War to other, defensible, borders in exchange for peace agreements. It also expressed a willingness to consider, alternatively, even partial withdrawals in exchange for states of nonbelligerence between itself and its Arab neighbors. Yet the Arabs remained steadfast in their uncompromising positions. They demanded that Israel return the territories it had captured in the Six Day War without anything in exchange, without any reciprocity—no peace, no recognition of Israel, and no negotiations or dialogue with it. The status quo and stalemate were becoming more firmly established.

It seemed, at least to the Arabs, that this state of affairs was convenient for Israel, which was taking advantage of its extended presence in the Sinai, the Golan Heights, and other territories to render that presence a permanent reality. It seemed as if the great powers and the international community were getting used to, and becoming reconciled with, the status quo.

After the death of Egyptian president Nasser in September 1970, Anwar Sadat acceded to the presidency. Sadat frequently resorted to threats of war, as a means of spurring on the diplomatic processes aimed at bringing about a settlement. Nevertheless, he had indicated no willingness to be satisfied with anything less than complete Israeli withdrawal. He declared that 1971 would be the "year of decision" between peace and war. Egypt demanded acquiescence with its terms, refused to consider Israeli demands for secure borders, and thus contributed to the stalemate—but neither did it go to war.

While still threatening Israel, Egypt decided in July 1972 to expel the advisors, technicians, and servicemen the Soviet Union had sent. The reason was Egyptian dissatisfaction with the small extent to which the Soviets had acceded to its demands, political and military.

The Arabs, above all Egypt and Syria, had come to sense that time was working against them, and they decided to go to war in 1973. It is possible that war could have been averted had Israel considered the possibility of ending the overall conflict by signing a peace treaty with Egypt consisting of the same terms, or even better ones, than those contained in the peace treaty signed after the Yom Kippur War. But that was not to be; Egypt took pains to prepare itself thoroughly for war. It made certain it would be able to rely on the Soviet Union for weapons and military equipment, and, as a guarantee against complete military collapse should its venture fail, on Soviet intervention to obtain a timely cease-fire. Egypt actively worked to undermine Israel's standing in the international arena and delegitimate it. The Egyptians nurtured an all-Arab coalition aimed at undoing the results of the Six Day War, in which the confrontation states had lost the Sinai Peninsula, the Gaza Strip, Jerusalem, Judaea, Samaria, and the Golan Heights.

In addition to pan-Arab aims, which had focused on the Palestinians and on Arab unity ever since the establishment of the State of Israel in the War of Independence, there were now the particular national interests of the confrontation states: the return of the territories Israel had captured in the Six Day War. In the meantime, the Palestinians and the terrorist organizations had risen in importance, and they put pressure on Arab governments to take meaningful action against Israel. Egypt and Syria at this time had been earnestly preparing for war, procuring the best weapons in the Soviet arsenal and building up their strength both in quantity and quality. The Soviet Union had had no intention of becoming involved in war but extended generous amounts of aid to Egypt and Syria in helping them to prepare for war. While the Soviet Union may not have encouraged Egypt and Syria to start the Yom Kippur War, it was to a great extent responsible for that war, because of the virtually unlimited military support it gave the Arabs. After war broke out, it did its utmost to influence the outcome, even to the extent of encouraging other Arab states to intervene.

As has been mentioned, after the Six Day War the Soviet Union helped Egypt and Syria to rehabilitate their armed forces, replacing the military equipment and weapons lost in the Six Day War, and then some. In 1973, the Soviet Union furnished substantial quantities of Scud surface-to-surface missiles, with a range of three hundred kilometers, in addition to the Frog surface-to-surface missiles, with a range of sixty-five kilometers it had previously sent. Furthermore, that year it also furnished Sukhoi-20 aircraft, advanced-model MiGs, various models of antiaircraft missiles, T-62 tanks, Sagger antitank missiles, RPG antitank rocket launchers, artillery, heavy mortars, bridging equipment to cross antitank ditches, and river-crossing equipment for the Suez Canal.

Israeli security policy after the Six Day War aimed at maintaining the strategic and territorial circumstances that that war had produced, pending a diplomatic settlement with the Arabs. The IDF continued to build up its forces, so as to deter the enemy and prevent war. Ongoing military activity, the war on terrorism, and establishing and nurturing good relations with the Palestinian population in Judaea, Samaria, and the Gaza Strip were also matters of central importance to security policy in this period.

Israel aspired to reach a permanent peace settlement with the Arab states on the basis of what had been termed "agreed defensible borders" ("strategic defense borders"). A basic principle was that it would never return to the lines of June 1967. Israeli policy aims in these years were to preserve the cease-fire and deter the Arab states from violating it. Israel declared its willingness to make every effort to achieve peace and security, and that it did not reject, nor would it reject, any serious dialogue toward that end. However, as long as the road to peace was blocked, it would continue to nurture the might of the IDF, wherein lay the guarantee of its security. The IDF had to allow the government freedom of action in advancing the national aims while deterring offensive initiatives by the enemy and any attempt to compromise Israel's sovereignty or harm its people, foiling offensive activity, and above all bringing a war, should one come, to a successful conclusion.

THE ROAD TO WAR

In the summer of 1972, the IDF General Staff concluded that since 1971—which President Sadat had declared would be "the year of decision" between peace and war—had passed with no political or military decision, and since there had been no change in the declared positions of the parties to the dispute, the Arabs must have become aware of Israel's military power and improved political position. Thus it was reasonable to assume that the status quo would continue over the coming year. This appreciation was also based on the seeming agreement between the United States and the Soviet Union to reach a settlement of the Middle Eastern dispute through negotiations. Israel assumed that the United States would continue to oppose Soviet expansionary efforts by, among other means, a strong Israel.

In the view of the Intelligence Branch, the conditions requisite for an Egyptian military option would not obtain before April 1973. If the Egyptians nevertheless felt the military option was open to them and went to war, the Intelligence Branch assumed, they would try to cross the Suez Canal with the aim of advancing to the Mitla and Gidi passes, some forty kilometers east of the canal.

Israel's national assessment of the situation was that in the light of changes in the Arab world, the most salient of which was the expulsion of Soviet advisors from Egypt, it would be reasonable to assume that in the coming year there would not be a war, although afterward war would certainly be a possibility. The IDF began a thorough examination of its operational preparedness, in the course of which many operational plans, both defensive and offensive, were completed, including many changes and improvements in the system of reserve mobilization. Particular emphasis was placed on the operational plans of the Air Force, in the light of the modern surface-to-air missiles being deployed by Egypt and Syria.

In early 1973, the IDF General Staff believed that the struggle between the great powers for advantage in the Middle East and expansion of their influence in the region would continue. However, because of their mutual deterrence, they would avoid military confrontation and try to avoid active involvement in the event that a Middle Eastern war did break out. The Arabs would be able to obtain modern weapons, ammunition, and political, economic, and moral support. Hence, the stability of the Middle East depended on the ratio of military forces between Israel and the Arab states. Since each of the superpowers would continue to defend its vital interests, they would find it difficult to cooperate; therefore, both would show inclinations toward policies that tended to preserve the status quo. Hence, significant political or strategic change could come about only through war.

The interests of the Soviet Union would require it to continue to extend military and economic aid to the Arabs; to cooperate with the United States to the extent of preventing a deterioration in the Israel-Arab dispute that could cause a clash between the superpowers; and to prevent, by political means and deterrence, the collapse of its Arab allies in the event of war.

The interests of the United States would induce it to extend economic and military aid to states that could help it to stabilize the region and prevent Soviet penetration and the radicalization of Arab regimes; to extend economic and military aid to Israel, with a view toward preserving the balance of forces so as to prevent the region from sliding into a general war and to preserve Israel's deterrence and ability to defend its existence; to initiate political arrangements that would prevent war; and to strive for a final settlement that would guarantee nonbelligerency and peaceful relations.

The IDF General Staff expected the economic and political power of the Arab states to rise, because of their oil. The United States and the states of Western Europe would be doubly dependent on Arab oil—because of their actual oil needs, on the one hand, and Arab purchasing power, which would rise because of their oil sales, on the other. The Arabs would have money to buy, and other countries would have an interest in selling, to keep the wheels of their industries turning; furthermore, they would be exposed to pressure, even blackmail, because of Arab oil. Hence, the Arabs would be surfeited with modern weapons systems. In the views of the General Staff, Israel, because of the rising costs of weapons systems, would find it increasingly difficult to ensure that the quantitative gap, disadvantageous to itself, would not widen in favor of the Arabs. Israel would find the economic burden of maintaining the existing ratio of forces increasingly difficult to bear in the future.

The General Staff classified enemy states in two groups:

1. The confrontation states: Egypt, Syria, Jordan, and Lebanon.
2. The permanent (or "natural") allies of the confrontation states: the Arab states of the Middle East and North Africa, which were liable to send expeditionary forces against Israel.

The financial resources were in the hands of the permanent (natural) allies, namely, in the hands of the oil-producing states, on which the confrontation states depended. Since the Arabs were far from realizing the principle of unity of aims, and since the divisions and the conflicts of interest between the regimes would continue to exist in the years ahead, the assumption was generally accepted that not all of the potential Arab economic and political power would be channeled into a common effort against Israel. The General Staff had assumed that out of the Arab world's enormous and varied wealth and arsenal, something would be allotted to general Arab aims. The confrontation states would be dependent on their rich allies, which would not make the lion's share of their resources, but only a small fraction thereof, available to them. While the confrontation states would have access to virtually unlimited manpower reserves, the material resources would be in the hands of their natural allies. Therefore, the Arabs would be able to make full use of their power against Israel only if they were able to unite and channel their entire national efforts toward attaining military superiority over Israel. Considering the contrasts in societies and regimes, there was (according to the General Staff appreciation) no danger of such unity materializing in the 1970s. At most, cooperation and mutual aid among the Arabs would rise.

In the General Staff appreciation, the following capabilities would be required of the IDF in the 1970s:

1. Full deterrent capability against the confrontation states and their permanent allies and partial deterrent capability—according to need, circumstances, and possibilities—against allies of opportunity.
2. The ability to defeat all the confrontation states, by conducting two main offensives concurrently—on the Egyptian front and the eastern front.
3. The ability to deliver preventive and retaliatory blows against the permanent allies of the confrontation states, so as to maintain Israel's deterrent capability in respect of them.
4. The ability to conduct offensives on all fronts, with the ground forces, against the confrontation states and their permanent allies, even without air superiority.
5. The ability to undertake general national tasks and maintain military superiority and flexibility, so as to afford the government full freedom of action in advancing the national aims.

In March 1973, reports began to be received concerning Egyptian and Syrian preparations for war. Pursuant to such reports, a decision was reached to implement an emergency program, designated "Blue and White," the aim of which would be to complete and accelerate IDF preparations for a possible war in the course of the year. These intelligence reports warned of an overall trend but did not specify any particular time frame for the outbreak of war. The main element in Blue and White was the acceleration of the IDF buildup and the bringing forward to 1973 of large segments of the work programs for 1974 and subsequent years. Accelerated establishment of optimal military power for a possible war also required increasing budgets, which the government duly authorized.

The operational plans of Egypt and Syria were known to the IDF, which also knew that if a war broke out at Arab initiative, its main participants would be Egypt and Syria. The enemy war aim was to break the political stalemate by the very act of going to war, to bring an end to the status quo in the Sinai and Golan Heights, and to force the superpowers to pressure Israel into withdrawing from the territories it had taken in the Six Day War. The main military aims of the Arabs, which derived from their war aims, were as follows:

On the Egyptian side—

a. To cross the canal, become established on its eastern bank, and exploit that success by capturing Sharm el-Sheikh and the western Sinai to a depth of approximately seventy kilometers, up to the line connecting Bir Gafgafa, the Mitla Pass, and Bir Thamada.
b. To inflict heavy casualties on the IDF and wear Israel down.

On the Syrian side—

a. To capture the entire Golan Heights and capture a bridgehead west of the Jordan.
b. To destroy the IDF forces on the Golan Heights.
c. To exploit the above successes by capturing areas west of the Jordan deep inside Israel, possibly up to Nazareth.

Israeli war aims were based on an appreciation of possible Arab modes of operation and on the assumption that war would be undesirable for Israel. The possibility of a war initiated by the Arabs led to the assumption that a war would commence with an Arab offensive, which the IDF would try to contain before going over, as soon as possible, to a counteroffensive. The Israeli war aim would be "to deny the enemy any military gain and to administer him a defeat involving the destruction of his forces and military infrastructure, so as to confer Israel with substantial military advantage, both in ratio of forces and cease-fire lines." The attainment of such an aim would enhance Israel's power of deterrence, prove to the Arabs that they could gain little glory in war, and strengthen Israel's hand in negotiations over cease-fire terms at war's end.

The operational objectives of the IDF and its operational methods naturally derived from the aims of the war. Differences of opinion prior to the outbreak of war at General Staff meetings, chaired by the minister of defense, focused on the aims of a war should such be forced on Israel. No one thought a war was necessary, but it was decided that if Israel had to fight one, it should derive the most possible benefit from it, capturing territory and improving the cease-fire lines. Yet another opinion was also offered: some opposed conquest of additional territories and thought it would be best to limit the duration and scope of a war so as to reduce the attendant political, military, and social damage. This viewpoint was rejected.

The minister of defense in the name of the government, ordered the IDF to prepare for a war with Egypt and Syria in the coming summer, on the basis of clear, unequivocal guidelines. From March 1973 until the outbreak of war in October, the activities of the IDF were dominated by these preparations, which included a wide range of tasks. All echelons of the IDF were involved, and many units brought forward their training schedules, particularly units that according to the original program would have undergone training only in 1974.

Many additional units and formations were established as part of the Blue and White program: a new armored division was established, which according to original plan was to have been established in 1974; the headquarters of another new division, which according to the original plan was to have been established in 1977, was put in operation on an improvised basis; existing divisions were reinforced with new battalions (over ten armored, artillery, and reconnaisance battalions), the creation of some of which had been advanced a year, of others by several years. The newly established units attained levels of operational capability comparable to veteran units in much less time than had been expected.

Thanks to Blue and White, the IDF entered the Yom Kippur War much stronger than it would have been in October 1973 on the basis of the original plan. It was an even stronger IDF than that which had been envisaged for 1974 or 1975.

Despite reservations about the method of defense in the Sinai, the General Staff continued its support for the line of strong points; in any event, they were there, and they drove home Israel's permanent presence on the banks of the canal. The General Staff recognized the validity of the anxieties, voiced by opponents of the strong-point concept, concerning the fates of those who manned them in the event of war, but it believed that if there were a perceivable threat, they could be evacuated. The defense of the Sinai was understood to be a mobile, armored campaign, in the framework of which the strong points would be integrated.

In the course of the summer of 1972, it was assessed that the ability of the IDF to cross the Suez Canal was doubtful, due to the lack of necessary equipment. Hence, the General Staff decided to undertake an emergency program to organize a canal-crossing engineering force, step up the pace of development and manufacture of the necessary equipment, and train assault engineer units. Thanks to the emergency program, the crossing of the canal proved feasible, from an engineering standpoint, in the Yom Kippur War. However, because the war broke out before completion of the canal-crossing engineering force, the actual crossing by the IDF took on the character of an improvised operation.

The emergency stores of the armored brigades and artillery battalions were moved closer to the expected zones of operations on the Golan Heights and in the Sinai in the period before the war. Improvements were made in fortifications in several sectors. On the Golan Heights in particular, extensive work on infrastructure was carried out, including the addition of many fortifications, obstacles, and communication lines, and the paving of 121 kilometers of roads for tanks and artillery. Numerous arrangements were made to shorten warning times, the process of mobilizing reserves, and preparations required for the movement of standing forces from the center of the country to the two fronts at short notice.

The Blue and White emergency program was completed by the end of August 1973, its success exceeding the most optimistic projections.

In the spheres of civil defense and emergency economy, Israel's staying power proved reasonably strong, and its national security doctrine adequate.

DEPLOYMENT FOR WAR

When intelligence was received in March 1973 to the effect that the Egyptians and Syrians intended to go to war that spring, the IDF began to watch their preparations very closely. In the spring, it became known that the president of Syria had requested delaying war until the autumn, because Syria had not yet received certain essential weapons the Soviet Union had promised, such as Sukhoi bombers, Frog surface-to-surface missiles, T-62 tanks, artillery, and tanks with bridging equipment for crossing Israeli antitank ditches on the Golan Heights. On 20 August, the General Staff learned to its consternation that the array of surface-to-air missiles that had defended Damascus had been moved forward to the Golan Heights. The IDF felt constrained to prohibit air traffic over the Golan Heights, except for agricultural spraying aircraft.

At the end of August, information reached Israel that a delegation of Soviet experts had come to Syria. They had conducted a survey of the Golan Heights and submitted to the Syrians a report to the effect that they could recapture the Golan Heights, given existing force ratios, within hours. The IDF also knew that the Syrians had conducted full-scale maneuvers for reconquest of the Heights.

On 30 August, it became clear to the General Staff that the Soviet Union had already delivered to Syria and Egypt the weapons systems that had been expected of it, including Frog missiles to Syria and Scud missiles to Egypt. The appearance of these missiles constituted an early warning, because in the appreciation of IDF intelligence the Arabs would refrain from embarking on all-out war only as long as they did not have the capability to attack objectives deep in Israel.

On 4 September, the Syrians began to reinforce their units along the Golan Heights front with artillery and infantry. On 13 September, Israeli aircraft conducted photographic sorties deep in Syria. On their way back, Syrian aircraft tried to intercept them, and in the ensuing air battle twelve Syrian aircraft were shot down. The Syrian armed forces entered a high state of readiness, as did the Egyptian armed forces, on land, air, and sea. On the same day, the Syrian military completed the deployment of its full order of battle on the Golan Heights. It was ready at its emergency positions, which could be used either as defensive positions or as jump-off points for attack.

The General Staff knew all this, as well as the operational details of plans for the Syrian offensive, and its order of forces. The same was true concerning Egyptian forces on the canal. Considerable preparations had been noticed along the front lines, and intelligence reports had repeatedly been received concerning the Egyptian-Syrian intention to go to war, their timetable, and operational plans. Along the canal, however, the IDF was taken in by an Egyptian deception that led Intelligence to believe that the Egyptians were conducting an exercise. At 2:00 A.M. on Friday, 5 October, information was again received to the effect that Egypt and Syria were preparing to attack Israel and that the families of the Soviet experts were leaving the two countries.

Despite the flow of information on Egyptian and Syrian military preparations, Israel relied until the morning of 6 October on a calculated risk (as it were) based on a sense of security—after all, it had the benefit of both strategic depth and the awesome firepower of the Air Force. Thus Israel put off mobilization of the reserves until the intentions of the Arabs could be further clarified. The drama was nearing its peak, the ground was already beginning to shake; the threat to Israel's security was increasing, the military preparations aimed at it were nearing completion, and the Egyptian and Syrian armed forces were waiting taut at their start lines; the Russian advisors and specialists had begun to evacuate Egypt and Syria, leaving the stage for the next act—and Israel still did not mobilize reserves. It continued to await yet further intelligence, contenting itself with ordering the highest state of readiness for all standing IDF forces. On Yom Kippur, at the last minute, the scales finally began to fall from the eyes of the IDF high command.

The last intelligence warning reached Israel on 6 October, at 2:40 A.M. According to this information, on that very day, in the evening, Egypt and Syria would attack Israel. It was only then that Israel began to consider that it had conclusive, unequivocal proof of a pending threat. The government received the report an hour, and the CGS two hours, after its original receipt. Another five hours, for a total seven hours after original receipt of the intelligence, passed before Israel decided upon mobilization of the reserves. As soon as the General Staff understood that war was a certainty, it requested permission to launch a preemptive air strike. The government agonized over the matter, reflecting an uncertainty influenced by two factors: the desire to avoid war, and the desire not to be perceived as the aggressor, so as to assure U.S. support. The prime minister and ministers, confronting the full force of the dilemma, elected against a preemptive air strike.

The General Staff had presented a plan for a strike on Syria alone, but the ministers had thought that it was for a massive attack, one that would seriously damage Syria's operational capabilities. The General Staff had set before the ministers a rosy picture: the Syrian air force would be destroyed within three hours, after which its system of surface-to-air missiles would be knocked out, leaving Israel's air force unlimited freedom of action in the ensuing battle against Syrian ground forces. The truth of the matter was that the proposed air strike, which the government did not authorize, had never been intended as a significant military blow. In fact, what had been under consideration was not a massive, comprehensive air assault against Egypt and Syria but only a strike on Syrian airfields—not on either Syrian surface-to-air missile deployments or ground forces.

The dilemma the Israeli government had to face, then, was whether to choose the military advantage that would accrue from a preemptive air strike, or the political benefits that could be derived from waiting, which might even avoid war. The decision was made against an air strike in order to derive the political benefits, and mainly because of the desire to avoid war. The prime minister, Golda Meir, told the Americans on the morning of Yom Kippur, 6 October, that the Arabs planned to attack that same day but that Israel would not be the first to open fire. She asked the United States to warn the Russians and Egyptians.

Because of a refusal to believe and a sense of security deriving from strategic depth and the firepower of the Air Force, a process began in mid-September of waiting for one more piece of intelligence, one more verification, almost until the shooting actually started. The telltale signs and threatening concentration of forces had not been enough. It was this paralysis, this suspension of military alertness, that had caused Israel to find out for itself what a Barbarossa or Pearl Harbor tastes like.

CHAPTER 21
THE YOM KIPPUR WAR, 1973

The war started on Yom Kippur, 6 October 1973, at two o'clock in the afternoon. The Egyptians and Syrians attacked simultaneously on the Golan Heights and in the Sinai. Under these opening conditions, only Israel's standing forces confronted the enemy, and most of its ground forces had not yet been mobilized. The assault commenced along the entire Sinai and Golan fronts. Some 150 Egyptian aircraft crossed the Suez Canal at low altitude into the Sinai, and some sixty Syrian aircraft crossed the cease-fire lines on the Golan Heights, to attack Israeli military targets. Immediately after the planes crossed the cease-fire lines, Egyptian and Syrian artillery began a heavy bombardment all along the Sinai and Golan fronts.

In the Sinai, the Egyptian frontline force of two armies (equivalent to two corps in the West), the Second and Third Armies, deployed along the entire 150-kilometer Suez Canal front. From the Mediterranean Sea to the Gulf of Suez, the assault was carried out by five infantry divisions, four independent brigades, some twelve commando battalions, and approximately 1,200 tanks. Supporting them were 1,500 heavy artillery pieces and mortars, along with some 450 other cannon and tank destroyers for breaching the Israeli fortifications and direct support in establishing bridgeheads—all told, some two thousand artillery pieces.

The Egyptian forces in the Canal theater on 6 October 1973 numbered some two hundred thousand combat troops. By nightfall that first day, some forty thousand of these troops had crossed the canal and established themselves on the eastern bank, between the Israeli strong points (defended positions).

Since the reserves had not been mobilized, the Israeli forces along the 150-kilometer front numbered, at the outset of the attack, only ten infantry, mechanized infantry, and reconnaissance companies, twelve batteries of artillery (fifty-two guns), 290 tanks, two batteries of Hawk antiaircraft missiles, and six batteries of air defense artillery. Along the entire front, the Israeli forces numbered 450 soldiers, who manned sixteen strong points and seven observation posts between the strong points. The distance between strong points ranged from five to fifteen kilometers. The strong points were manned by between twenty and sixty soldiers each, and the observation posts by from five to ten. This was the total military "strength" Israel had deployed along the line of contact with the Egyptian forces that crossed the canal. Under these circumstances, and with the ratio of forces described above, whatever meager armored forces the IDF had available were compelled to shuttle back and forth all along the canal, fighting desperately to check the tide—something they tried to accomplish with mere companies, or even platoons or individual tanks.

Each of the five Egyptian divisions managed to cross the Canal and establish a bridgehead in the sector allotted it on the eastern bank. These bridgeheads linked up with one another, eventually forming a continuous strip along the entire front. The Egyptian troops were under almost no artillery fire during their crossing; furthermore, the firepower of the Israeli Air Force was blunted to a considerable extent by Egyptian antiaircraft fire. Facing only token opposition, the Egyptian crossing of the Canal was like a one-sided live-ammunition exercise.

At 5:30 P.M., at the approach of dusk, the Egyptians commenced landing helicopter-borne commandos deep inside the Sinai. Their job was to cut road axes to prevent Israeli reinforcements from being brought up to the canal front, capture Abu Rodeis, and hold territory along the Gulf of Suez coast until the main Egyptian forces that had crossed the canal could move south and link up with them. The commando units and helicopters failed. Of the forty-eight Egyptian helicopters that tried to ferry forces into the Sinai, twenty were shot down by Israeli combat aircraft or ground fire. Many of the helicopters crashed before the troops they carried could disembark. Commandos that did manage to land were killed, captured, or scattered. About half of the Egyptian helicopter-borne commandos that set out that day were killed.

The 450 Israeli troops in their strong points along the canal were subjected to withering fire. The strong points did not hold up the crossing. Their fire did hit a boat here and there and cause casualties, but the Egyptian plan called for circumvention of the strong points in the first place. It was only after the Egyptian assault forces had a foothold on the eastern bank that they allocated forces for a direct assault on the strong points.

At the beginning of the war, the Egyptians had to contend only with the troops in the strong points and whatever armored units and artillery batteries happened to be in the Sinai. The Israeli Air Force went into action without letup, in an attempt to check the flood tide of enemy divisions crossing the canal. Each of the strong points fought alone. They were distant and cut off from one another, and the handful of surrounded troops in each fought for their lives against an Egyptian onslaught that was supported by a massive artillery barrage. The massive shelling and the direct fire from tanks on the west bank across the canal destroyed the Israeli trenches. At most strong points, the commanding officers were killed in the initial stages of fighting.

Israeli tanks rushed to the canal line and strong points to relieve some of the pressure, and they fought tenaciously. The handful of IDF artillery batteries on hand gave whatever aid they could, although their fire was extremely sparse. They had to disperse their fire along the entire width of the front and were often compelled to allot single guns to provide fire support that had little chance of being effective.

Attacks by the Air Force on enemy forces crossing the canal disrupted Egyptian bridgeheads and efforts to bring forces eastward over the canal, but they could not check the tide. The 450 men in the strong points, the 290 tanks, the fifty-two artillery pieces, and combat aircraft exposed to surface-to-air missiles (SAMs) did not have a chance to prevent the crossing or stop the five Egyptian infantry divisions and the thousands of artillery pieces and tanks that were assaulting them. Yet despite it all, the defenders stood their ground. They were not able to prevent the enemy advance, but they inflicted losses on the forces that attacked them.

Not a single strong point fell in the first twenty-four hours of the attack. Nevertheless, instead of constituting firm bases of support for the mobile units in the field, and upon which the maneuvering armored units would be able to rely—as had originally been assumed by supporters of the strong point method of defense—the strong points were actually a burden. Their survival was the goal that dictated the moves made in the difficult early days; the need to protect them, help them, and extricate men from them were the considerations that spurred on the tank forces, which fought suicidal battles on their behalf.

By midnight on 6 October on the Egyptian front, 180 IDF ground troops had been killed. Four fighter aircraft had been shot down on ground-support missions, with three pilots killed and one captured, and another five aircraft damaged. All told, some 150 tanks had been engaged on the canal front, until rear-echelon brigades from Bir Thamara and Bir Gafgafa were brought up; of these, some eighty were knocked out—fifty were destroyed and abandoned, and thirty others damaged and evacuated.

Because of the qualitative superiority of the IDF, the Egyptians did not have a chance against it in armored and aerial combat. Hence, they avoided setting overly ambitious operational goals, such as the conquest of the Sinai Peninsula. Such a move would have required Egypt to conduct a war of movement, and in such a war its armored divisions would have been dealt with decisively by those of the IDF. In any case, they could not have undertaken such a move, because in order to do so they would have had to leave the protective antiaircraft umbrella they had deployed along the canal front. Without such cover, their ground forces would have been at the mercy of the Israeli Air Force. Crossing the canal and taking control of it had not involved a war of movement and maneuver by armored formations.

The crossing and consolidation of bridgeheads by the Egyptians on the eastern bank had been performed by infantry divisions and had not been dependent on the outcome of armored operations. They were satisfied with being able to defend themselves from Israeli armor by digging in and using the plethora of antitank weapons at their disposal. They concentrated enormous quantities of tanks, tank destroyers, antitank guns, recoilless guns, and antitank missiles, forming a continuous array of arcs of antitank fire, an array that was dense to the point of saturation. Large quantities of RPGs, recoilless guns, and missiles had been brought over to the eastern bank and organized into fields of fire that were thickened by overlapping fields of fire of tanks, tank destroyers, artillery and missiles on the western bank, which provided cover for the crossing and for the forces dug in on the eastern bank.

Thus the Egyptians realized that they could not face the IDF on land, in combat between tanks; forgoing mobile armored warfare, they pinned all their hopes on a stationary battle, the mainstay of which is antitank capability. So it was in the air as well, where air defense systems were the central component in Egypt's plan for aerial combat. Egypt had 155 antiaircraft missile batteries, fifty-five of which were deployed along the Canal front, and a hundred in the interior of Egypt. In addition to its anti-aircraft missile batteries, Egypt had the infantry-borne SA-7 missile (the "Strella") as the antiaircraft weapon of its ground units, as well as thousands of artillery pieces and heavy machine guns used for air defense, some of them radar directed. As the Egyptian Air Force lacked the capability to protect its ground forces against the Israeli Air Force, Egypt relied on a massive array of antiaircraft missile batteries. Under the circumstances of stationary warfare, it was an effective alternative to air power. The area protected by this air defense array extended from eight to ten kilometers east of the canal—in other words, roughly to the point at which the Egyptian mobile artillery was emplaced.

In contrast to the Egyptians, who were aware of their limitations and had drawn up their operational plans accordingly, the IDF found itself impotent in the air because it did not want to recognize the limitations of air power under these circumstances. Since the reserves had not been mobilized on time, the IDF's meager ground forces in the Sinai were not able to contain the massive Egyptian assault. The Air Force had to come to their aid. The simultaneous attacks in the Sinai and the Golan Heights forced the Israeli Air Force to divide its efforts between two fronts. Worse yet, the Air Force had to attack the Egyptian forces crossing the canal before a planned, concentrated attack had been made on the system of antiaircraft batteries, which the basic operational plans of the IDF always called for. Air support then, under these circumstances, was relatively meager. Nevertheless, the contribution of the Air Force in providing cover for the ground forces and annihilating the Egyptian commando force was substantial: in the first day of combat, IDF aircraft and antiaircraft batteries shot down fifty Egyptian and Syrian combat aircraft and helicopters. The Air Force successfully protected the ground forces from air attack and played a decisive role in neutralizing Egyptian commando forces that were flown into the Sinai by helicopter for raids deep in Israeli territory.

On the Golan Heights, the Syrians attacked along an eighty-kilometer front, from Mount Hermon in the north to the Yarmuk River in the south. The front-line Syrian force comprised three reinforced divisions, totalling fourteen infantry and armored brigades, and another seven battalions of commandos and paratroopers. The first assault wave consisted of forty-five thousand troops and 930 tanks. They were supported by 157 batteries of artillery, with a total of 942 artillery pieces.

Facing the Syrians along Golan front were 230 IDF soldiers, who manned ten defended positions. The positions were from three to six kilometers distant from one another and overlooked the minefields and antitank ditch that ran along the front line, although they did not control them with fire. Each position had some twenty soldiers. A support company was stationed in Kuneitra, and five observation posts were stationed along the front line. An infantry platoon was stationed on the hill of Tel-Zohar. Sixty soldiers were stationed at the Mount Hermon strong point, which afforded a view several dozen kilometers into Syrian territory, but only fourteen of the sixty were combat troops; the remainder were Intelligence or Air Force specialist personnel. The Mount Hermon strong point consisted of three guard posts, one ordinary observation post, and one artillery observation post. The layout of the ten positions was reinforced by two armored battalions (seventy-two tanks), which were deployed along the line of positions on the El Al-Rafid road. All told, a total of ten infantry and mechanized companies, 177 tanks, and eleven batteries of artillery with forty-four artillery pieces were deployed on the Golan Heights.

As on the Egyptian front, so too on the Syrian—Israeli air power was to a great extent neutralized and could not bring its enormous firepower to bear. As on the canal, here too it was the ground forces that bore the main burden of containing the onslaught. Syrian antiaircraft fire was heavy, and on 6 October the Israeli Air Force was able to fly only thirty-two attack sorties.

The Syrians had deployed thirty-six antiaircraft missile batteries. Of these, twenty-five were on the Golan front, and eleven were deployed to defend the Syrian interior, around Damascus and else-where. The effective defensive range of Syrian air defense missiles, even under an altitude of five hundred meters, extended eight kilo-meters into the Golan Heights. In addition to antiaircraft missile batteries, the Syrian forces possessed individual portable antiaircraft missiles (Strella), and thousands of antiaircraft guns and heavy ma-chine guns, some of them radar controlled.

The Syrian attack into the Golan Heights began immediately with the commencement of fighting. The first wave, consisting of three infantry divisions reinforced by several armored brigades with some six hundred tanks, involved two operational efforts, one in the northern Golan and one in the southern, extending between them along the entire width of the front. Israeli armor was forced to split its efforts, as in the Sinai, against large enemy tank forces. The Israeli tanks fought in small groups, and at times even as individual tanks. Syrian helicopter-borne commando forces captured the Mount Her-mon strong point in the initial stage of the assault.

As in the Sinai, the handful of Israeli troops on the Golan Heights absorbed the full impact of the enemy assault. By morning of the second day, they had suffered over a hundred casualties. The de-fended positions held their own, except for three that were evacu-ated; in their advance, the Syrians by-passed the Israeli positions. They managed to effect deep breakthroughs, and there was a danger that with their overwhelming quantitative superiority they would capture the entire Golan Heights. However, thanks to the high qual-ity and professionalism of the IDF forces, and the heroic efforts of the Air Force on the critical night of 6–7 October, the IDF managed to check the Syrian advance in the central Golan. That first night of the war, the first reserve tank forces arrived, and by 10:00 P.M. they were already engaged in the fighting. The Syrians, for their part, also committed an additional armored division to the battle.

The Yom Kippur War commenced under extremely difficult con-ditions for Israel, because the reserves had not been mobilized on time and the Air Force was not able to provide effective fire support for the ground forces. The initial stages of the war were almost tantamount to Case All—concurrent attacks by the Syrians on the Golan and Egyptians in the Sinai, as the reserves mobilized under fire. Nothing went according to the book. The "original sin" of the Yom Kippur War was that the reserves were not called up in time, and this caused all subsequent military problems and frustrations during the war. The IDF was forced to enter battle in an improvised manner. Instead of sending them out properly equipped and organized, as tightly knit organic units and formations, the General Staff had to send its forces to the front piecemeal. Instead of sending tanks and other armored vehicles to the front on tank transporters and trains, it hurried them off on their own tracks. Going thus into battle would be a mistake under ordinary circumstances, entailing as it does the erosion of the machinery of war even before the test of combat. However, under the circumstances of the opening stages of the Yom Kippur War, this improvisation enabled the IDF to conduct an effective defense.

The reserves got to the Golan Heights within a day of the outbreak of fighting, which was ahead of the timetable set in IDF mobilization plans. They went into action on Sunday, 7 October 1973. One reserve brigade had already gone into action on the night of the first day (the night of 6–7 October). According to the IDF's standing readiness plans, only 36 percent of all tanks, self-propelled artillery, and heavy engineering equipment were to head for the Sinai and Golan Heights on their own tracks, with the remainder being brought up by track transporters and trains. However, on 6 October 1973, 82 percent of such equipment were on the way to the Sinai and Golan Heights on their own tracks. According to basic mobilization plans, reserve forces intended for the Sinai were supposed to get there and complete their deployments in eight days. In the actual event, most reserve formations reached the front in the Sinai between noon on Sunday, 7 October, and dawn on Monday, 8 October—in other words, in two days. According to plan, the aggregate distance travelled by tanks on their tracks was supposed to amount to some twenty-seven thousand kilometers, while in actual fact it totalled 209,000 kilometers.

At the outbreak of fighting, there was a widespread feeling that a shortage of ammunition existed in Israel's ground forces, although in fact there were sufficient quantities, except for one type. The feeling of scarcity derived from the way the war had begun: calling up the reserves in an improvised manner, as the fighting progressed, led to the control of logistics at the various command levels also being improvised, which in turn led to problems in the flow of ammunition to the fighting forces. Israel Military Industries manufactured ammunition during the fighting at an accelerated pace, making a significant contribution to the war effort. IDF requirements for ammunition stockpiles were appropriate to what its national security doctrine called for, and to a considerable extent were proved adequate even for a long conflict.

At dawn, after the first critical night between Yom Kippur and Sunday, 7 October, the IDF high command decided to reinforce the two divisions intended for the Golan Heights with the General Staff Reserve, an armored division, which was duly sent to the heights from the center of the country on Sunday. On the morning of Monday, 8 October, the IDF's three armored divisions launched a counterattack, inflicting heavy casualties on the Syrians and evicting them from the Golan Heights; by 10 October, the Golan Heights were once again entirely in the hands of the IDF, although the Mount Hermon strong point remained under Syrian control. On 11 October, the IDF went over to a general offensive into Syria itself, hitting the Syrian Army hard, along with expeditionary forces sent by Iraq, Jordan, and Morocco. The IDF captured a large salient inside Syria, and fire from its artillery reached the outskirts of Damascus. On the night of 21–22 October, the IDF recaptured the Mount Hermon strong point.

On 8 October the IDF also launched a counteroffensive in the south, with the aim of throwing back the Egyptian forces that had crossed the canal. The counterattack failed, and Israeli armored forces suffered heavy losses. On 14 October, Egyptian armored divisions crossed the canal and launched an armored offensive aimed at reaching the passes at Bir Gafgafa, Gidi, and Mitla, with the intention of relieving the pressure of the Israeli offensive of 11 October in the north against Syria. In the intensive tank-versus-tank battles that ensued, Israeli armor decisively defeated Egyptian armor, destroying some two hundred Egyptian tanks at little cost to itself. When Egyptian armor exposed itself to engage Israeli armor in a mobile battle, it did not have a chance.

Henceforth, the initiative passed to the IDF, and the Egyptians went over to the defensive. On the night of the following day, the IDF crossed the canal, bringing the battle into Egypt itself. On 23 October, IDF armored divisions encircled the Egyptian Third Army, on the southern sector of the canal, and reached kilometer 101 on the road to Cairo.

In the Yom Kippur War, Israeli ground forces fought a war of the few against the many, not only in numbers but in firepower, as well.

Firepower from the various categories of enemy artillery was unprecedented in its magnitude and poured down relentlessly on IDF forces. Enemy artillery fire caused more IDF combat casualties than any other type of fire, while enemy troops were not, in the offensive stage of their operations, under effective fire. The IDF did not have much artillery, since it had relied on air power as an alternative to artillery. Toward the end of the war, during IDF offensives on both the northern and southern fronts, conditions were created that permitted Israeli aircraft to provide more effective fire support. By the morning of 9 October, Syrian stocks of antiaircraft missiles had been depleted. The Air Force took advantage of the opportunity thus presented and, enjoying freedom of action, launched intensive and effective attacks on Syrian forces. However, within twenty-four hours the depleted Syrian missile stocks had been replenished by a Soviet airlift, as Antonov aircraft brought in new quantities of missiles.

In the south, the skies opened up to the Israeli Air Force after Israeli tanks crossed the canal, and in their advance attacked antiaircraft missile sites in certain sectors. The Air Force took advantage of the breach in the Egyptian air defense wall and launched concentrated attacks on air defense batteries, destroying many of them, thus regaining command of the air.

THE WAR AT SEA

With the outbreak of war, Egypt and Syria imposed a naval blockade of Israel. However, the Israeli Navy had control of the Mediterranean arena and was able to preserve freedom of navigation. During the war, some two hundred ships entered and left Israeli territorial waters, guarded by Israeli Sa'ar 4 missile boats. Syria and Egypt had 28 missile boats, eight destroyers and frigates, twelve submarines, and over a hundred torpedo boats and patrol ships, against which Israel had a naval force of fourteen missile boats and twenty-five patrol boats. The Arabs' superiority in quantity was of little use to them. Control of the maritime arena remained with the Israeli Navy, thanks to the offensive operations of its missile boats.

In naval battles, the enemy fired some fifty Soviet-made surface-to-surface missiles, not one of which hit its target. Israeli missile boats also fired some fifty surface-to-surface missiles, of Israeli manufacture, and scored at least twenty hits, sinking seven Syrian and Egyptian missile boats. The superiority of the Israeli Navy was due to the high quality of its combat personnel, the quality of its combat doctrine, and the weapons and countermeasures against naval missiles that Israel had developed.

The Egyptians were able to maintain their blockade of the Red Sea, because Israel did not have any missile boats there. Nevertheless, the Israeli Navy's Red Sea Command maintained control of the Gulf of Suez and Gulf of Eilat with Dvora patrol boats, and Israeli naval commandos attacked enemy naval vessels in their Red Sea anchorages, sinking two missile boats. (Naval commandos sank a third missile boat in Port Said on the Mediterranean.)

The Israeli Navy performed brilliantly in the war. It defeated enemy fleets in combat, inflicting heavy casualties, and thwarted their attempts to impose a blockade of Israel's Mediterranean coast. Furthermore, it foiled enemy attempts to land forces for offensive operations against important objectives on Israeli-controlled sectors of the Gulf of Suez coast, where he intended to establish himself.

THE CEASE-FIRE

Egypt and Syria were not able to attain their military objectives in the war. Their armed forces were badly mauled, despite their quantitative superiority over the IDF and the initial circumstances of the war. At the outset, the Egyptians managed to capture a strip ten kilometers wide on the eastern bank of the Suez Canal. The IDF recaptured part of that strip, crossed the canal, overran large areas on the western bank, and, destroying considerable Egyptian forces, advanced twenty kilometers into Egyptian territory, where it took control of a large area that stretched from Isma'ilia southward to Jabil Athaka. IDF forces encircled the Egyptian Third Army and the city of Suez. The Egyptians, though, achieved an important objective on the ground: they retained control of two bridgeheads on the eastern bank of the canal. Israel captured and retained control of large areas in Egypt and Syria, and its forces positioned themselves near their capitals, on the axes of approach to Damascus and Cairo.

When IDF forces crossed the canal, President Sadat of Egypt announced that Egypt would be prepared to accept a cease-fire only on condition that Israel withdrew from all the territories it captured in the Six Day War. When it became clear to him two days later that Israeli armored divisions with close to a thousand tanks were threatening his armies and were even liable to advance on Cairo, he pleaded for an immediate cease-fire to save his forces, forgoing the condition that Israel withdraw from the territories it had captured. It was only because of massive American pressure on Israel that the Egyptian Third Army was not annihilated. At this time, President Assad of Syria ordered his army to dig in for the defense of Damascus.

On 24 October 1973, a cease-fire between Israel, Egypt, and Syria went into effect, in accordance with a UN Security Council resolution and under pressure from the great powers. At that stage, IDF forces were already only 101 kilometers from Cairo and forty-five from Damascus. No territory that had been under Israeli control before the war remained in Syrian hands, while Israel had captured, and established itself in, a salient inside Syria.

The Syrians and Egyptians did not honor the cease-fire agreements, and wars of attrition developed in both the north and the south. After long and difficult negotiations, at the center of which was the United States, separation-of-forces agreements were signed, between Israel and Egypt in January 1974, and between Israel and Syria in May 1974. In the wars of attrition between the cease-fire of 24 October 1973 and the implementation of separation-of-forces agreements, 166 Israeli servicemen were killed and some one thousand wounded. Pursuant to the separation-of-forces agreements, the IDF withdrew from the Suez Canal zone up to the road parallel to the canal, and a UN emergency force was deployed between the Israeli and Egyptian forces. Limits were also placed on the forces the belligerents were permitted to keep adjacent to the separation zone. Egypt lifted its naval blockade of the Bab-el-Mandeb Straits, at the entrance to the Red Sea. The agreements stated that they constituted first steps toward peace.

In the agreement with Syria, Israel made concessions in a number of sectors, especially in Kuneitra, which the Syrians claimed they intended to rebuild. Israel did not agree to give up military positions it occupied when the cease-fire agreement was drawn up. It did not agree to withdraw from areas overlooking Kuneitra and Rafid. As in the Sinai, a separation zone was established on the Golan, and limits were placed on the military forces the belligerents were permitted to maintain adjacent to it.

CASUALTIES

Estimates of enemy casualties were: 15,600 dead, 35,000 wounded, and 8,700 captured and interned in IDF POW camps. IDF losses in the war and the subsequent war of attrition, up to the separation of forces were: 2,656 dead, 7,251 wounded, and 301 captured. The enemy lost 440 combat aircraft, against 102 for the IDF. A total of 2,250 enemy tanks were destroyed or captured, compared to IDF losses of 400 tanks, and another 600 that were damaged, repaired, and put back into service. The enemy lost 770 artillery pieces, and Israel 25.

Israeli Navy missile boats, Air Force planes, and naval commandos sank twelve enemy missile boats. Not a single IDF missile boat was lost. Likewise, the Israeli Navy sank over thirty enemy vessels of various types—torpedo boats, patrol boats, and armed fishing vessels that were to be used for landing forces on the Suez coast.

CONCLUSIONS

There was an outburst of public fury in Israel after the war. It was directed at everything that touched upon the war, including the way the mobilization had been conducted, the movement of forces to the front, and the state of emergency stores of the reserve formations. Such frustration and anger blurred one of Israel's greatest national accomplishments in the war: that it had been able to mobilize under fire, equip forces and move them to the fronts, conduct a defensive that contained massive offensives on two fronts, and finally, on both fronts, go over to the offensive.

The Air Force, which had been intended to provide cover for the mobilization and deployment of the Army, and to help the standing Army in containing the enemy until the reserves were deployed in force, could not effectively provide such support, because of the massive enemy deployment of antiaircraft missiles. The Air Force, which according to its original plans would first attain air supremacy by neutralizing the antiaircraft missiles and guns along the canal and on the Golan Heights, and only then to provide massive fire support for the ground forces, was forced to change the order of its tasks and first aid the standing army in containing the momentum of the enemy assaults, both north and south. Air Force pilots fought courageously to halt the enemy on the ground. They suffered heavy losses, but the enormous firepower of the Air Force, upon which Israel had based its national security doctrine, yielded only limited results because of enemy antiaircraft systems.

For years, the IDF had deluded itself, and the civilian leadership, into thinking that the Air Force would be able to solve most of Israel's military problems. After the Six Day War, the Air Force had coined a new phrase: no longer "support and air-ground co-operation," but "participation" in the land battle. The Air Force claimed that destruction of the enemy air force was not sufficient; the role of the Air Force was also to operate in the land theater and "pave the way for the armor." The Air Force had to provide IDF ground forces freedom of action and clear the way for their advance. In the Yom Kippur War, it was sometimes the Armored Corps that paved the way for the Air Force.

It was not because of the government's decision on the morning of the outbreak of war that the Air Force was not able to thwart the strategic and tactical moves of the enemy and alter the course of the Yom Kippur War with a preemptive air strike; it was because of the limitations of air power, which derive from the nature and effectiveness of modern enemy antiaircraft systems. Even if Israel's political leadership had not dismissed the possibility of a preemptive strike on the day the fighting began, Egypt, both its forces and strategic infrastructure, would have remained unscathed, and so too the Syrian Army, and its antiaircraft missile force. Assaults on a few Syrian airfields (with greater or lesser degrees of success) could not have destroyed in advance the momentum of the massive Arab assault on the Golan and the Canal.

For Israel, the Yom Kippur War almost became a war of existence. The reasons for this were:

1. Despite the fact that there was a threat and that the government and General Staff had followed what was transpiring "in real time," reserves were not mobilized until Yom Kippur morning—because of the idea that the Arabs did not intend to attack, and because of the confidence Israel had in its strategic depth and the power of its Air Force.

2. The IDF was weak when the war broke out, because Israel's small standing military forces alone were compelled to contain the thrust of the enemy assault on the Golan and Sinai. Furthermore, not only was the IDF quantitatively inferior—with the forces conducting defensives, before the arrival of the reserves both north and south, pale reflections of

the full power of the IDF—but IDF firepower was extremely weak as well. The enemy's attacking forces encountered only sporadic Israeli fire. Israeli firepower in land battles had traditionally been based on that of the Air Force, in its role as flying artillery.

3. The enemy, who was well aware of this, had wisely planned an almost static war, under skies well defended by modern antiaircraft missiles and air defense artillery. Control over the tactical land battle was thus denied the Israeli Air Force, which could not effectively support the ground forces. Under these conditions the IDF was compelled, even after the reserves arrived and were thrown into battle, to conduct an extremely difficult defensive battle in the face of immense enemy firepower.

No wonder, then, that Israel was forced to fight a war of improvisation and attrition, one that tested its staying power, from the standpoint of the heavy casualties it suffered, the sustainability of its morale, and the adequacy of its material stocks. Mounting daily casualties among tank crews and tank losses left the IDF at the height of the fighting, without any reserves, and it was obviously growing progressively weaker on land. As for the Air Force, in the early stages of the fighting Air Force headquarters realized that losses in aircraft and pilots had already reached a critical level, one that could not long be sustained.

Concerning the attainment of air superiority and the defense of Israel's skies, all expectations of the Air Force were fully realized. Throughout the war, the Air Force provided effective air defense for the country. Under Air Force cover, the IDF was able to mobilize bring forces up to the front, and deploy with complete immunity from enemy air attack. While the Israeli Air Force conducted mainly offensive operations throughout the war, the air forces of Egypt and Syria were mainly engaged in their own self-defense.

Thanks to the qualitative superiority of the Israeli pilot and of the Air Force's combat doctrine, weapons systems, and command and control, the Egyptian and Syrian air forces were defeated in every air battle. Of the aircraft Israel lost in combat, only eight were shot down by enemy aircraft; all the others were shot down by missiles and air defense artillery. Most enemy aircraft lost in battle, though, were shot down by Israeli aircraft. For example, on the opening day of the war, 6 October 1973, at 2:00 P.M., an air battle took place over Shar el-Sheikh between two Israeli and twenty-eight Egyptian fighter aircraft (16 MiG-21s and 12 MiG-17s); seven enemy planes were shot down. On 23 October, at 10:15 A.M., an air battle commenced in Syrian airspace involving twelve Israeli fighter aircraft and thirty-two Syrian MiG-21s. Nine MiGs were shot down. On 24 October, at 1:10 P.M., a force of twelve Israeli fighter aircraft encountered nineteen Egyptian MiG-21s. In the ensuing battle, eleven Egyptian aircraft were shot down. In none of the above engagements did Israel lose a single aircraft.

Even in the early days of the war, the IDF high command sensed that the moment was rapidly approaching when the war would become one of national survival. It was only when the IDF went over to the offensive that Israel was extricated from the trap of a defensive war of attrition and removed the chance the Egyptian and Syrian forces had of defeating the IDF. As in previous wars, so too in the Yom Kippur War, the enemy was defeated by the IDF, once it went over to the offensive and set out to effect a decision rather than let itself be worn down trying to contain the enemy.

From the standpoint of the quantitative ratio of forces, Israel fought in the Yom Kippur War, as always, as the few against the many. The Jewish population of Israel numbered some three million, while the populations of Egypt and Syria alone numbered some forty-four million. Furthermore, there were many millions more in other Arab countries whose expeditionary forces participated in the fighting.

Militarily, the Arab war effort was based on the opening of two fronts, the Sinai and Golan; on the military power of Egypt and Syria; and on reinforcements from the expeditionary forces of other Arab countries. Indeed, expeditionary forces from the following countries also participated in the fighting: Iraq—two divisions, with eight armored and infantry brigades, over five hundred tanks and 180 field guns; Jordan—one armored division, with two armored brigades and 170 tanks; Libya—one armored brigade, with a hundred tanks; Algeria—one armored and one infantry brigade, totaling 130 tanks; Morocco—one infantry and one armored brigade, with thirty tanks; Sudan—one infantry brigade; and Saudi Arabia—an armored car battalion. Air reinforcements were also sent, as follows: to Egypt—squadrons of fighter aircraft from North Korea, Libya, Iraq, and Algeria; to Syria—squadrons from Iraq and Pakistan.

Politically and economically, the Arab war effort was based on Saudi Arabia and the other Arab petroleum-producing states, which put pressure on the West and the Third World. This pressure, increased with application of the "oil weapon," led to Israel's international isolation.

The quantitative ratio of military forces, on land, in the air, and at sea, between Israel and Egypt, Syria, and the expeditionary forces that reinforced them were, in most areas—manpower, main weapons systems, combat formations—approximately one to three, to Israel's disadvantage. The ratio in the area of antiaircraft missiles was one to thirty-seven.

The United States provided Israel with aircraft and operated an air "train" that brought it vital equipment and munitions. Some supplies were also sent on Israeli El-Al aircraft and by sea. Most of these supplies reached Israel after the war, but even so they were important, replacing aircraft and tanks lost, and replenishing stocks of ammunition spent. The American air train did not have a direct impact on Israeli military capability in the war, but it was of strategic importance in that it made clear to the Soviet Union and the Arabs that the United States would not stand by and do nothing while the Soviets sent massive amounts of weapons to Egypt and Syria, as they did by air and sea. The Soviets flew in some eight hundred supply flights of the Antonov-20 aircraft, which has a twenty-ton capacity, and of Antonov-22s, with eighty-ton capacities. During the war, Syria received some 150 MiG-21s, as well as surface-to-air missiles, antitank missiles, and some eight hundred tanks. Syria also received four missile boats after the war ended.

The quantities of aircraft Egypt received from the Soviets during the war were sufficient to make up for its losses. In addition to aircraft, Egypt also received batteries of surface-to-air missiles, air defense artillery, and hundreds of tanks.

The general Arab war aim, as has been mentioned, was to break the political stalemate in the Arab-Israeli dispute and bring about a dynamic political process; the Arab military aims in the war were limited. They did not delude themselves that they could defeat Israel militarily and evict it from the areas it had captured in 1967, to say nothing of annihilate it. The Arabs did attain their general war aims—that is, their political aim. The United States began an intensive diplomatic effort, and Israel had to withdraw from all the areas it had captured inside Egypt and Syria in the Yom Kippur War. It was not able to improve the cease-fire lines; the opposite proved to be the case. Furthermore, the war put in motion a process whereby Israel began to give up areas it had captured in the Sinai and Golan Heights in the Six Day War.

The enemy had been able to inflict painful losses on the IDF and wear Israel down, but by war's end it was apparent that despite their initial advantage, Egypt and Syria were on the verge of military defeat. From a professional standpoint, they are to be commended for their choice of a war aim, their war plan, and their military and political preparations. The Arab plans for the Yom Kippur War can be included among the classics of the art of war. However, their actual conduct of the war was not impressive. As in previous wars, Israeli command capabilities at all levels outmatched those of the Arabs, and the quality of Israeli fighting men proved superior to that of their enemies on land, in the air, and at sea. They fought, as always, the few against the many, and they demonstrated intelligence, courage, motivation, and maintenance of the aim. They were the few in quantity and the many in quality; each soldier was a "force multiplier," with the wounded continuing to fight, and when one fell in battle, his comrades taking his place. Many Israelis who were overseas returned home to fight. The wounded, after leaving hospital, returned to fill the depleted ranks.

Israel's war aim was to thwart that of the Arabs, prevent them from attaining any military gains, improve its cease-fire lines, defeat the Egyptian and Syrian armed forces, and destroy as much of their forces and infrastructure as possible. These war aims were only partially achieved.

Israel's qualitative military superiority, on land, in the air, and at sea, is especially noticeable in view of the initial circumstances of the Yom Kippur War, with its small standing armed forces holding their own on two fronts against the full military might of Egypt and Syria.

The enemy forced Israel to conduct a static war of attrition, forcing Israel to rely on its limited staying power. As a result of that and of the loss of its air-based firepower in the land battle, Israel lost its operational and strategic balance on the first day of fighting and was not able to regain it. Nevertheless, it managed to hold its own in a defensive war, contain and then repulse the enemy assault, and eventually go over to the offensive, on both the northern and southern fronts. As in its previous wars, so too here: Israel's offensive assault power is what decided the issue militarily. Egyptian morale at the war's conclusion was high. The Egyptians considered the very fact of starting the war and of maneuvering Israel into a difficult situation a victory; furthermore, they attained their overall political war aim.

Due to the circumstances the war was conducted in and the stand taken by the United States, Israel was denied an overall victory. Israel's military victory could not cover up the failure of the IDF to anticipate the war on time, to mobilize the reserves, and to deploy in full force in the Sinai and Golan Heights. The people of Israel felt a deep sense of frustration. There were those who thought that Israel had for years been conducting foreign and defense policies that "invited" the war, and that when it came, the IDF disappointed them; it failed to mobilize in a timely way, and it suffered heavy casualties. Protest movements sprung up in Israel denouncing the political and military leadership, and a commision of enquiry was appointed to investigate the war and the events leading up to it. Israel's self-image was seriously marred, and the prestige of the IDF declined.

CHAPTER 22
SUBSEQUENT WARS

THE WAR IN LEBANON, 1982

The Palestinian terrorist organizations continued their acts of violence, in Israel and abroad, after the Yom Kippur War. They came to constitute a kind of sovereign entity within Lebanon, making themselves entirely at home in that country and taking part in its civil war. The head of the Palestine Liberation Organization (PLO) maintained his headquarters in Lebanon. The various Palestinian organizations derived their support from the masses of Palestinian refugees, large concentrations of whom lived both in refugee camps and the cities. They had become well armed, including with long-range multiple rocket launchers ("katyushas") of Soviet origin. The katyushas enabled them to shell settlements throughout the northern part of Israel from deep inside Lebanese territory. They would infiltrate into Israel over its northern border and commit acts of terrorism, including the taking of hostages and indiscriminate murder. The shelling of settlements would sometimes force their inhabitants to sleep in air raid shelters, disrupting life and seriously damaging the morale of the people. Tourism was hurt. Matters had come to the point where inhabitants of the north fled to the center of the country to wait for the storm to abate. Even in periods of relative calm, whether achieved by U.S. mediation or the effectiveness of IDF deterrence, the inhabitants of the north lived under a constant shadow; at any moment, the rockets could once again strike, spreading indiscriminate death and destruction among the people.

In June 1982, the government of Israel decided to launch a military campaign, "Operation Peace to Galilee," to take control of extensive areas of Lebanon. The aim of the operation was to push the Palestinians several score kilometers away from the Israeli border, beyond the range of their long-range multiple rocket launchers. In the beginning, the government enjoyed wide public support. However, what began as a limited campaign expanded into a war against not only the Palestinian terrorist organizations, but also their supporters and allies, the Syrians.

The IDF and Syrian armed forces fought ground and air battles. The Israeli Air Force destroyed Syrian surface-to-air missiles and shot down over eighty modern, Soviet-made fighter aircraft. Israeli ground forces advanced into the heart of Lebanon and captured its capital, Beirut. During the fighting, the Israeli Navy landed large armored and infantry forces south of Beirut. What began as a punitive expedition against terrorist organizations became a real war and a bone of contention in Israel. A board of enquiry was established to investigate the circumstances surrounding, and responsibility for, the massacre of Palestinians in Beirut by Lebanese-Arab Christian militiamen.

As IDF casualties mounted and the dynamic of the war led to its constant expansion, as Arab was massacred by Arab, and as international criticism of Israel mounted, the parliamentary opposition in Israel, which at first had enthusiastically supported the war, including in votes, began to criticize the government bitterly. A protest movement came into being with broad public support, and the political and social atmosphere in Israel began to resemble the frustration and anger that had come over the country in the aftermath of the Yom Kippur War.

In a certain respect, the war in Lebanon resembled the Sinai Campaign. Both had been intended to smash guerrilla and terrorist efforts aimed at Israel, reflected in fire across the border, raids, and indiscriminate murder. Yet from another standpoint, the two wars were different. The essential difference was that the Sinai campaign had been perceived by Israelis, albeit with a certain degree of hesitation, as a preemptive war; during the war in Lebanon, in contrast, the prime minister of Israel had declared that "wars of choice" are also legitimate, not just "wars of no choice."

The Lebanon-based terrorist organizations were hit hard, and the head of the PLO and his staff were forced to leave Lebanon under American guarantee, and relocate in Tunis. The IDF withdrew southward to a security zone along the Israeli border inside Lebanon. The war in Lebanon left unpleasant sediments in Israel. Perception of it as a "war of choice" had undermined the national consensus.

THE *INTIFADA*, 1987–1993

The *Intifada* (the uprising) broke out formally on 9 December 1987, although its roots lay in the traditional popular opposition of Israeli Arabs (the Palestinians) and of the Arab world in general to the return to Zion of the Jewish people and to their settlement in the Land of Israel. That opposition had become exacerbated by the protracted occupation.

The Palestinians' violent struggle against the Jewish population had broken out on various occasions even before the War of Independence, whether because of political developments and events, or provocations and agitation. At times this struggle had taken the form of such outbursts as riots, involving agitated mobs, and at times of attacks by armed bands on Jewish transport and settlements. In the War of Independence, the Palestinians had waged a bitter war against the Jews. They and the invading Arab armies were defeated, yet ever since, the Palestinians have persevered in their opposition to Israel. They have remained in refugee camps, refused to be resettled in Arab lands, and nurtured the hope, while waging a terrorist war against Israel, of returning to their former homeland and supplanting the state of the Jews.

Until the Six Day War, the Arabs of Gaza had lived under Egyptian occupation, and those in East Jerusalem, Judaea, and Samaria had been ruled by Jordan. In the Six Day War, Israel had captured these areas from Egypt and Jordan. Ever since, hatred of Israel and a desire for vengeance kindled in the hearts of the Arabs; with the Six Day War, as the Israelis became conquerors and settlers, the yearnings of the Palestinians for national independence took on added force.

By the late 1980s, the conditions for a rebellion had ripened over a long process, and the Palestinian pressure cooker had become ready for an explosion. Economic and social pressures among the Palestinians had become aggravated and had accompanied their deep sense of political frustration. They feared that Israel and Jordan would reach an agreement at their expense, thus sealing their fate, given Israel's refusal to negotiate with their representative leadership, the PLO, and given the establishment of Jewish settlements in Gaza, Judaea, and Samaria.

It is largely because of the *Intifada* that Israel has been obliged to recognize the PLO as the representative of the Palestinian people, to recognize a Palestinian national entity, and to agree in principle to a division of the land west of the River Jordan between the two peoples. In 1993, an agreement was signed between Israel and the PLO to end their conflict. At the time, the Arab population of Judaea, Samaria, and the Gaza Strip numbered some 2.4 million.

Despite the Israeli-Palestinian rapprochement, the animosity of the generality of the Palestinians toward Israel has not abated, and the extremists among them have continued to wage a campaign of sabotage and murder against the people of the state of the Jews.

THE GULF WAR, 1991

In January and February 1991 during the Gulf War, between a worldwide coalition led by the United States on the one hand and Iraq on the other, the Iraqis fired some forty surface-to-surface missiles at Israel.

Most of those missiles were fired at the Tel-Aviv area but caused little damage. Most of the damage they caused was psychological and to morale. They caused tension and panic, and some of Tel-Aviv's inhabitants left with their children to find refuge outside the danger zone. This was similar to the reaction of people of northern Israel during the katyusha attacks, although the people of Tel-Aviv acted more on the spur of the moment than the more experience-hardened northerners.

The missiles fired at Israel were the forerunner of the modern strategic threat that would leave its imprint on Israel's national security thinking and determine the nature of its future strategic deterrence.

The two elements of conventional warfare are mobility and firepower. Mobility is traditionally considered the decisive element.

However, from the first day of the Gulf War, firepower has been its most decisive element. The Americans won the war virtually without casualties. They "swamped" strategic objectives in Iraq—infrastructure and land, air, and sea forces—with electronic energy and fire. Iraqi forces were not able to participate actively in the war.

That kind of war cannot be fought between similar countries. A spectacle like Iraqi gall, ignorance, and insanity is unusual; the "U.S.-Iraqi War" deserves a place in the annals of the international relations of the late twentieth century, but not among the classics of the art of war.

One must not draw mistaken conclusions. Everything is relative: compared to the United States, Iraq is a paper tiger. Nevertheless, awesome airpower, a large fleet, armored divisions, and a half million soldiers were needed to defeat it. Relative to Israel, Iraq is not a paper tiger but a Middle Eastern power. Israel has no chance of attaining the kind of superiority the United States attained, either in firepower, manpower, or economic and technological resources. Israel must invest its finest intellectual and material resources in its wars, for they are always fateful and of existential importance to it.

Israel did not lose anything of its deterrent power, even though it did not respond to missile attacks on itself. The United States pressed Israel not to intervene in the war, so that the Arab members of the anti-Iraqi coalition it had put together would not abandon it. Israel acceded to the American request.

The U.S. war in the Gulf shows that even a world power needs international support and domestic concurrence for a war effort. The Gulf War waged by the United States also showed, in bold relief, the importance of strategic planning, of thorough preparation, and of the principle that tactical, operational, and military considerations derive from the level of political-strategic considerations, serve it, and are subordinate to it. One more lesson: Even a world power that sets out to attack a small, nonmodern state must take various constraints into consideration and is not immune to the limits of power in determining its objectives. This is all the more so for a small state.

It is because of the extraordinary quality of its Air Force that Israel enjoys superiority in the air. The Arabs have been trying to bridge that qualitative gap by means of sophisticated and modern air defense, in order to defend themselves against the Israeli Air Force, on the one hand, and to develop attack capabilities against

Israel by means of surface-to-surface missiles, on the other. A war cannot be decided by missiles alone. However, missiles and the threat they represent have become an increasingly important factor in the conduct of war.

CHAPTER 23
NATIONAL SECURITY DOCTRINE IN THE TEST OF TIME

The Six Day and Yom Kippur Wars were historical turning points for Israel, bearing on its fate and its relations with the Arab world. The outcome of the Six Day War had altered geopolitical, national, and strategic reality, as well as Israel's national security doctrine.

After that war, Israelis began to deceive themselves to the effect that they could shape reality as they saw fit. The people became divided, and the consensus that had existed since the War of Independence concerning national goals and the country's borders dissipated. At the same time, in Egypt, Syria, and Jordan, not only the pan-Arab goal, namely the Palestinian problem, united the Arabs against Israel but immediate national goals—the return of the territories conquered by Israel: the Sinai, the Golan Heights, and Judaea and Samaria on the west bank of the River Jordan (the West Bank).

The Arab world was in a state of shock after the Six Day War, its peoples in a state of crisis. Israel, on the other hand, which before the war had been in a severe economic recession and whose people had been low in spirit, after the war enjoyed prosperity and underwent a technological and industrial revolution. Its economic and military strength continued to grow. The prosperity was the result of the optimism that took hold of the people after the victory, which in turn led to increasing investment and rising demand, and hence to economic growth. The number of emigrants from Israel declined, and immigration to it rose. With the increased immigration, housing construction underwent a boom. Defense outlays also rose. The IDF grew and became an increasingly sophisticated military force. Even the embargo on weapons to Israel contributed to increased economic demand, because of the need to increase the rate of domestic development and production of weapons. Furthermore, there was the additional expense of maintaining an occupation of the territories.

In the years prior to the Six Day War, money from the Jewish people, as well as reparations from Germany, had financed the State of Israel, including its defense expenditures. In those days, Israel had difficulty in obtaining weapons, because the various powers refused to sell to it, and whatever it had been able to obtain had to be paid for in full. It was only after the Six Day War, in the 1970s, that Israel began to receive significant financial assistance, both military and economic, from the United States. At the outset, this assistance was extended partly as a grant and partly in the form of loans, but from the mid-1980s it has been given entirely as grants. A foreign government bears part of Israel's defense expenditures. Along with the benefit Israel has derived from such aid, there has also been damage: "easy" money has had a negative impact on different aspects of life in Israel, even on military thought and professionalism. Instead of investing efforts to develop leadership, and impart the educational and professional skills required to solve problems that arise in various military and defense-related areas, the IDF has come to seek easy solutions—often based on investment in costly equipment—that frequently prove ineffective. Another deleterious development since the Six Day War has been the supplanting of Jewish labor by cheap Arab labor in construction, agriculture, the services, and industry. The replacement of Jewish with Arab muscle has also had negative ramifications in social and national security matters.

In the aftermath of the Yom Kippur War (and in the period prior to it), a sobering process began among both Israelis and Arabs. In Israel there has been an increasingly widespread feeling that it is not possible to keep all the territories captured in the Six Day War and at the same time to preserve the political status quo. The Arabs, for their part, have come to realize that the chance of imposing their will on Israel is negligible; even in the Yom Kippur War, which they had waged under optimal conditions, from their standpoint, they had suffered a military defeat. They have learned that they must abandon the path of war and take that of a political settlement of the dispute with Israel. Egypt was the forerunner on the political path to a settlement.

NATIONAL GOALS

The main historical significance of the Six Day War is that until then, Israel's overall political war aims focused on the preservation of its existence and on the 1949 armistice lines as the basis for peace agreements with the confrontation states. Those aims were clear, simple, and agreed upon, and their validity was self-evident. Israeli national security doctrine, which had derived from those war aims in the 1950s, was valid until the Six Day War.

The results of the Six Day War—the conquest of Judaea, Samaria, the Gaza Strip, the Sinai, and the Golan Heights—brought about a complete change in the national goals of the State of Israel. After the war, the leaders of Israel, who before that war had felt that the country faced an existential threat and was forced to fight a war for survival, indicated a change in national goals.

The IDF's conquest of the West Bank, of the Sinai, and the Golan Heights had given Israel the strategic depth it had so lacked in the past; an enormous sense of national power pervaded the people, producing a profound sense of self-confidence. It was against this background that an inclination developed to see in the conquest of territories beyond the 1949 armistice lines an expression of "the realization of the yearnings of the Jewish people." Realistic political appreciations were now superseded by pretentious security concepts regarding "Greater Israel" and "strategic depth and strategic security borders." The assumption that from now on Israel would enjoy freedom of choice, permitting it to make geopolitical decisions as it saw fit, came to be accepted by a majority of the people. Questions concerning limits that would qualify such freedom of choice bothered but few in the country.

There have certainly been instances in the history of wars leading to the expansion of a nation's borders. What was not legitimate was the pretentiousness of Israeli leaders who after the war denied that on 5 June 1967 Israel had gone to war to defend its very existence. They argued that in truth Israel had fought to realize a yearning of the Jewish people—to inherit all the land of Israel. It is worth stressing that what we have here is not the fog of history, a failure of memory developing in the national awareness over generations, or the operation of mechanisms of national repression. On the one hand, we are speaking of an understandable turnaround, the result of the intoxication of victory, a sense of salvation by a whole nation among which existential fears had suddenly been superseded by a feeling of absolute, conclusive security. On the other hand, it was a demagogic phenomenon and an act of irresponsibility by the national leadership, which had not only not endeavored to dampen the appetite for territorial expansion but had encouraged, nurtured it.

The leaders had not learned that there is no way of altering the overall national balance of power in the Middle East and that it is impossible to hold all the conquered areas of western Israel indefinitely, with their Arab inhabitants. Instead of maintaining the original national goal—striving to end the conflict and reach agreement over permanent borders of peace—and turning the victory into a lever for a political settlement; instead of holding onto portions of the country that had been captured as a deposit, most of which would be returned after secure borders had been agreed upon; instead of this sensible course, some of the people and their leadership nurtured illusions.

The national goals had split; the people had become divided and involved in a controversy over beliefs and opinions. Some continued to adhere to the original national goals, but some of them to "Greater Israel"—the annexation of all of the land west of the Jordan, or most of it, to the State of Israel. There was no argument with the basic Zionist idea, as formulated at the end of the nineteenth century and from which Israel's essence derives. There remained general agreement concerning the unity of fate of the Jewish people, which necessitates Jewish sovereignty and the defense of that sovereignty at all costs, a basic matter for which Israelis are willing to sacrifice their lives. However, the sense of unity of goals was undermined after Six Day War, leaving only a sense of unity of fate. As a consequence, other points of previous agreement and values became undermined, including the national consensus on security, strategy, military aims, combat doctrines, the task of leadership, and motivation. Loss of unity over goals has damaged the capabilities of the national leadership. The nation has become a divided nation, as the national goal is no longer implicitly understood and common to all; the task of leadership has become increasingly difficult.

The Arab side has undergone the opposite change: agreement and motivation have become stronger. In this respect, it would be difficult to exaggerate the importance of the Israeli occupation and its impact on the determination of Egypt and Syria, which had fought for the Sinai and the Golan Heights in the Yom Kippur War. The controversy over Greater Israel did not only touch upon considerations of the military aspects of Israeli-Arab relations, but also upon the essence of the state of the Jews, its image and purpose. Ought Israel aim to expand its boundaries so as to attain "strategic security borders" that would give it strategic territorial depth but also a large Arab population, rendering it in essence a binational state? Or would a smaller state be preferable, one with "demographic security borders" that divide the two peoples and guarantee Israel's continued existence as the state of the Jewish people?

Between the Six Day and Yom Kippur Wars, no single logically consistent line ran through the concepts "national goals," "political thought," and "military thought." Military appreciations of the situation, for both the short and long terms, no longer derived from defined national goals but rather from assumptions, wishes, desires. Instead of military strategy deriving from policy, operational thought from strategy, and tactics from operational thought, the process became confused to the point where the order was actually reversed. Even worse than the confusion in political and military thought between the Six Day and Yom Kippur Wars was the undermining of the national consensus, the creation of a deep split among Israelis concerning the justice of their country's position. The people became divided over the simple question, "What are we dying for?" That is the most penetrating question relating to national security—since it deals with the main component of power and the secret of Israel's military superiority—motivation and morale.

The Six Day War had been forced upon Israel; it was clearly a "war of no choice." The world was astounded by Israel's victory; its international image and its self-image soared. But Israel then sank into a national security lethargy, into a worship of the political status quo. It preferred to create established facts on the ground, military and civilian. World opinion turned against Israel. Various countries and international institutions came to see Israel as a state that retained its conquests and repressed another nation. The Arabs put pressure on the international community, used their influence, and hurt the interests of anyone who maintained close relations with Israel. Thus, Israel found itself increasingly isolated. It almost became a pariah state.

By the early 1970s, it had become apparent to the Israeli government that the Arabs would not sit with their hands folded. There were two possibilities: either a dynamic political process aimed at finding a solution to the conflict would get under way, or the Arabs would go to war. Many in the government and General Staff believed that Israel was in a strong position, politically and militarily, and that if there was a war, the Arabs would be able to extricate themselves from it only by the skin of their teeth; not only would Israel's position not become weaker, it would actually be enhanced. The government came to the view that it would be war that eventually materialized.

DEPTH

Basic Israeli national security doctrine prior to the Six Day War had not only posited the offensive as the preferred mode of conducting battle, along with taking the fighting deep into enemy territory and structuring forces accordingly, but also taking the initiative, meaning "preemptive war." The principle of initiative derived from the assumption that the optimal manner of combat is the complete, immediate offensive, without an initial defensive stage. However, in the aftermath of the Six Day War, in which strategic and operational depth was acquired, the IDF forwent the offensive as an absolute mandate of national security, as well as the desire to be the initiator, or preemptor, of war.

An assumption gained currency that the enormous strategic advantage derived from the conquests of the Six Day War—the depth conferred by the spaces of the Sinai, the West Bank, and Golan Heights—would henceforth afford the government maximum political flexibility, complete freedom of action. Political considerations would no longer be subject to military constraints; henceforth, Israel could permit itself not to take preemptive military initiative. In the face of incipient threats along its borders, it could permit itself to await military developments and conduct a defensive if the enemy attacked. The imperative that Israel must take the initiative and deliver the first blow was purged from national security thinking.

Furthermore, until the Six Day War the IDF had adhered to the principle of rigid defense, since the task had been to hold ground, not give it up, even at the price of forgoing opportunities to destroy enemy forces. Until the Six Day War, an Arab attack would have directly endangered vital strategic objectives in Israel; hence, the IDF could not have allowed itself to conduct a flexible defense, maneuvering with the aim of destroying large enemy forces at the expense of lost of territory. The strategic depth acquired in the Six Day War made it possible to conduct flexible defensive battles. The IDF could permit itself to lose ground as a means of destroying large enemy forces with minimal attrition of its own forces, yet continued to adhere to the method of rigid defense. Just as in the political sphere, where Israel did not consider territory captured a deposit to be held for bargaining, so too in the military realm: the IDF did not exploit its new strategic depth in favor of the method of flexible defense, which affords the greatest economy of force.

After the Six Day War, when the entire Sinai, West Bank, and Golan Heights came under Israeli control, the IDF General Staff heaved a sigh of relief and informed the government that Israel had at long last reached the "promised land"—it now possessed the strategic depth it had so coveted. Henceforth, the government would be able to conduct policy with flexibility, because it was now militarily permissible for Israel to conduct a defensive in the initial stage of a war and go over to the offensive later. The country was no longer in the confining circumstances it had suffered until the Six Day War, when it had had to base its hopes on its assault power and a short war, in order to avoid a war of attrition.

The position of the General Staff would have been correct in the context of a war for the defense of existense, for survival, but it was incorrect in any other context. Israel's new territorial goals and its behavior on the ground took the wind out of the sails of strategic depth. According to the idea the IDF now embraced, it had to prevent a large-scale canal crossing, come to the aid of the strong points along the Suez Canal, and remain steadfast along the canal, instead of exploiting depth, conducting a flexible defense, and maneuvering with the aim of destroying Egyptian forces deep in the Sinai, beyond the range of the static Egyptian infrastructure of artillery and air defense. The matter was even more pronounced on the Golan Heights and in Judaea, and Samaria, where settlements had been built along the borders; in other words, in those areas not only was strategic depth canceled, but tactical and operational depth as well.

In the Six Day War Israel had pushed the enemy away from its borders, and then it had pushed itself up against its new borders—within range of enemy observation points, artillery, even small-arms fire. The situation had become dichotomous: there was and was not strategic depth—at one and the same time! There was existential national depth, and yet there was no depth to defend the settlements and conduct optimal defensive operations based on mobility and flexibility, the purpose of which would have been plain—the destruction of enemy forces. Thus was emptied of any significance the most important advantage conferred by combat doctrine when one's side has strategic and operational depth.

The most critical mistake resulted from an incorrect understanding of the concept of strategic depth. The IDF perceived the expanses of the Sinai and Golan Heights correctly as a force multiplier and guarantor of existence and national security. Hence, it had contented itself in the Yom Kippur War, both intentionally and by intuition, with an inadequate ratio of forces on both fronts, knowing that with strategic depth it would be able to win a war of existence. However, success in war does not derive merely from an overall victory in a war for existence. It is possible to absorb painful blows, heavy casualties, even defeats, both military and political, even when existence does not hang in the balance. Strategic depth is irrelevant when there is no possibility of exploiting it to outmaneuver the enemy, as part of defensive operations, into a position where one can destroy his forces at the price of lost ground. The tasks undertaken in the Yom Kippur War did not make possible such use of strategic depth; the IDF undertook to conduct a rigid defense of the Suez Canal line and the line of fortified positions and settlements on the Golan Heights.

Strategic depth was important for the defense of national existence and should have been exploited. In that respect, the feeling of security among the nation's leadership, civilian and military, was well founded. However, that depth was irrelevant in the context of a rigid defense of every piece of ground under IDF control. The mistake of the IDF was to continue to think in explicit existential terms, as it had been accustomed to doing before the Six Day War. The IDF high command had not become psychologically aware that in a "normal" war, one that takes place in an arena affording strategic depth, one may suffer terrible blows, even be defeated in war, without putting national existence in the balance.

FIREPOWER

Israel's employment of its airpower in the War of Attrition, in the final analysis, contributed to an enhancement of Egypt's ability to deal with the Israeli Air Force and neutralize it in critical stages of the Yom Kippur War. Abundant deliveries of Soviet air defense systems in the wake of deep Israeli penetration raids into Egypt in the War of Attrition, Soviet command of those systems in Egypt, and the development of appropriate combat doctrine had enabled Egypt to plan for the Yom Kippur War so that the Israeli Air Force would not be able to prevent a canal crossing. The Egyptians had acquired combat experience in the War of Attrition fighting alongside the Russians and approached the Yom Kippur War well trained and with self-confidence in their proficiency in air defense.

Even in the War of Attrition a tocsin had been sounded, as Israeli aircraft had had to contend with Soviet surface-to-air missile batteries. Yet the Israeli Air Force did not understand that something fundamental, something substantial, had begun to change and that it was losing part of its ability to provide tactical air support for the ground forces. The IDF had continued to believe that in the future it would still be able to avail itself of the awesome firepower of the Air Force, a firepower greater than that of all the Arab armed forces combined.

It was in the Yom Kippur War that the painful sobering-up was experienced, and at, of all moments, the low ebb of the IDF's fortunes on the battlefield. Just when the Army most needed the overwhelming superiority of Air Force firepower as "flying artillery," it was not available.

Neutralization of the airplane as the main platform for bringing firepower to bear in tactical ground engagements was the first discernible crack in the IDF's traditional combat doctrine, as derived from Israeli national security doctrine. It took the Yom Kippur War to drive home fully the seriousness of the new reality of modern aerial combat. It became clear that Israel had prepared for the previous war in the air rather than for the next one. In this war, Israel had lost the superiority it had enjoyed for many years in firepower for tactical land battles, a superiority embodied in air power. The IDF had entered the war without realizing that because of the firepower of air defense systems, superiority in tactical firepower had passed from Israeli aircraft to Egyptian and Syrian artillery.

Egyptian and Syrian artillery were formidable opponents for the IDF in the War of Attrition and Yom Kippur War. The ratio of artillery forces was to Israel's disadvantage, and the relative importance of artillery in determining the characters of these wars and their outcomes was substantial. Such things have happened before in military history; armored assaults have been broken solely by artillery fire. Enemy artillery fire would disrupt the operations of IDF tank and artillery units, forcing them to move to alternative positions. Enemy counterbattery fire would be directed at IDF artillery batteries, inflicting heavy casualties. IDF batteries under such fire would be forced to move to new positions, in some cases two or three times in succession. There were cases of batteries having to move before completing their assigned tasks, with men killed and equipment damaged while they were in transit. There was one case of an artillery battalion that was unable to complete 50 percent of its tasks because of counterbattery fire. At times, massive artillery fire would be rained down on tank units for hours on end, forcing the tanks to move to new positions, where they would be further harried by massive artillery fire. Tank crewmen would be killed and wounded, tanks damaged and destroyed. In one instance during the operations to halt the Egyptian assault in the Sinai, a tank battalion was subjected to three hours of artillery pounding. The battalion suffered twenty dead and wounded and three tanks completely destroyed.

EARLY WARNING

In the War of Independence, Israel's capacity for early warning was not put to the test. Neither was it in the Sinai Campaign in 1956, because Israel had initiated the operations. The early warning capability of Israeli intelligence, according to the pure definition of the concept of "early warning" in Israeli national security doctrine, was first tested in 1960—and failed. On 18 February 1960, Egyptian forces began moving into the Sinai, without Israeli intelligence being aware of the fact. Only after four days did it become clear that Egyptian forces had deployed in the Sinai. When the fact became known, the General Staff did not bother itself with the question of intentions; it immediately deployed the standing forces in the south of the country to meet the threat. That action was taken in accordance with Israel's national security doctrine, which states that the

IDF is to deploy in sufficient force in the face of a threat and endeavor to deliver a preemptive blow should the enemy not back down. National security doctrine holds that the enemy must know the principles upon which Israeli doctrine is based, including that Israel is not able to keep forces mobilized for long without a decision of the issue. If someone wants war, he will get it; if someone does not want war, he will take heed, back down, and not test Israel. The Egyptians did not want war; they backed down and withdrew from the Sinai. They knew the principles of Israeli national security doctrine. The incident became known as "Operation Rotem."

On the eve of the Six Day War, the Intelligence Branch again grappled with intentions and again failed. It had claimed that as long as the Egyptians were involved militarily in Yemen, they would not send forces into the Sinai, and that in any event there was no need to worry about Egypt intending to attack Israel. Reality was to prove Intelligence wrong: the Egyptians did move into the Sinai. The strategy chosen by the Egyptians was to send their forces into the Sinai openly, accompanied by much fanfare. The ability of Intelligence to warn of the formation of a threat was not proved, in any event. Furthermore, its attempt to furnish early warning of intentions failed. On 14 May 1967, Egyptian forces moved openly into the Sinai, and the IDF, true to Israeli national security doctrine, reacted immediately by concentrating part of its forces in the south of the country, in proportion to the perceived severity of the threat. Whether the Egyptians had intended to go to war from the beginning or were gradually drawn into an ad hoc decision to commence hostilities—to which effect they had made a deliberate and conscious declaration when they announced closure of the Straits of Tiran to Israeli shipping—they were not deterred and did not back down in the face of Israeli mobilization and deployment opposite their own forces. In the period 20–26 May, the Egyptians brought additional, strong forces into the Sinai. These developments, along with the fact that the enemy had not withdrawn even when the IDF had deployed opposite him, were sufficient to induce Israel to mobilize its reserves and deploy the IDF in full strength along all fronts. The General Staff then proceeded according to national security doctrine, and Israel launched a preemptive strike.

In the period between June 1972 and October 1973, the concept of early warning became confused with the concept of warning of enemy intentions rather than that of possibilities open to the enemy.

This confusion of security doctrine, and deviation from it, explains much of the blow Israel sustained in the Yom Kippur War. In June 1972, the General Staff conducted its annual appreciation of the situation. The chief of the General Staff Branch told the chief of Intelligence to prepare in writing an authoritative appreciation of the prospects for detecting early warning, with regard to the capabilities of the Intelligence Branch. Within a few days a document was submitted outlining the prospects for obtaining early warning of incipient threats from the various confrontation states. Regarding Egypt, for instance, the report stated that in the event of an Egyptian offensive, the IDF could expect several days' advance warning on the basis of various indications. However, if in such a period the Egyptians conducted an exercise, the capacity for early warning would be disabled, because it would not be clear whether what was being observed was an exercise or a deception.

Such assertions concerning the prospects for early warning of a threat posed by various states were not based on intentions but on the formation of a threat. On the other hand, the document asserted that the possibility of obtaining early strategic warning of intentions was doubtful. However, it transpired in the Yom Kippur War that even when Israel had very dire early warning of intentions, even the most conclusive and authoritative of such early warning, there was still gnawing doubt about the degree of certainty that war would actually break out. For all practical purposes, the government and General Staff treated the certain early warning of intentions as just one more indication. In the Yom Kippur War, Intelligence provided, for the first time in Israeli history, complete military early warning of a threat and had thus fulfilled its explicit role in national security doctrine. Yet the government and General Staff waited for more intelligence on intentions, not content with the intelligence, detailed and authoritative to an unprecedented degree, that they had come into possession of concerning the dire military threat hovering over Israel.

Despite the terrible threat that had become obvious from Egyptian and Syrian military preparations, despite their deployment in full strength opposite Israel in offensive positions, and despite the "conclusive" information from a source of the highest authority on Yom Kippur morning concerning the intention to attack Israel that very day, the Israelis continued to haggle over the extent of reserve mobilization. Had everyone relied before the event on traditional doctrine concerning early warning—in other words on early warning of a threat—history might possibly have taken a different course.

Blame for the surprise should not be laid on the Intelligence Branch, since it furnished full early warning according to the criteria of Israeli national security doctrine. The very essence of the doctrine of early warning had become confused in the general consciousness, in the period prior to the Yom Kippur War.

The chief of Intelligence had indeed said that the probability of war was low. Yet he and his staff had furnished unequivocal and authoritative early warning of threats, based on a variety of military preparations in Egypt and Syria, and other indications. The failure to call up the reserves on time is usually explained away by claiming that the prime minister, the minister of defense, the CGS, and the General Staff all awaited the word from one man—the chief of the Intelligence Branch. While the chief of Intelligence was mistaken in his appreciation of Syrian and Egyptian intentions, he had not misled anyone. Everyone was immeasurably more influenced by information concerning Egyptian and Syrian intentions to attack Israel, by the seriousness of the looming threat, and by the potential danger it posed than by the subjective assessment of the chief of Intelligence and some of his officers. In the days preceding war, while importance had been attached to the chief of Intelligence and his views, those views were not decisive (in contrast to what it became customary to say after the war). The minister of defense and CGS did not await his every utterance with bated breath, nor did they consider his appreciations "stone from Sinai" or in any way unimpeachable. In the light of incoming information about Egyptian and Syrian intentions to go to war, the actual concentration of Egyptian and Syrian forces, and the hasty departure of the families of Soviet advisors from Egypt and Syria on the eve of the attack, the government and General Staff had been anxious over the possibility of war, and the awareness of its likelihood guided their every step.

The blame for failing to anticipate war properly ought not be pinned on Intelligence. The chief of Intelligence and his subordinates had erred about enemy intentions; yet it was not because of their error that Israel did not mobilize its reserve military forces, nor did that error serve as the basis upon which the government and General Staff decided their moves at the approach of war. On Friday morning, the day before war broke out, the chief of Intelligence described the full extent of the threat to a meeting chaired by the prime minister and attended by a large number of ministers and the CGS. He told the gathering that the Egyptians and Syrians were deployed, ready, and from a technical standpoint, capable of launching an attack at any moment, although he believed the probability of such to be low. The CGS said that the Syrians and Egyptians had the technical capability to attack and that there was no proof they had no intention of doing so, although if they did intend to attack, he believed, there would be additional indications. Hence, he recommended not mobilizing reserves for the time being. He believed that if they did intend to attack, Israel would have twelve to twenty-four hours' advance warning. The chief of Intelligence and the CGS had been aware, then, of the existence of a threat. On that day, the CGS ordered the highest state of alert in the IDF.

The fate of a nation does not hinge on the appreciation or the mistake of a single man. All those at the above meeting decided, for the time being, against mobilization. Four of them have been chiefs of the General Staff (past and present), and two others were ministers with impressive experience in national security affairs. The ministers were fully aware of the seriousness of the situation. They knew that from a technical standpoint, the Egyptian and Syrian armed forces were able to launch an attack at any moment and that intelligence had been received indicating the intentions of those two states to go to war.

Responsibility for the serious deviation from the dictates of Israeli national security doctrine, and the creation of a precedent whereby reserves are not called up in the face of threatening enemy deployments on land, in the air, and at sea, in the north and south, rests with Israel's entire national leadership, civilian and military. It does not rest with the Intelligence Branch, which for the first time in Israel's history had provided warning in accordance with the full requirement of national security doctrine—early warning of threats.

The national leadership erred in being oblivious to political reality, which had tilted to Israel's disadvantage, both worldwide and in the Middle East. In the days before the outbreak of war, Israel's national leadership erred in its appreciation of the ratio of forces on the ground; instead of mobilizing Israel's full military power in the face of the unprecedented threat, it contented itself with the standing military forces and the Air Force. There was a pervasive sense of confidence that in the event of war, standing IDF forces alone would be able to contend with the enormous quantitative superiority of the

Egyptians and Syrians, thanks to Israel's strategic depth. Furthermore, the General Staff believed that the awesome firepower of the Air Force would make up for the enemy's quantitative superiority.

Reliance on strategic depth was not well founded. For all practical purposes, there *was* no depth. The IDF had been charged with a rigid defense; its task had been to defend the borders, in the north and south. Now, it was impossible to check enemy offensives and contain them close to their jump-off positions. Neither was reliance on superior firepower well founded, since for all practical purposes, such superiority did not exist, due to enemy air defense missile systems. Because of the glaring quantitative inferiority of standing IDF ground forces, in the north and south, and because of limits to the freedom of action by aircraft, the regular Israeli Army and Air Force stood alone in the breach in the early days of the war; they fought heroically, and they suffered dreadful casualties.

In the Yom Kippur War, Israeli intelligence had discerned Egyptian and Syrian war preparations on time but did not believe the Arabs intended to launch an all-out war. The government and General Staff had monitored the deployment of Egyptian and Syrian forces at threatening jump-off positions, but still permitted them, in complete violation of national security doctrine, to attack Israel while its military forces were not mobilized, its servicemen at home or synagogue on this holiest of days in the Jewish calendar. The national security doctrine had not failed; what had failed was the IDF's adherence to it. Israel "voluntarily" entered the "staying power" trap the Arabs had set for it.

In the spring of 1973, intelligence had been received concerning Egyptian and Syrian intentions to go to war, although no actual threat had formed in the field; hence, despite the intelligence concerning intentions, the reserves were not mobilized then. On Yom Kippur, the reserve forces were not mobilized, despite the clear threat in the field as well as intelligence concerning the intentions of Egypt and Syria to go to war.

There was a denial of the national security doctrine—a distortion of the concept of early warning and disregard of an absolute imperative of that doctrine, namely, that when Arab forces are concentrated and constitute a threat, Israel must mobilize its reserve forces forthwith and be prepared to meet that threat. The government and General Staff had not sufficed with an early warning of threats, as required by national security doctrine. They had sought an early warning of intentions, a concept foreign to Israeli security doctrine, in that it requires a state of alert in the face of the formation of a serious threat in the field. However, even when early warning of intentions of unprecedented—and immediate—seriousness was received, the government and General Staff did not heed it. Israel can only hope that in the future, the Intelligence Branch will give early warning of the formation of military threats as it did in October 1973.

LEADERSHIP

Leadership is the power to unite people and move them toward attainment of a common goal. In organizations and institutions, the division of work is defined, as are the responsibilities and authorities of the various levels and functions. However, authority alone does not suffice. Channels of communication, centers of decision making, and power do not necessarily coincide with formal hierarchical structures. Hence, formal authority delegated to the individual, whether he attained his position by force of law, election, or appointment, is not sufficient. It is the *power* of leadership that is capable of realizing what formal authority cannot—moving men and influencing them.

Leadership is relative. Someone may be accepted as a leader by one group and not by another. Furthermore, the same person, in the same group, may be accepted as a leader in some circumstances but be rejected in others.

In the past, military leadership in Israel was relatively easy, because the unity of existential goals was unchallenged, deriving as it did from a very potent sense of unity of fate. The Arab threat had brought about a unity among the people. The unity of the existential goal was not in doubt. It constituted the national "Archimedean point." In the past, the national consensus on matters relating to survival overcame differences over beliefs and opinions. The leadership enjoyed the benefit of a convenient background of unity of fate and unity of goals, which was implicitly understood by all.

In the War of Independence, there was a complete consensus over national security. In the 1950s, in the period of the retaliation raids, fissures appeared in the national consensus over the morality of such raids, which caused casualties among Arab civilians. That proved but a passing episode, though, as operations against civilians were immediately suspended, and the retaliation raids focused on military objectives. But protest motivated by morality was then replaced by opposition based on questions of efficacy: opponents contended that it is not in the nature of such raids to deter the enemy but to extend the area of friction. Supporters contended that such raids did constitute a deterrent factor, proving to the enemy that in the long run his guerrilla warfare and terrorism would gain him nothing. The argument had been over means, though, not ends. A similar controversy took place over the Sinai Campaign.

After the Six Day War, the nation became divided over more than national goals. There was also a controversy over national security. Some argued that Israel no longer faced an existential military threat, since it had so convincingly demonstrated its military superiority and acquired significant strategic depth. Furthermore, it enjoyed the image of a country with powerful strategic and technological deterrence. The Yom Kippur and Lebanese ("Peace to Galilee") wars were attended by deep feelings of frustration and sharp criticism of the national leadership, political and military.

These controversies, the false sense of security, and the undermining of confidence in the national leadership led to a weakening of motivation. Furthermore, they undermined the erstwhile national consensus in national security affairs. As a result, the burden of political, social, and military leadership in Israel has become increasingly heavy.

Past differences of opinion over the role of the state, against the background of the status quo and political deadlock, were essentially academic. However, with the coming of the era of political dialogue in Israeli-Arab relations, and the peace process, the argument ceased to be theoretical; it became practical and bitter, and highly divisive. Peace involves painful compromises. A fateful era has commenced in Israel's life, an era that requires inspired national leadership that can unify the people and move them to new horizons.

CONCLUSIONS

In the Yom Kippur War, the armed forces of Syria and Egypt, augmented by the expeditionary forces of seven other Arab states, assaulted Israel, whose forces had not been mobilized or fully deployed for battle. Because of that, the IDF was thrown out of its operational equilibrium and forced to conduct a defensive war of attrition in the face of awesome firepower. An obvious conclusion to be drawn is that if with even such a ratio of forces and under such circumstances the IDF won a military victory, the Arabs certainly could not hope to defeat the IDF under normal circumstances, with the IDF functioning properly.

A few days after the conclusion of hostilities in the Yom Kippur War, on 1 November 1973, General el-Gamasy, head of the Egyptian military delegation to the negotiations with Israel on implementation of the cease-fire agreement, at Kilometer 101 on the Suez-Cairo road, told the deputy chief of the IDF General Staff that Egypt would not give up its claim to a single square inch of its territory; it insisted on complete return of all the areas Israel had captured from Egypt in the Yom Kippur War and the entire Sinai, which it had captured from Egypt in the Six Day War. Nevertheless, the Egyptian general went on, Egypt wished to commence a process that would eventually lead to ending the historic conflict and the establishment of a full peace between itself and Israel.

It had taken a state of protracted war, involving terrorism and border clashes, campaigns and full-scale wars, for the Arabs to understand that there was no military solution to the conflict.

Israel's leaders lost their self-confidence in the Yom Kippur War, because of events preceding the war itself and during it, but above all because of the accusations and protests directed at them by groups across the spectrum of Israeli public opinion. They felt they had lost their favor with the people, the spirit of whom was no longer as stout as it had once been. They began to doubt whether the people were willing to continue to make sacrifices, as well as to doubt their nation's staying power. Many began to entertain doubts as to whether Israel could persevere in a state of war with the Arab world, in the light of the increasingly heavy burden that entailed.

A peace treaty was signed with Egypt. The Egyptians recognized Israel and established full diplomatic relations with it. It was a dramatic, astounding, historic event, one that presaged the beginning of the second stage of the Return to Zion, that of reconciliation with Israel by neighboring peoples and their adjustment to the fact of its existence. Israel returned the Sinai to Egypt, agreed to grant the Palestinians autonomy, and undertook to discuss permanent solution to the Palestinian problem within three years, to come into force five years after the establishment of autonomy. Negotiations on Palestinian autonomy failed. The allotted time passed, and the Palestinians eventually revolted (the *Intifada*). In the meantime, the Soviet empire collapsed, and the foundations of the modern world changed. The Oslo Accords with the Palestine Liberation Organization (PLO) were signed.

Israeli national security doctrine lost its balance after the Six Day and Yom Kippur Wars. It was no longer appropriate to the basic strategic parameters that obtained after each of those wars. Specific Egyptian and Syrian national goals came into being (the Sinai and Golan Heights), and the reality of the Israeli occupation and settlements eventually led to the *Intifada*.

The main criterion by which the validity of Israeli national security doctrine, as formulated after the War of Independence, ought to be judged is the extent to which it fulfilled the expectations of those who formulated it. One may say that the doctrine indeed met most of what was expected of it and fulfilled its purpose completely. It was intended to attain what apparently was impossible—Israel's survival of repeated attempts to exterminate it by a variety of means: full-scale wars, limited wars of attrition, terrorism, and sabotage. From the Atlantic Ocean to the Persian Gulf extended the wide expanses of a sea of hatred, which enjoyed strategic depth, large populations, and petroleum-based wealth. Beyond the Arab expanses that surround Israel are the countries of the Third World, partners of former Soviet Russia and its satellites in their hostility to Israel.

Israel's national security doctrine posited that the very extent to which its national interest is existential and vital serves as a force multiplier of the nation's might; the power of the struggle for its existence has been infinitely greater than the power of the negative, aggressive interest of the Arab states. The assumption was that lack of choice for the Jewish people yielded motivation, courage, willingness to sacrifice, and a power of national spirit immeasurably greater than those of the Arab nations. Furthermore, there was not only unity of Jewish fate but also unity of goals. Israeli national security doctrine also assumed, aside from the advantage of existential motivation, the superiority of Israeli quality, and given Israel's qualitative edge and its technological and scientific deterrence, over Arab quantity in the entire range of critical spheres—human, moral, scientific, and technological. Israel relied on the fact that since Arab opposition to it was not based on the elements of necessity and lack of choice, the Arabs would not be able to extract from themselves the full measure of power, of body and spirit, when the chips were down. Hence, there was always the chance that they would reconcile themselves to Israel's existence, taking into account that as long as they adhered to their goal of exterminating it, Israel would manage to thwart their attempts.

Therefore, the transition from the stage of war to that of a peace process and reconciliation with the state of the Jews, whether it proves permanent or only temporary, is an outcome of the principle, which underlies Israeli national security doctrine, of frustrating attempts to destroy it. Such a transition commenced when Egypt signed a peace treaty with the state of the Jews. Whether the process of peace and reconciliation will succeed is not certain. The third stage of Israeli integration in the region, if and when it materializes, is beyond the horizon of peace. There is a chance to end the conflict with the Arabs, but not certainty of it. The danger of war has not passed—hatred of Israel permeates the Arab peoples, and a willingness to reconcile themselves with the Jews is far from them. The war of terrorism against Israel and the Jews continues. It was not the conquests of the Six Day War that caused Arab hatred, but the opposite—it was their hatred that made Israel a conqueror.

The peace agreements with the Palestinians and Arab states, as dramatic, significant, even fateful, as they are—and indeed they are exceedingly important—are still political agreements between governments and leaders. Only acceptance of Israel by the broad mass of the Arab populations can guarantee an end to the historical conflict and put that peace on a firm basis.

To the sum total of factors that complicate Israeli-Arab relations and inhibit the development of a true, stable peace must be added the fact that no Arab state is a democracy. For the time being, the establishment of peace reflects the interests of Arab governments and regimes that are not necessarily stable; they do not reflect the will of a broad spectrum of Arab opinion. As in war, so in peace, there is no symmetry between Israeli society and the Arab peoples. The yearning for peace and the perception of it as a self-justifying end rather than as a means are not mutual.

The Jewish people has been struggling for its right to security, independence, and freedom. In the course of the wars, guerrilla warfare, and terrorism imposed upon it, by the Arabs and others, Israel has fought desperately in self-defense. While Israel has stumbled on the road to its survival, making some mistakes, both moral and practical, in a broad historical perspective it has been on the defensive, fighting for its very life. While others have tried to destroy it, Israel has wanted to destroy no one, and it has never believed that the end justifies the means.

In both full-scale wars and campaigns of attrition, Israel has shown the Arabs that they will not be able to impose their will on it by force. Israeli national security doctrine, in all the various parts that it comprises, including its various combat doctrines, has served it well and has gotten the better of continuous Arab hostility and Arab efforts to undermine its very existence, in every possible sphere and every possible way. Israel's national security doctrine has not disappointed from a professional standpoint. It has been adequate, well founded, and reliable. It is only when Israel has diverged from it that Israel has been punished. The State of Israel has known both successes and failures.

The wars the Arabs have waged and their process of waking up to reality, to the point of willingness to make peace, have exacted (and continue to exact) a high price: tens of thousands of Jews, including hundreds outside Israel, and over a hundred thousand Arabs, have been killed or wounded in the Israeli-Arab conflict since the War of Independence.

There is no small state whose existence is guaranteed beyond doubt. Small states can be destroyed. They are subject to potential threats, and their survival depends to a great extent on their relations with other states. In general, the shadow of existential danger hovers over small states; this is especially true for the state of the Jews. There are those who have wanted to destroy it from the day it was established, and there have been actual attempts toward that end. A lesson of past wars is that no reliance should be placed on other countries' coming to Israel's assistance and saving it. It was a lesson Israel had experienced with particular immediacy in the Six Day War.

The Yom Kippur War turned into a war of existence because Israel ignored its national security doctrine; the IDF did not mobilize on time and deploy to meet the threat, neglected the principles of a preemptive war and the offensive, and did not take note of the loss of the Air Force's ability to provide tactical fire support for the ground forces.

An important lesson from Israel's wars to preserve its existence is that it must be able to deter and be strong enough to defeat its opponents by force of arms. It must adhere to an appropriate national security doctrine, it must employ all its power should its enemies wage war against it—and it must show goodwill and broad-mindedness when they come to discuss peace.

CHAPTER 24

NATIONAL SECURITY IN THE FUTURE

A NEW NATIONAL SECURITY DOCTRINE

The principles of Israel's national security doctrine and the basic IDF concepts concerning fighting doctrine, organization, and structure were set in the 1950s. Israeli military thinking since then has consisted essentially of marginal comments on military thinking that was formed at that time. The basics have remained unchanged.

That doctrine has proved itself over the decades. It has fulfilled its mission and attained its goals, but it is no longer relevant. The need has arisen for a thoroughgoing change and the development of a new national security doctrine. The reasons for this are:

1. The new military technology will enable hostile countries, both distant from Israel and near, to attack it from within their own territories, by means of strategic deterrent weapons based on surface-to-surface missiles and other modern systems. At the operational and tactical levels, modern air defense systems are liable to severely limit the ability of aircraft to provide fire support for ground forces on the battlefield of the future.

2. There is no way of knowing the nature of the world order in the twenty-first century. Neither can one know in advance what Middle Eastern developments will be in such areas as the peace process between Israel

and the Arabs, the spread of Islamic fundamentalism, or the relative importance and nature of relations between states in the region.

3. Looming over the horizon of national, and regional, security is the possible acquisition by militant Islamic states of weapons of mass destruction. With the shadow of such a nonconventional threat hovering over the Middle East, the concept of art of war will be replaced by an art of mutual deterrence—mutual neutralization resulting from the "balance of terror" that would prevail among the states of the region. Such a reality, a dangerous reality, is liable to be uncontrollable.

STRATEGIC DETERRENCE

Since the establishment of the State of Israel, it has been possible to shell settlements and other objectives in the country with artillery and to mount air raids against them from bases in the neighboring confrontation states as well as in their more distant allies. The answer to this threat has been the deterrent power of the Israeli Air Force. Arab states have feared the response of the IDF. They knew that attacks on objectives in Israel, whether from land, the air, or sea, would incur massive IDF retaliation on land, as well as air attacks on centers of government, infrastructure, and, if there were no choice, population centers; such attacks could eventually undermine the political stability of aggressor states. Whenever enemy aircraft did try to penetrate Israeli air space, they were shot down by Israeli fighters. Israel's air superiority was absolute.

Israeli defense doctrine always attached overriding importance to strategic considerations, over those of a tactical or operational nature. The IDF General Staff has favored the air arm in the allocation of resources, mainly because it has been its principal strategic arm, in addition to its role of protecting the country's air space. Defense doctrine has also assigned the air arm the role of "flying artillery" in support of the ground and sea forces. The Air Force has been the vehicle with which the IDF has been able to attack vital strategic objectives in enemy territory and defeat enemy air forces, preventing them from attacking objectives inside Israel or its ground forces.

While the strategic firepower of Israel and the Arabs was based on their air forces, as long as Israel maintained air superiority, it possessed an effective strategic deterrence. Hence, total war never broke out between Israel and the Arabs after Israel's 1948 War of Independence. Neither have the Arabs been able to mount significant air attacks on Israeli ground forces or airfields.

This state of affairs could very well undergo significant, and strategically critical, change in the future: Arab states have already come into the possession of surface-to-surface missiles, the arsenals of which they are liable to expand continually as well as enhance qualitatively. It may very well be that with surface-to-surface missiles, attacks on population centers and military objectives inside Israel will be possible, not only from the confrontation states and states near them but from their most distant allies as well. Thanks to developments in military technology, the Arabs and their allies have access to various types of relatively inexpensive surface-to-surface missiles that can be launched over long distances. With their economic power and political weight, states in the region will be able to procure missiles from various sources throughout the world, virtually without limit. Should long-range missiles be stockpiled in the Middle East, the ratio of forces between Israel and the other states in the region in the sphere of strategic firepower would be altered; with such missiles, the other states in the region would be able to reduce their traditional inferiority to Israel in the sphere of strategic firepower. They could conceivably hit Israel's airfields and disrupt the operations of its air force, attack population centers and military emergency stores, and disrupt the mobilization of reserves and the functioning of the rear-echelon systems. They could surprise Israel by preceding the movement of forces with the stage of fire, or by subjecting it to missile attack from the territory of distant states, which extend from North Africa to the Persian Gulf and beyond, as well as from the confrontation states. Some of the more distant states lie beyond the effective range of fighter-bombers; in respect of such states, air power would not be a principal strategic deterrent factor.

This development in the Middle Eastern arena constitutes the main conventional military problem confronting Israeli national defense at the approach of the twenty-first century.

The rules of warfare in the region will be different in the future. A future war is liable to be a total war, and its outcome will not be decided only by the results of operations on land, in the air, and at sea; the issue will also be decided by each side's staying power and capacity to absorb blows in the exchange of strategic fire, and by its ability to force the issue in that exchange. Such capacity is conditional upon the ability to employ varied means of intercepting missiles, to hit launch facilities and critical strategic enemy objectives, both civilian and military, and above all to deliver painful, massive deterrent blows to enemy population centers in retaliation for attacks on one's own population.

Air power is vitally essential, but it can no longer serve as Israel's sole deterrent and strategic bulwark. If a strategic revolution does take place in the region, it will characterize the battlefield of the future and pose a danger to Israel. Such a revolution will be brought about by long-range missiles in the possession of states both near and distant; they are liable to undermine Israel's historical deterrent capacity. Neither innovative tactical technologies, including precision weapons and smart munitions, nor its monopoly on air power will secure Israel in the face of these new strategic threats.

In the past, Israel would meet new threats by adjusting its defense doctrine to changing circumstances; it would change areas of emphasis in combat doctrine, weapons systems, and organization, as required. Such measures are no longer adequate—what is now required is a thoroughgoing overhaul of Israeli defense doctrine.

When distant allies of the Arab confrontation states used to participate in wars against Israel only by sending expeditionary forces, it was sufficient for the IDF to decide the issue with the confrontation states, because it was from their territory that expeditionary forces had to operate. In the new reality, the IDF will have to deter those distant states directly, since they will be able to attack Israel directly from their own territory, without any connection to the confrontation states, which would not even have to participate in the fighting.

These new threats are liable to limit the ability of the Israeli Air Force to fulfil its strategic role. Israel has enjoyed a monopoly on strategic deterrence over the years. Thanks to the qualitative superiority of the Israeli Air Force and its firepower, Israel has been able to reach objectives deep inside the territory of the confrontation states and spread havoc and destruction. Enemy air forces have not been able to overcome Israel's and mount deep-penetration raids inside Israeli territory. In the age of long-range missiles, a new strategic reality is likely to come into being in the Middle Eastern arena. The Israeli Air Force will not be able to prevent long-range missiles launched in distant countries from hitting Israel. Such missiles are liable to confer on the Arabs an effective strategic deterrent force, one that will dispossess Israel of its monopoly on strategic deterrence. The race will no longer be for monopoly, but rather for mutuality—for the maintenance of mutual deterrence.

The Air Force will remain, even in these circumstances, Israel's basic strategic deterrent force, although it will no longer be its only one. In response to the missile threat that has appeared on its national defense horizon, Israel must also be able to rely on other long-range offensive forces and weapons systems. In addition to developing offensive deterrent capabilities against strategic objectives throughout the region, defensive systems to neutralize and destroy missiles must also be developed; likewise, Israel's capacity to absorb passively an assault must be enhanced. Missiles are a new dimension and a new challenge, and Israel must prepare itself accordingly.

The Air Force must continue to be given priority in allocation of resources over the ground forces, but not over the development and maintenance of satellite-based early warning systems or over alternative means of conventional strategic deterrence. What is required is a new national security doctrine. As long as air power constituted Israel's strategic deterrent arm and the backbone of its national security doctrine, modification of that doctrine and improvisation were possible. However, one cannot change or shift the center of gravity of a building that rests on a single, central beam, if that beam can no longer bear the weight placed upon it. In a like manner, the Air Force can no longer be Israel's strategic backbone.

FIRE POWER IN LAND WARFARE

The idea that aircraft were the principal platforms of firepower, both strategic and tactical, was valid until the Yom Kippur War. In the ground battles of that war, the IDF lost its superiority in firepower, because of modern antiaircraft systems. Attacks on Israel by Iraqi surface-to-surface missiles in the 1991 Gulf War also foreshadowed the expected end of the hegemony of air-based firepower in strategic deterrence. Even before the Yom Kippur War, a number of IDF commanders took note of the expected future changes and recommended preparing for them. They argued that the aircraft had been "knocked off its pedestal" and felt that because of its range, it could no longer serve as the sole platform of strategic deterrence. Furthermore, because of modern air defense systems, it could not continue to be the main platform of firepower in tactical land combat. The IDF General Staff decided at the time to "concentrate on the present" and defer to a later date any discussion on the significance and impact of technological developments on combat doctrine.

Ever since their appearance in warfare, aircraft have been affected by the unreliability of the weather. From the 1970s on, its freedom of action has also been limited by modern air defense systems. Furthermore, in an age of surface-to-surface missiles, the airfields on which it must land and take off are subject to missile attack and may be neutralized for periods of time. These factors limit the ability of aircraft to provide fire support in tactical land combat—thus the importance of accelerating the pace of the development and procurement of other modern weapons systems, so as to ensure IDF superiority in firepower in land combat.

DEPTH

In order to achieve peace and to avoid becoming a binational state, Israel will not continue to hold large parts of the territories it took in the Six Day War. Hence, it will lose the benefit of strategic and operational geographic depth. The concept of strategic depth generally relates to geographic expanse of land, although the sea also constitutes strategic depth, provided that naval forces exist to exploit its surface and depths. The role of the Israeli Navy must be altered from that of an auxiliary force to a strategic deterrent force. Israel's Navy is relatively small quantitatively, yet it must be great qualitatively if it is to compensate for the lack of geographic depth on land. The concept of depth is sometimes understood superficially. Strategic depth has many dimensions, such as geography, demography, politics, allies, common interests, and international support. The Jewish people, as an ally of Israel, form part of the nation's strategic depth, while the demographic weight of the Arabs and that of the Islamic peoples who are their natural and reliable allies constitute their strategic depth.

Given its lack of significant "horizontal" geographic depth, and given the nature of threats it can expect to confront, Israel must nurture, and learn to rely on, all components of the strategic depth that it possesses. The concept of depth in modern warfare is also "vertical," extending not only over land, over the expanses and through the depths of the sea, and into the air, but also into space. In the age of modern warfare, the concept of depth is three-dimensional, involving volume, not merely area. Future military power, in time of peace as in war, will depend on large-scale investment of the nation's economic resources and on accelerated scientific and technological development.

RISKS AND MILITARY POWER

The basic strategic factors in the Middle Eastern arena are in a constant state of flux; alongside modern military technology and Arab wealth, which have been creating new circumstances in the region, a process has been developing that constitutes the basis for the hope that peace will prevail between the State of Israel and the Arab states. Formal peace agreements, if not accompanied by genuine reconciliation between the peoples of the region, contain hidden dangers. Threats to Israel from Arab states or organizations are liable to be serious even without war, if they see peace as "war by other means." What may develop in the best case is a state of political, economic, and cultural warfare against Israel, or in the worst, warfare involving low-level, chronic military activity and violations of internal security. The advantages of peace are clear, even if it is only a formal peace that falls far short of genuine rapprochement. Yet at the same time, peace also involves the loss of operational and tactical depth, and the creation of conditions convenient for harassment and terrorism.

Israel must prepare itself for the expected new reality. The substantive military problems it faces are not those of the techno-tactical "battlefield of the future" but rather those of the battlefield of the present, on which the battles for Israel's very existence are being conducted—a battlefield that is real, revolutionary, and dangerous. Here is where Israel's new national security doctrine must focus.

Not even richer countries than Israel can build up the ultramodern armed forces of the future all at once. The structure of armed forces will continue to consist of both traditional and innovative elements. Economic constraints preclude equipping the IDF at a reasonable pace with modern weapons systems. However, as long as the conflict continues, as long as there is no genuine reconciliation with Israel, the IDF must under absolutely no circumstances compromise on two matters: its capacity for the strategic deterrence necessary for the country's survival, and the firepower it can bring to bear on strategic objectives in the confrontation states and their allies.

There are those in Israel who call for a "small, smart military." But as long as there is no general peace in the region, as long as the fires of hatred of Israel continue to burn among the Arab peoples, Israel needs a large military. It must be among the larger armed forces of the world, relative to population; it must contain a large conscript and reserve military, along with a small permanent cadre of specialists. What the IDF requires is not to become "small and smart" but to rely, as in the past, on military wisdom. Those who seek a small military need not worry: the IDF is small in any event; there is no need to cut it down to size. It is not possible to divorce a discussion about Israel's military might, including the size of the IDF, from Israel's national and foreign policy goals; the subject at hand is not of a professional military nature but of a strategic, political one.

Reduction of the military budget is to be avoided. If and when the regional conflict ends, the threats to Israel are removed, and the stage of integration into the region is reached, it will be possible to divert fewer resources to defense. But even then, an adequate national military strength will be a necessary condition for defense of the peace, and when that is violated, for defense of the country. Israel cannot compete with the Arabs in quantity. Accordingly it must maintain technological superiority, exhaust its scientific capabilities, and find innovative solutions, both quantitative and qualitative, to its strategic problems. These can be solved only by the most advanced technologies and daring weapons systems, even at the expense of the tactical and operational levels.

It is customary to define modern precision weapons as having a high probability of destroying pinpoint targets—with one or a few shots, destruction of a target is assured. This is in contrast to ordinary artillery, for example, which is a "statistical" weapon—a large number of projectiles are fired over a wide area to increase the probability that some of them will hit the target. It is a mistake to think that as weapons systems become more precise, war itself becomes more "mathematical," more precise. War has always been statistical, and the outcome of conventional wars has been, is, and will continue to be dependent on national goals and on the overall ratio of forces between nations—in both quantity and quality—and on leadership.

Replacement of an existing arsenal is a very expensive and lengthy process. Innovative weapons systems enter service and take their rightful places in a military arsenal gradually. When these new weapons systems pass practical tests of their worth, they become ordinary, even "old," and in short order more up-to-date ideas and weapons systems are introduced to supersede them. Hence, the old and the new constitute a mixture that shapes the art of war. That is the dialectic of warfare. An outstanding example of such a process is the aircraft carrier in the Second World War; war at sea in the future seemed to belong to aircraft carriers, but battleships were not phased out until the carriers had actually proved themselves. Real wars are always waged by divisions that actually exist in the field, not new ones that still exist only in the mind, or weapons that are still on the drawing table or being tested in theoretical war games. Hence, war in general is "old fashioned."

Concerning the limits of power, what is important is the provenance of resources, not just their quantity. Ever since the Yom Kippur War, the government of the United States has taken the place of the Jewish people as the main economic support of the State of Israel. A necessary condition, although not a sufficient one, of national security is military power based on economic power. Israel's flight into the shelter of U.S. economic aid, as an alternative to putting its own house in order economically and becoming self-reliant, is no indication of moral strength; neither is it conducive to motivation. It is also plain dangerous. Allies, of course, are not to be made light of, certainly not the political, economic, and deterrent aid extended by the United States, for which Israel owes a debt of gratitude. However, the aid extended by the United States should be an augmentation of Israel's own strength and that of the Jewish people; it should not be an alternative to them. Beyond that, in the final analysis, Israel's relations with the states of the region and the prospects for peace with them are no less important than relations with distant allies.

Israeli security depends upon the national ethos and on whether the Jewish people can preserve their state. The shadow that hovers over its security is that not only of modern military technology but of the self-image of Israeli society, its efficiency, and the degree of its motivation. Security depends on high productive capacity, on technological innovativeness, and the technologies of the future, such as those related to space. The military might of the IDF will be in direct proportion to Israel's inventiveness, the development of its infrastructure, and its technological and industrial capacity. Relations with the countries of the world, above all the Arab states and the United States, are also very important to national security, as is the setting of realistic national goals, goals that can unite the people and maintain the highest possible degree of motivation.

THE STATE OF THE JEWISH PEOPLE

The territories captured in the Six Day War are important to Israel's security. They could serve as platforms for harassment of Israel with fire, causing harm to its people and property, for disrupting life and undermining the sense of personal safety. It is by such circumstances of constant friction between two neighboring peoples in constant contact with each other that the extent of necessary current military activity is determined. The main factors in this regard are the nature of the underlying relations between the peoples, the efficacy of Israel's military deterrence, the positions taken by the Arab leadership, its ability to impose its will on the Palestinian population, and geography and topography. Indeed, there is also military significance to geographic space, in that it provides the security of depth.

Israel enjoyed strategic depth when it controlled the Sinai Peninsula after the Six Day War, while the depth afforded by the West Bank and Golan Heights is operational. Both have very considerable national security value. Yet despite that value, even if Israel were freely given the choice of annexing those territories, with their Arab populations, for the defensive depth they afford, it would still be an open question whether such a course would be desirable. And the answer is in the negative: the Zionist goal is a national Jewish state, not a binational one.

The bitter lesson of Jewish history is that the Jews must never rely on others, never live defenselessly among others, never be at their tender mercy. It is only under Jewish governance that the rights and freedom of the Jews may be assured; this is an eternal fact, and without it there could never have been a Zionist movement. At the same time, one must bear in mind that minorities live in Israel as of right, not on sufferance; their rights are inalienable. Israel is a national state, but the difference between that and a binational state is relative, one of degree. Israel belongs to all its people, including its minorities—and all have equal rights. However, its essence as the state of the Jewish people is determined by its language, its collective historical memory, and the heritage and culture of the majority of its people. Their national self-image is what determines its identity.

Hence, there is no security value in the annexation of Arab populations that reduce, or even cancel, the Jewish majority. Such an annexation contradicts the goals of Zionism. Basic goals must be adhered to; if the preservation of the state of the Jews involves risk, that risk must be confronted. Under no circumstances, though, must the unique Jewish character of Israel be forgone or retreated from. Israel must avoid the paradox of ceasing to *be* the state of the Jewish people in order to *defend* the state of the Jewish people. Every foot of ground, every hill, is important for the defense of the country, even in the age of missiles, but the state of the Jewish people is more important. The entire advantage gained from annexing all of the captured territories (if that were possible) would be canceled because of the Arab population there.

All Jews agree that the Jewish people has a right to the land of Israel. However, there are those who claim that just as it was right to take Arab-settled areas away from their inhabitants during the 1948 War of Independence, it would be permissible to do so now as well. Such a position is incorrect, both morally and practically. The Zionist idea is just: the existential Jewish choice, both personal and national, brought about the Return to Zion. Most of the land was desolate, its inhabitants few in number. The Jews had no intention of dispossessing the Arabs from their homes and land; they wanted to live alongside them.

It was the Arabs who waged a life-and-death war against the Jews, despite decisions by the League of Nations and the United Nations, and despite recognition by the nations of the world of the right of the Jews to their land, to establish a sovereign state in it. The Arabs consistently refused the various compromise proposals raised over the years, while the Jews agreed to most of them. In the War of Independence, the fate of the Jews in Palestine hung in the balance. The Arabs fought not only for territorial and political ends but against the physical existence, individual and national, of the Jewish people in the land of Israel. Three years after the Holocaust, there was another attempt to exterminate physically an entire community of Jews. The Arabs forced a war of life-and-death on the Jewish population in the land of Israel and were defeated. Israel does not owe them an apology for thwarting their homicidal scheme.

At that time, it was just and morally defensible to dispossess the Palestinian Arabs, because the existential goal, and only that goal, justifies such means; such means could not be fairly criticized, given the violent opposition of the Arabs and their continuing effort to annihilate Israel and its Jewish population. The existential solution, considering the circumstances of the Jewish people in the Diaspora, which included persecutions, pogroms, and massacres, was embodied in the Zionist idea of freedom and independence—the state of the Jewish people. With the realization of that just idea, the chapter in the history of a people without a state, who were constantly at the mercy of others, also came to an end. As long as the Palestinians do not intend or have the power to threaten Israel's very existence, however, the former moral justification no longer obtains. That is because only the aim of existence itself may justify means—but even then, not all means.

With the establishment of the State of Israel and its consolidation, a new historical period commenced, one subject to different values and terms of reference. The principle of overall historical perseverence and continuity remains valid, but from the standpoint of the history of the criteria of values there commenced, with Israel's establishment and its ability to defend itself, a new Jewish national history. From here on, what has been under consideration has no longer been the lesser evil: the ends have ceased to justify the means.

SECURITY AND PEACE

An existential threat hovers over Israel and not the Arab peoples. Therefore, while Israel must take Arab wishes into consideration, it must refrain from bending over backward to satisfy them at any price. There are two kinds of existential "red lines." The first relates to national security, to Israel's ability to defend its very existence. The second relates to the ultimate national goal that Israel must be a Jewish, not a binational, state. Israel's national existence is conditional upon both these elements: national security and the ultimate national goal. Defensible assets that are essential to survival and that can, to a degree, serve as alternatives to defensive depth lost through territorial compromise must be held on to, without compromise. If their appetite is such the Arabs even insist on "the poor man's lamb"—changes in the pre-1967 borders that are critical from the standpoint of Israeli national security, and other important changes, such as those relating to water and land—their demands must be unequivocally rejected. Israel must vigorously oppose all attempts to increase the Arab minority in its midst by virtue of the Palestinians' claim of a "right of return"; it must not recognize the rights of Palestinians to work permanently in Israel, or grant unqualified work or entry permits, or the like. Arab demands such as these do not indicate a genuine desire for reconciliation with Israel, and acceding to them would pose an existential threat to Israel.

Arrangements pertaining to borders, assets, and rights that militate against the risks of peace are of infinitely greater value than temporary security arrangements meant to avoid the dangers of war. National security borders must be based on two elements: geography and demography. Such borders provide defense against both external attack and internal dangers. Various dangers lie in wait for Israel: war, terrorism, subversion, and agitation, both domestic and external, that could arouse irredentist tendencies among some of its people. The demographic border is more important than the geographic one.

Israel must not be patronizing, or put on airs of bearing a message or being a light to the region. It must not be arrogant. It must honor territorial, economic, and cultural commitments, and borders. Israel must act as a democracy, even if others are not democratic.

If and when the third stage of the Return to Zion is realized, the stage of political integration into the region—integration and not assimilation—and Israel is accepted as one of the states of the region, the sufficient condition for its optimal national security will also obtain. But the end should not be rushed. Cooperation with other states must be the result of a natural, gradual process of peoples moving toward one another over the axis of time, not one of either using elbows or being obsequious.

Until that day comes, Israel's security will hinge on its qualitative and military superiority. As long as the likelihood exists of an automatic coalition of the Arab states forming against Israel, and as long as Arab terrorism against Israel and its people continues, Israel cannot disarm. Only if a strong, stable peace prevails and the balance of military power is no longer something that is automatically measured between Israel and the other states of the region, only then will it be possible for Israel to reduce its military strength and cease to devote its best resources to remaining constantly on guard.

The process of reconciliation with Israel and the transition to a state of peace involve the return of land to the Arabs and the loss of territorial depth. In other words, Israel will be weakened in certain respects, and it must be compensated with various means for early warning and alert that would enhance its military power, above all its military technology. Arab opposition to alternative early warning and alert systems indicates an attempt to undermine Israel's national security and its capacity for self-defense.

Staying power in war is not measured only in terms of a nation's capacity to defend its existence directly. Painful enemy blows and military setbacks, and the attainment of limited military or political aims by the enemy, can also indirectly undermine Israel's existence over the long term. The danger lies in the accumulated loss of life, damage, and destruction, and of the erosion of material and political assets that weaken morale as well as Israel's image, both external and domestic, and lessen its determination and power to deter. Deterrence against such indirect existential threats must be based on varied means that are suitable to specific threats, and on a flexible national security doctrine.

Above all, the most basic, most vital, condition for Israel's national security is its internal strength. Internecine strife within Israel is liable to weaken it. The unity of fate has long been conferred on the Jewish people: over the ages, everywhere they have been, their enemies have always seen to that. But unity of goal has not necessarily been their lot. Unity of fate and unity of goal are in tension with each other. It is important that there be basic unity in Israeli society concerning the State of Israel's character as a Jewish, Zionist, and democratic state. It is absolutely vital that there be a consensus on national security—basic, existential matters must be beyond political differences.

One cannot know if time is working for Israel or against it. There was no way of predicting when the Arabs would take the path to peace, or the mass immigration from Russia, or the disintegration of the Soviet empire and the end of the Cold War. The Middle East is a powder keg, and not just because of the Arab-Israeli dispute. It is rich in oil, and rich nations live beside poor ones. There are conflicts of interest among the Arabs themselves. There is no way of knowing whether the future will unfold a reality dominated by economic and political struggles or one dominated by war and revolution, regional and worldwide.

The Jewish people must, and can, be prepared to defend its existence by any means—this is a categorical imperative, and its denial is immoral.

For the time being, the nature of Israeli-Arab relations requires that Israel, through no fault of its own, rely on its sword and maintain a strong, effective deterrent capability against the missile threat, as well as the potential threat posed by various weapons of mass destruction. It is not only relations with the Arab world that preclude a relaxing of preparedness; other Muslim states are also liable to threaten Israel's existence. The present historical phase, at the conclusion of the twentieth century—marked by dialogue between Israel and the Arabs and attempts to establish a comprehensive peace in the region—requires Israel to remain on guard even more than in the past. Territorial concessions and the loss of deterrent and defensive depth will force Israel to rely on a large military and to develop and maintain deterrence systems based in space, on land, in the air and at sea, as well as up-to-date long-range strategic weapons systems. Progress toward ending the conflict in the region and creating conditions conducive to reconciliation between Israel and the Arabs requires the nurturing and consolidation of Israel's national security, including one of its most important elements—peace.

INDEX

About the Author

ISRAEL TAL is the Assistant Minister of Defense for Israel. In February 1942, he joined the British Eighth Army, Jewish Brigade, to serve in the Western Desert on the Italian Front. He served as the Commanding General, Armored Corps Command during the 1967 war and as the Vice Chief of the General Staff of the Israeli Defense Forces in the 1973 Yom Kippur War.